DEATH BY RENTAL CAR:
HOW THE HOUCK CASE
CHANGED THE LAW

DEATH BY RENTAL CAR: HOW THE HOUCK CASE CHANGED THE LAW

BEN KELLEY

Foreword by Ralph Nader

VOX JUSTITIA BOOKS
Pebble Beach, California

ISBN: 0692559132
ISBN 13: 9780692559130
Library of Congress Control Number: 2015955518
Vox Justitia Books, Pebble Beach, CA

This book is dedicated to the Houck family

CONTENTS

FOREWORD

THIS IS THE gripping story of two young women – sisters aged 24 and 20 – whose promising lives were snuffed out in a fiery, traumatic instant collision by their Chrysler PT Cruiser with a semi-truck on a California highway and the tenacious effort by their parents and attorneys to hold accountable the rental car company that ignored a government recall for a lethal defect and the manufacturer that made the car.

The story of *Death By Rental Car* has many dimensions that readers would do well to absorb in their own roles as motorists, car owners and, especially, car renters. I've known Ben Kelley over his forty-five years of work in traffic safety as a meticulous researcher and communicator. He is ideally suited to go through the masses of evidence, the conflicting assertions, the nearly six years of pressure on the young women's parents and relatives and come out with this compelling story of corporate evasion and duplicity driven by a legal strategy of attrition.

Carol and Charles Houck saw beyond their own personal tragedy when they pursued a lawsuit to bring to light the hard knuckle practices of Chrysler and Enterprise Rental. They saw their lawsuit as a tool to advance the public's right to know what both Chrysler and Enterprise Rental wanted kept secret. Drivers and passengers on the roads were in danger. Secret settlements from Chrysler and Enterprise Rental to the Houcks would not help these other passengers and drivers. Such secrecy is counter to the principles of humanitarianism. The parents were able to memorialize the lives of their daughters by trying to save those of many more people through their efforts to gain proper disclosure of the defects.

What makes this book so engrossing is Mr. Kelley's refusal to summarize what deserves detailed explanation. You'll read key excerpts from the exact transcripts of key depositions, see how Enterprise Rental's corporate parent tries to escape the responsibility for its subsidiaries, and learn how Chrysler used the bankruptcy laws not just to escape its creditors, but to escape those whom it harmed with pending cases in court.

You'll read what a difference dedicated, persistent personal injury attorneys, on contingent fees, can make in a constricted civil justice system, which for all its warts and obstructions keeping many justified claims from going forward is without peer in the world. You'll become able to see through the avaricious propaganda of the corporate wrongdoing lobbies who want Americans to think it is easy to use the courts to shake down these corporate defendants.

Finally, you'll be so impressed, I believe, by Carol Houck's mission, which is to obtain state and federal legislation that requires rental car companies to fix recalled vehicles before renting them out. She'll need your help with your legislators. She established the Raechel & Jackie Foundation to encourage creative expression and environmental stewardship that improves the quality of life for youth. She says "the mom in me knew there were going to be other kids, and, by golly, I wasn't going to let Raechel and Jackie die in vain."

There are passages in this resonating book that standing alone justify it belonging to your library, including the remarkable letter that 17-year-old Raechel wrote to her parents entitled "Yin and Yang." It is an insightful, poetically composed tribute to parenting by a youngster who was wise beyond her years. This book portrays an irreversible tragedy from which emerges an indomitable human spirit of preventative care for others.

Ralph Nader
Washington, D.C.
March 8, 2015

PREFACE

BARBARA BOXER WAS not happy. Glaring down at the witness, voice edged with exasperation, the California senator again asked whether the witness supported a law that prohibited recalled cars from being rented or loaned until their defects were fixed.

"Do you support a law like that?" she asked for the second time, and again did not get a straight answer.

General Motors CEO Mary Barra was clearly unprepared for the question. Caught off-guard, stammering, staring up at Boxer from the witness table, she looked like the proverbial deer caught in the headlights – not an inapt simile for the nation's most powerful auto executive.

It was April 2, 2014, and Barra was testifying under oath at a Senate hearing into GM's decade-long cover-up of a deadly ignition switch defect, one that could cause millions of cars to shut down on the highway, lose all power and crucial safety protections – including air bags – and end up crashing. Belatedly GM had agreed to recall and fix the cars, but not before the defect had caused hundreds of crashes, at least thirteen of them fatal. Pummeled for hours by questions from Boxer and other subcommittee members, Barra had been attempting to show that GM had the situation under control. So far her answers had largely failed to satisfy the subcommittee.

Barra, a long-time senior executive at the giant car company only recently elevated to the CEO slot, had been briefed about the defect by GM's lawyers and PR people before the hearing. Thus she was able to field most of the questions thrown at her by subcommittee members, although often with hedged "we're working on it" answers and "I'll find out and let you know" assurances. But Boxer had opened a new line of interrogation, one which had caught Barra off guard.

Barra tried to mollify the senator. If there was a safety issue with a GM car, she said, the company would "ground" the car – i.e., not sell it until the defect was corrected. But that was already required by law, and didn't apply to rental car companies. Barra's answer was irrelevant. Boxer cut her off. "No, no!"

The senator asked yet again: "Do you support a proposed law by Sen. McCaskill and myself that will say recalled cars like yours can no longer be rented or loaned?" She raised her voice and spaced her words to give them emphasis, further underscoring the question with chopping motions of her hands. "Do. You. Support. A. Law? Yes or No?"

Barra tried another deflecting answer. "Conceptually, it makes sense. I would like to understand…"

Boxer: Well, conceptually is not the question. Do you support the bill?
Barra: I haven't read it.
Boxer: Well, you should since you were the CEO of GM when we got an email from your organization that you're a part of – the Auto Manufacturers' Alliance – opposing the bill. So you already were CEO. This is the new GM, and you opposed the law.

Clearly angered, Boxer gave up trying to get a straight answer. The auto industry's trade association was against the proposed law, and Barra had signed on to that opposition, not "conceptually" but in fact.

Barra fell silent as Boxer lectured her on why the rental-car recall bill was urgently needed, why the issues underlying it "run deep."

"You should know that my constituent, Cally Houck, lost her two daughters, Raechel, 24, and Jackie, 20, in a tragic accident caused by an unrepaired safety defect in a rental car they were driving. So Senators Schumer and McCaskill – we wrote the Raechel and Jacqueline Houck Safe Rental Car Act."

Boxer refused to accept Barra's refusal to support a bill that would "make sure that no one – no one – would die the way they died." Speaking "woman to woman, I am very disappointed because the culture that you are representing here today is the culture of the status quo." In disgust, she ended her interrogation of the GM CEO.

The U.S. Senate bill to outlaw rentals of unrepaired recalled cars had been introduced by Boxer and her colleagues in 2012, but the tragedy that took the lives of the Houck sisters had occurred nearly nine years earlier, on October 7, 2004. Driving on northbound Highway 101 in California, they had been killed in a head-on collision with a tractor-trailer. Their car, a Chrysler PT Cruiser rented from Enterprise Rent-A-Car, had been recalled for a safety defect that could cause an engine fire, but the corporation had failed to repair it.

The cause of the crash, occurring during daylight hours on a busy stretch of highway, seemed likely to be recorded in highway fatality statistics as a simple matter of "driver error" resulting from what the investigating police officer would call an "unsafe turning movement" by the driver. But then, through the perseverance of the sisters' parents and the unremitting efforts of a small Los Angeles law firm that waged a five-year court battle against Enterprise, the true nature of the crash and its staggering implications for national auto safety policy emerged.

This book tells the story of the Houck case and its consequences. It is about a lonely and seemingly hopeless fight by a bereft family and their lawyers against a behemoth auto rental company and a huge car manufacturer. It is about corporate callousness and abuse of power. Finally, it is about a long-undiscovered legal loophole that for decades put millions of rental car customers at risk of death or serious injury on the highways of America until finally, on December 4, 2015, the *Raechel and Jacqueline Houck Safe Rental Car Act* was signed into law.

1

THE TRIP HOME

SEPARATELY OR TOGETHER, the Houck sisters, Raechel and Jacqueline, had made the Santa Cruz-Ojai drive often enough that by the fall of 2004 it was second nature. Southbound from Santa Cruz, where they'd been living on and off for four years, you follow Route 1 down the edge of beautiful Monterey Bay until the turnoff onto Route 156 below the marina at Moss Landing. That takes you inland a few miles to southbound Route 101. After 250 miles of mixed terrain – big and small towns, lush vineyards, cattle ranches, seaside resorts, oil wells, colleges, an army base, a prison – 101 brings you to Santa Barbara, the self-proclaimed American Riviera.

Just south of Santa Barbara, after ten miles of stunning Pacific Ocean views, you turn inland on Route 150, which winds its scenic way up into the hills of the Los Padres National Forest, then down past Lake Casitas for the last switchback leg into the mountain-ringed Ojai Valley.

Ojai, home to artists and actors, retirees and spiritual seekers, also was home to the Houck girls.

Raechel Houck had reserved a rental car for the sisters' drive from Santa Cruz to Ojai on Monday, October 4, 2004. Jacqueline, her younger sister, owned an older car but they didn't think it was sound enough for long-distance travel. A rental car would be safer, more reliable for the trip to Ojai and back. An Enterprise Rent-A-Car outlet, called the Capitola branch because it was near the border between Capitola and Santa Cruz, was located on Soquel Avenue, about two miles from the bungalow the sisters shared with Jacqueline's boyfriend, Caleb Stevens, in the Opal Cliffs neighborhood of Santa Cruz. That was where Raechel had reserved the car.

Enterprise wasn't the only car rental agency in town – there were Hertz and Avis offices and some smaller local agencies – but the sisters knew that Chuck Houck, their father, was familiar with Enterprise; the Mercedes dealership in Calabasas, where he worked as a service manager, had a close connection with Enterprise and often used it to provide loaner cars for customers having their vehicles serviced or, on occasion, fixed under defect recall notices.

Enterprise's famous slogan is, "We'll Pick You Up." Two Enterprise employees, Ian Burnham and Alisha Jensen, collected Raechel at the bungalow and drove her to the rental company's office. They hit it off right away – they were all in their twenties, and Burnham and Jensen thought Raechel was "really nice."

The three young people chatted for a while before turning to the rental agreement. At 24, Raechel Houck was old enough to sign for the car, but there was a problem: recently returned from a long stay in Europe, she had no credit cards and no auto insurance. Chuck had sent the girls money to cover the rental so she wanted to pay in cash. But since Raechel was a cash customer, Enterprise policy required her to fill out a "cash/debit card qualification" form. She listed her place of employment as Catalyst Beach Bar and Grill, where she'd been waitressing for a few weeks since returning from Europe. (Her sister Jacqueline, an aspiring painter, already had been waitressing at Santa Cruz restaurants for many months while she worked at selling her art.) Raechel was listed as the only driver.

The rental almost didn't happen. Raechel "didn't have much money," Alisha Jensen recalled. "I remember she came in with a lunchbox purse, and she was counting her last pennies.... The truth is, she just didn't qualify..." The on-site manager, Andrea Avecilla, approved her anyway, "because she was such a nice girl, she lived locally, and seemed trustworthy..."

There was a surprise bonus for the girls. Instead of the cheaper car that Raechel had reserved, she was given a silver 2004-model Chrysler PT Cruiser for the same price. Not that there was a choice; it was the last car on the lot.

The PT Cruiser had been a hot seller for Chrysler since its introduction in 2001 as a "chop-top" retro entry into the new-car market. *Edmunds.com* had praised its "Hollywood style... fun to drive." *Cars.com* had gone further: "Only a few cars make a visual statement that's as strong as the PT Cruiser's proclamation. Imaginative and distinctive styling may be the main attraction... The PT Cruiser's terrific handling is confident and nimble." In federal crash tests the PT Cruiser had done reasonably well. The product, aimed at the youth market, had quickly achieved cult status.

"Wow," Raechel told her mother later, "they upgraded us!"

California's central coast weather that day was at its autumnal best – balmy, free of rainstorms, never warmer than seventy degrees or chillier than fifty. On some days at that time of year you could hit soaring temperatures along the route, particularly around Paso Robles and King City, making travel less than comfortable. Happily for drivers along the 101 on October 4, this was not one of those days.

There was much for the two young women to talk about on the drive south. In the national news, a riveting development in the 20-month-old Iraq War had been announced – a CIA report that found no evidence in Iraq of the Weapons of Mass Destruction claimed by the Bush Administration as a major justification for the U.S. attack on Iraq. And with Presidential elections just a month away, news media were reporting that Democratic contender John Kerry was outperforming President Bush in their televised debates. Locally, it had been an exciting weekend; Santa Cruz had celebrated its two hundred thirteenth birthday a day earlier, with a bash that included a huge fireworks display at Main Beach, not far from the house where the girls were staying.

But more important than the news were the family and friends they'd be visiting in and around Ojai, what they'd been doing recently with their lives, their plans for the near future. The sisters, described by those who knew them as "best friends" and "inseparable," were drawn to foreign travel.

They had made a European trip together in 2002, spending six months in Spain. Jacqueline had then returned home; Raechel had gone on to Italy to work and study. Their mother, Carol "Cally" Houck, like a third sister in her closeness to the girls, had visited Raechel there. Less than two months before their drive south, Raechel had returned to Santa Cruz. By now her Italian was so fluent that she was thinking of applying to the Italian Cultural Institute in San Francisco for certification as an interpreter, then building a career based on using the language.

In the near future Jacqueline, an accomplished equestrian, was planning to go to Costa Rica with her boyfriend Caleb, whose family lived there. In Costa Rica she intended to paint, teach art to children, and use her skills as a horse trainer and riding instructor. She and Caleb might get a small piece of property and have some horses. "I can start teaching some kids how to ride," she'd tell her father.

Their Ojai visit would allow barely enough time to see and catch up with friends and family. There was Cally, of course, their mother, friend and companion for all seasons. Jacqueline had seen her recently – just a few months earlier, actually, on the Fourth of July weekend. Cally had driven up to Santa Cruz to visit her daughter and see the Santa Cruz fireworks display, famed as one of California's more impressive pyrotechnic events. Greg, the girls' younger brother, had been with her. Raechel hadn't seen her mother or father since returning from Italy, although she'd talked with each of them on the phone every few weeks and kept in constant email touch, both while in Italy and after returning to Santa Cruz. The last time the whole family had been together was Thanksgiving a year earlier.

Cally and Chuck had divorced in 1999, so trips home usually meant visits to two households, both of them held close in the sisters' affections.

Cally now lived in Oak View, a few miles west of Ojai. She'd gotten a law degree in 1994 and maintained a solo practice in Ojai's Meiners Oaks neighborhood. Chuck and his second wife, Victoria, lived in Agoura, an hour's drive southeast of Ojai, with Victoria's two children by a former marriage. Greg lived on and off with both parents. On this trip the sisters planned to stop first in Ojai and stay with their mother overnight, then on Tuesday go to their father's place, returning to their mother's on Wednesday and heading back to Santa Cruz on Thursday, October 7.

Besides catching up with family – two families, actually – there was a host of long-cherished friends to see. For Jacqueline, there were the "stable rats," as she affectionately called the many horse-riding enthusiasts to whom she'd grown close over her years of equestrian training, both as a competitor in show events and eventually as an apprentice trainer herself. There was Laurie Canty, her trainer at Ojai's Rancho Royale stables. There were long-time friends at the Ventura County Saddle Club, where she'd often competed in events.

For Raechel, in addition to catching up with friends and family there was a special purpose for the Ojai visit. One of her closest pals, Brenna Carlson, was getting married later that autumn and had asked Raechel to be a bridesmaid. On this trip she planned to have a long visit with Brenna and get fitted for her bridesmaid's dress. She also planned to talk with her father about borrowing his cabin retreat at Big Bear Lake in the San Bernardino National Forest, three hours inland from the coast. It was quiet, remote, a good place to think about her plans for the future.

The girls reached Ojai midday and went to their mother's law office to say hello. From there they went to see a close family friend, Nancy Mason, whose daughter Melissa had been a classmate and pal of Raechel's since third grade. Melissa was away at college but Nancy, a hairdresser, had the day off. It had been awhile since she'd seen the Houck sisters; it was, Nancy recalled, a wonderful visit. "We hung out for the afternoon, talked about everything." Nancy noticed that their rental car was a PT Cruiser, still something of a novelty at the time. "I was excited about it," she recalled.

That night the sisters stayed at their mother's house. The next day they'd drive south to visit their father and his new family, then back to their mother's house on Wednesday. In between they'd catch up with as many of their school friends as possible. It would be a hectic but happy time. They'd leave for Santa Cruz on Thursday morning; the PT Cruiser was due back at Enterprise that evening.

2

The Defect

IN APRIL 2004, Chrysler mechanical engineer Jesus Francisco Trevino was alerted to an alarming safety problem, one that would consume virtually all his professional attention for the next few months.

Trevino, who had joined Chrysler a year earlier, was based at the manufacturer's Technical Center in Auburn Hills, Michigan, where he was assigned to work on the design of power steering systems for four Chrysler models – Neon, Stratus, Sebring, and PT Cruiser. Mexican by birth, he held degrees from Technologico de Monterrey and Carnegie Mellon University. He was equally comfortable speaking English with colleagues at the Tech Center and Spanish with the staff at Chrysler's facility in Toluca, Mexico.

The problem had shown up in one of the models Trevino was assigned to work on – the PT Cruiser. It seemed that something in the design of the vehicle's power steering system could allow highly volatile fluid to escape from a high-pressure feeder hose. If the fluid dripped onto a hot surface, it would ignite, causing an under-hood fire. This in turn could cause a fire in the passenger compartment. The most likely hot surface, given the location of the hose, was the vehicle's catalytic converter. Catalytic converters reach on-the-road temperatures of well over 1000 degrees Fahrenheit.

"When I was informed of this [fluid leakage] issue, [management] asked me to put all other of my engineering tasks as a second priority," Trevino said later. "They decided that my time was better spent focusing on this issue." He recalled that his supervisor, Sarah Harding, a Chrysler quality control executive, told him that "we had an issue that sometimes this hose was being abraded and sometimes these abrasions caused leaks. She wanted me to investigate why this was happening and she wanted for me to investigate how we could solve it... These two specific questions I was responsible to answer."

Although the leaks also could disable the car's power steering – and thus cause partial loss of driver control - the bottom-line issue was fire, a dreaded hazard anytime but more so when it erupts in a moving motor vehicle. Fire was not mentioned to Trevino, however; he was told euphemistically that the leaks could cause "thermal events." He knew what that meant.

This was Trevino's first involvement with a potential safety defect. As he was turning his attention to the PT Cruiser "thermal event" problem in April, a government investigation of the same hazard was already underway. On March 15, the National Highway Traffic Safety Administration (NHTSA) had initiated what is called a Preliminary Evaluation (PE) – the first step in the agency's process to determine the existence of auto safety defects. The investigation covered model years 2001, 2002 and 2003. It would shortly be expanded to cover 2004 models, which had the identical design flaw.

"PE04028," as the investigation was labeled, was triggered by complaints from owners of 2001-2003 PT Cruisers reporting that the engine compartments of their vehicles had burst into flame. Some of the complaints reported total destruction of PT Cruisers by fire due to the leakage of flammable power steering fluid from abraded hoses onto hot surfaces. In PE04028, NHTSA engineers and lawyers would evaluate the complaints, seek more information from Chrysler, and, if warranted, upgrade the PE to an Engineering Analysis (EA) – the final step in determining whether a recall is warranted.

NHTSA's defect investigation and notification powers date from early in the history of the auto safety regulatory program. The initial Federal statute setting up the program, Public Law 89-563, enacted in September 1966, required that manufacturers must notify vehicle owners of "any defect" in their vehicles which "relates to motor vehicle safety," and do so "within a reasonable time" after the defect is discovered. Since then there have been changes in the law and in NHTSA's regulations carrying it out – importantly, manufacturers now are required to repair any such defects at their own expense – but its purpose remains intact.

Under current practice, manufacturers generally decide to initiate safety defect recalls without waiting for an order from NHTSA. They may do so on the basis of such factors as complaints received by the company, by NHTSA, or by both, as well as evidence developed by the agency's technical staff or by engineers within the company itself. Although these company-initiated recalls are referred to as "voluntary" by industry and NHTSA personnel, they are simply instances of a company's correcting a violation of law prior to being ordered to do so. Between 350 and 600 recalls are carried out each year, most of them "voluntary." These involve anywhere from 8 million to 30 million motor vehicles and components annually.

Trevino apparently had not been told by management that as part of its PE04028 probe, NHTSA on March 25 had sent Chrysler a detailed interrogatory about the PT Cruiser fire hazard. Addressed to Stephan Speth, Chrysler's director of vehicle compliance and safety affairs, and signed by Jeffrey Quandt, a senior staffer in the agency's Office of Defects Investigation, the interrogatory stated that NHTSA had received nine reports of engine fires in 2001 PT Cruisers alone. "None of the owners reported any prior warning of fire," it said. "Two of the incidents resulted in injuries to the drivers, one due to burns on the driver's head and both due to smoke inhalation. At least seven of the nine incidents involved vehicles that were totaled and one involved a vehicle that incurred $8,000 of fire damage."

The interrogatory directed Chrysler to submit to NHTSA a long list of documents, including all reports it had received of deaths, injuries, property damage, fire, or lawsuits which "may relate to the alleged defect in MY 2001-2003 PT Cruisers vehicles," consumer complaints, warranty claims, lawsuits, and field reports from dealer or other sources; the number of PT Cruisers manufactured in those model years for sale or lease in the U.S., and the manufacturer's "assessment of the problem, with a summary of the significant underlying facts and evidence."

It also instructed Chrysler to "describe in detail" its criteria for collecting this information within the company. (Manufacturers have been known on occasion to abuse discovery requirements by arbitrarily limiting the scope of their searches for internal defect-related documents sought by NHTSA investigators or by plaintiffs during discovery in injury lawsuits, thereby concealing key, possibly incriminating information.) Further, the NHTSA interrogatory asked for samples of both new PT Cruiser power-steering component parts and "field return components exhibiting any failure mode related to the alleged defect in the subject vehicles." Chrysler was directed to produce the information and parts within six weeks.

Proceeding independently of the NHTSA investigators, Trevino began looking at real-world PT Cruisers in an effort to find the problem and determine how he could meet Sarah Harding's mandate to "solve it." Working with Harding and Chrysler lab technicians and designers, he secured fifty exemplar cars from the company motor pool and from other Chrysler employees who owned PT Cruisers. He ran them on the Tech Center test track, examined them on hoists in the mock-up garage, and dismantled and studied their power steering fluid hoses and brackets in search of a key to the defect's cause.

His first conclusion was that engine roll – the slight side-to-side movement of the engine block while a car is in motion - was causing the power steering system's pressure hose on some PT Cruisers to rub against the crankcase. "So we knew it was a problem with the engine rolling and pulling and hitting against this this hose," he said later. "I don't remember the exact moment that I saw the, this interference happening, but I think during the course of our first vehicles that we were examining we saw that there was a correlation between the edge of the crankcase and the way the abrasions were on the steering hose."

An initial idea proposed by some Chrysler engineers for dealing with the problem was to put a rubber or foam grommet, or "doughnut," around the hose to alleviate the friction. "We shot that down rather quickly," Trevino recalled, because the grommet would not hold up for long and the friction problem would reemerge. Trevino then considered the possibility that the solution would require a longer hose, to eliminate contact between it and the crankcase. But after further study he decided that "the overall length of the hose was correct. It was just the effective length between the last bracket to the steering gear rack, which was not long enough to accommodate engine roll... The complete hose length was correct. The brackets were correct. It was just that with the manufacturing variation we should have established our tolerances... so that we could make sure that, that this length was long enough to accommodate engine roll... It was a defect, it was, was, a mistake on the, on the way we established the tolerances of this hose."

Two hose-clamp brackets secured the hose to the rear of the engine. Most of the time the hose and bracket design "worked perfectly fine," Trevino decided, but in some "rare instances," contact would occur between the hose and the crankcase because of the incorrect tolerances. This could lead to abrasion of the hose and fluid leakage. He hadn't been involved in the initial design and he didn't know who had been. But he now knew how to fix the defect it had led to: move the brackets to create more slack in the existing belt.

Once Trevino had concluded that the positioning of the brackets was critical, "we went ahead and issued an Interim Authorization Approval (IAA), which is a kind of change notice, to relocate these brackets." The IAA established new positions for the hose brackets, using so-called "geometric distance and tolerance" measurements that Trevino had developed for the components. These would ensure sufficient space between the hose and the crankcase and eliminate the potential for an abrasion-and-leak hazard.

The assembly point for the PT Cruiser was Chrysler's plant in Toluca de Lerdo, Mexico, an hour's drive southwest of Mexico City. On the day the IAA was issued, Trevino flew to Toluca with his blueprints of the new geometric and tolerance measurements, his notes, and a copy of the IAA. He spent three days working with engineers and technicians at the plant to develop and apply the bracket relocation procedure for PT Cruisers that were still on the assembly line or already in the warehouse. He approved 90 hours of overtime for staff work needed to implement the defect fix, at a cost of $2,250. Then he returned to Michigan.

Trevino's fix would apply to nearly half a million PT Cruisers, model years 2001-2004, that were in production, in dealership inventories, or already sold to individual customers and corporate fleet buyers such as Enterprise Rent-A-Car.

As Trevino was implementing the fix, Chrysler officials and NHTSA investigators in Washington were moving closer to a recall of the affected vehicles. On May 7, Speth sent a detailed response to NHTSA's interrogatory of March 25, consisting of a cover letter and attachments. The one-page cover letter stated, rather opaquely, that "the most likely source contributing to the reports included in the inquiry is related to routing of the high pressure power steering hose on certain powertrain combinations of the subject vehicles." The words "leak" and "fire" were not used. Chrysler "will continue to investigate this alleged issue and provide updates as they become available," the letter concluded.

The letter's 12-page attachment was more revealing. Describing the "alleged condition" as "a possible under-hood fire," it disclosed that Chrysler knew of "a total of 218 customer complaints, which include seven NHTSA reports (VOQs) that may relate to the alleged condition... a total of 118 relate to power steering leaks and 100 suggest a vehicle fire." When lawsuits, field reports and legal claims related to the "alleged condition" were added in, it said, the total rose to 279. No deaths or serious injuries had been reported so far.

For the condition to occur, the attachment said, three circumstances were needed: It was necessary that the power steering fluid "leak under high pressure in a specific air/fluid proportional mix," that the fluid's path allow it to "contact the exhaust manifold or catalyst surfaces during a state of elevated temperature," and that there be "unique air flow characteristics" near the heat source. What those characteristics had to be was not specified.

"Based on preliminary evaluation and investigation," the attachment concluded, Chrysler "has determined that in rare instances, the routing of the high pressure power steering hose on certain powertrain combinations of the subject vehicles (2.4LK naturally aspirated gasoline engine with automatic transaxle) may contribute to a possible under-hood fire... Because of the unique manner in which an under-hood fire develops and gradually progresses in the affected vehicles, it is not likely that the condition would result in death, injury, or vehicle crash." It made no mention of Trevino's fix and its implementation at the Toluca plant. Nor did it mention the hazard associated with a driver losing control of the vehicle due to loss of power steering.

On June 18, Speth sent a second letter to NHTSA. It reported a slight increase in the number of records of incidents that "may relate to the alleged condition," based on Chrysler's "recent conversations" with a NHTSA investigator assigned to the case. The conversations apparently had convinced Chrysler that NHTSA would push for a recall of the defective PT Cruisers, for on the same day, NHTSA closed its investigation with a one-page document revealing that two weeks earlier Chrysler had "notified NHTSA of a safety defect in MY 2001-2005 PT Cruiser vehicles equipped with naturally aspirated 2.4l engines and automatic transaxles (Recall 04V-268)" and now would "instruct owners to bring their vehicles to a dealer to have the power steering hose assembly inspected and relocated, or replaced, as necessary..."

Chrysler had now admitted to a safety-related defect in PT Cruisers manufactured and sold over a five-year period – a hazard that imperiled the lives of drivers and passengers travelling in those vehicles by exposing them to fire. It was compelled to recall the vehicles and fix the problem at its own expense, or be in violation of federal laws and regulations.

On September 9, five months after assigning Jesus Trevino to find a fix for the problem and three months after acknowledging to NHTSA that the problem constituted a safety defect, Chrysler notified the agency that on September 20, 2004 it would begin a general recall – "DaimlerChrysler Recall D18" – of 435,000 PT Cruisers with the suspect power steering hose configuration. Notices would be sent to all vehicle owners, alerting them to the fire hazard and directing them to "contact your dealer right away to schedule a service appointment." At the dealer, thirty minutes would be required to inspect the hose. "Replacement, if necessary, will require another hour." At the same time – as required by law – Chrysler dealers would be instructed not to sell recalled PT Cruisers until their defect had been fixed.

But the manufacturer did not wait until September 20 to send defect notifications to fleet owners of PT Cruisers. Also on September 9, it emailed alerts to officials of more than fifty fleets, including those operated by governments, major corporations, public utilities, and car rental agencies who had purchased PT Cruiser models from Chrysler.

One of the recipients was Bob Agnew, Enterprise Rent-A-Car's national service manager.

3

THE CRASH

SINCE ARRIVING IN Ojai on Monday, the Houck sisters had been kept busy with visits to friends and family. On Monday, after visiting Nancy Mason, they spent the evening with their mother. The next day they drove south to Westlake Village to see their father, his family, and their brother Greg. On Wednesday morning they returned to Ojai for more visits with friends.

That evening Jacqueline had dinner with Laurie Canty, her equestrian trainer, and Laurie's husband Billy. Raechel joined a group of friends at Billy O's Restaurant & Saloon in nearby Ventura for a farewell visit. The next morning she stopped in to see a few friends in Ventura and Ojai. Just before heading for Santa Cruz she dropped by Nancy Mason's nearby beauty salon to say goodbye. Nancy told her, "Come back before the wedding, I'll do your hair."

Raechel and Jacqueline Houck left Ojai midday Thursday, Oct. 7 for the 300-mile return trip north. The weather was clear; traffic on northbound 101 was moving well. If all went smoothly they'd be in Santa Cruz in time to drop off the rented PT Cruiser at Enterprise that evening.

For the first 150 miles or so the trip was uneventful. By 4:30 p.m. they had passed the town of Paso Robles, in San Luis Obispo County, and were more than halfway home. Shortly before five p.m. they passed the turn-off for the town of San Miguel, where a stark, lonely ruin of a Spanish mission bell-tower flanks the highway, and crossed the border into Monterey County.

At a point a few miles north of San Miguel the highway transects Camp Roberts, a forty-two-thousand acre military reservation whose terrain along 101 is dominated by rolling hills, grassland, and scrub trees. The Nacimiento River, flowing westward across Camp Roberts into Lake Nacimiento, passes under 101 near this point. The roadway along this stretch is flat and straight, with a speed limit of 70 miles per hour for cars, 55 miles per hour for trucks. Northbound and southbound vehicles, travelling in two lanes each way, are separated by a 30-foot-wide grassy median. A rest area serving northbound travelers lies slightly beyond the river crossing. Another, serving southbound traffic, lies a mile further on. Nearby is the small town of Bradley.

As the Houck car approached the northbound rest area, something went horribly wrong.

Carlos Woods was driving a southbound Freightliner Century tractor pulling a refrigerated trailer. His co-driver Richard Woods, who was also his cousin, was napping in the sleeper berth behind the driver's seat. The 18-wheeler had left Salinas with a partial load of produce a few hours earlier and was headed south to Los Angeles to pick up more freight for Gorvack Transporting, the Florida company that owned the rig. Moments after Woods passed the southbound rest area, he recalled, it happened:

"I saw some smoke and that got my attention and I looked over to the left and by the time I looked over to the left I seen a car turned like an angle and start heading towards the median, so I knew something was wrong, so I locked the brakes up on it, on the truck... And by then they had got in the median... I'm already on the brakes all the way down, just sliding. And basically the car kept sliding across kicking up dust... I just knew it was just going to come on over towards me, so I steered right to try to steer away from it."

The Houck PT Cruiser had suddenly and, it seemed, inexplicably veered leftwards off the northbound roadway and was hurtling across the median toward Woods's oncoming truck. Woods wrestled to redirect the truck away from the car's trajectory, but it was too late. In a split-second the two vehicles met head-on. It sounded to Woods like "everything just blew up." The violence of the crash broke the truck's windshield; shards of glass flew into his face. When his vision cleared he could no longer see the PT Cruiser.

"Well, after the impact it just, like a cloud of smoke, fire, by then the truck had went from the shoulder of the road over to the median and we was trying to get out but the doors were jammed at first. And we finally got the door open, and we got to get out on the passenger side. And once we got out on the passenger side we got, ran over towards the shoulder trying to figure out which way the car went because we really couldn't see anything at that time," Woods recalled.

Esther Kosty was on her way north to her home in King City, about 30 miles north of the crash site, from her job as office manager at a vineyard management company near Paso Robles. She was leaving the northbound rest area after a brief stop. As she drove down the rest area exit ramp and was preparing to merge into 101 traffic, she heard "a big boom, crash" and saw "a PT Cruiser embedded in the front end of a semi... It was in the median, between the northbound and the southbound lane." The PT Cruiser was engulfed in flames.

Kosty pulled her car over to the shoulder of the ramp and dialed 911. She tried to tell the dispatcher where the crash had occurred but, shaken by the sight of the burning car, she couldn't remember the name "Camp Roberts." In frustration, she yelled that the crash was in the median in front of a rest area near a military camp. As she watched, someone jumped from the passenger side of the truck and ran. Another motorist appeared with a fire extinguisher but after trying to approach the crashed and burning vehicles, he backed off. As Kosty watched, "Things were exploding... The whole thing was inflamed [sic]." The fire "had gone all the way through" the car. As the fire grew more intense Kosty heard more explosions from the direction of the crash.

A few hours earlier Denise Schafer and her friend Candy Lindquist, en route from Los Angeles to Spokane, had stopped in Santa Barbara for lunch and some shopping. After leaving Santa Barbara on northbound

101, they had become vaguely aware of a silver PT Cruiser in the cluster
of traffic around them. "You know, as you drive sometimes you're, you
know, with the same pack of cars, and you know, we would pass them
and then they would pass us." She'd noticed the PT Cruiser in particular
"because you don't see them very often."

Schafer had lost sight of the PT Cruiser when, as they neared the
northbound rest area, "all of a sudden I saw – as I was driving I saw
the semi-truck sliding into the median, and I thought at first it was the
truck, the semi-truck, on fire, the cab on fire. And then it was Candy, my
friend, who – passenger, who said, 'it's the PT Cruiser.' And that's when
I realized that it was the PT Cruiser in the front of the semi-truck... The
next thing that I remember are the two men who were in the semi-truck
jumping out of the truck."

The PT Cruiser had plowed under the front end of the 18-wheeler.
Schafer could see that the car's rear tires "were just right up against the
grill of the semi... It was just totally in flames."

She pulled over to the right side of the road – "Everyone was pulling over" – and called 911. The dispatcher told her they knew about the
crash and the police were on their way. Then "I got out of the car and
wanted – I guess Candy said that it's the PT Cruiser, and so I got out of
the car to, in craziness thinking that maybe there was something someone could do." The two women were moving toward the median with
the idea of somehow helping but "by that time, you know, people were
saying to get back and stuff, so we never really went over there. And it
was obvious there wasn't anything we could do, unfortunately."

The first police officer to arrive on the scene was Russell Deases, who
worked out of the California Highway Patrol office in King City. Assigned
to patrol a 25-mile stretch of 101 that took in San Miguel, Bradley, and the
rest area, he had been on the road since 2 p.m. At a few minutes before
5 p.m., heading north on 101 not far from San Miguel, he saw "a large
column of black smoke" ahead of him.

"Upon cresting a rise in the roadway just south of the fire, I observed
a big rig and another vehicle fully engulfed in flames in the center

divider. As I reached for my radio microphone, dispatch advised me of the head-on collision." He reached the scene moments later, but "I was unable to get close to the vehicles due to the intensity of the fire."

Within minutes, firemen and equipment from the Camp Roberts Fire Department and the California Department of Forestry station in Bradley had arrived. Soon they were followed by four more CHP officers – Douglas Finch, Darrell Mackinga, William Stratman and Anthony McFarland – and Detective Andrew Kopicki, an investigator from the Monterey County coroner's office. A CHP helicopter circled overhead; an officer in the 'copter took pictures of the site. Ambulances arrived and stood by to transport any injured survivors of the crash.

The trailer of Woods's rig was sprawled across most of southbound 101. The tractor jutted into the median, the PT Cruiser partially buried under its nose. Police closed the southbound lanes to traffic while the firefighters attempted to bring the blaze under control. Woods and his cousin were standing, stunned, by the side of the road. After they assured Deases there were no other occupants in the burning truck cab, an ambulance took them to Twin Cities Hospital in San Luis Obispo to be treated for minor injuries.

By now the police officers had cleared the area of bystanders and Deases was assessing the crash based on witness statements and the post-collision location of the PT Cruiser, labeled "Vehicle #1" in his subsequent report, and the 18-wheeler, or "Vehicle #2":

"For reasons unknown, Vehicle #1 swerved to the left and crossed over the dirt center median into oncoming traffic... and a head-on collision occurred in the no. 2 [outer] lane of southbound US 101. Both vehicles became engulfed in flames as they continued to travel southbound. Vehicle #2's momentum forced both Vehicle #1 and Vehicle #2 across the #2 and #1 lanes into the center divide where they both came to rest...Vehicle #1 (PT Cruiser) was located in an upright position under Vehicle #2's (Freightliner) engine compartment which was fully engulfed in flames facing in a northwesterly direction upon my arrival. Vehicle #1's passenger compartment (roof and all four doors) had been compressed back into the rear seat. Vehicle #1's engine compartment, firewall, and hood were pushed back into the front seating positions. All four of Vehicle #1's tires had been incinerated completely in the fire."

The truck's tractor and cab also were "fully engulfed in flames" and sustained "total fire damage." Its passenger compartment had melted and burned in the fire. "All interior items (seats, sleeper bunks, storage area and dash) were incinerated... front tires had been incinerated completely." All that remained of the tractor was the engine block, protruding frame, and front axle and wheel assemblies.

Visible within the PT Cruiser were the bodies of Raechel and Jacqueline Houck, pinned under the truck's engine compartment – "badly damaged traumatically and burned," according to Kopicki of the coroner's office. "I removed the bodies from the wreckage with the assistance of the firemen and the Coroner's contracted removal service personnel." Both bodies were burned beyond recognition. In the scorched remains of a wallet in Raechel's pocket, the officers found enough of her driver's license to provide them with identification.

When autopsies were performed the next morning the coroner would determine that both sisters had died of "massive blunt force injuries" that were "virtually instantly fatal." The fire had not caused their deaths, he concluded.

The last CPH officer to arrive at the scene, Michael Schad, had not gone on duty until 8:30 p.m. that evening, some three and a half hours after the crash. Schad was directed to go to the crash site and prepare a factual diagram – a schematic mapping of the vehicles' location and measurements; location of physical evidence such as skid marks, road and median dimensions, and roadway terrain leading up to and away from the site. When he arrived he found that although firemen were still there, the fire had been put out. He watched as tow trucks lifted the semi up and off the PT Cruiser and took away the car's burnt-out remains. Then he walked the scene, making spray-paint marks at key points on the ground. "Once the roadway was clear and traffic had – the roadway was clear of the emergency vehicles as well as the other CHP officers and the tow trucks, the traffic thinned out quite a bit, and I believe it was – as I recall later in the evening, probably ten or eleven, I started making – I believe I may have finished with all the paint marks... I tried to make sure I painted the whole scene before I took measurements."

By now it was dark and Schad needed a flashlight to continue his work. He was unable to precisely diagram the point at which the PT Cruiser had come to rest, which had earlier been marked with orange spray paint by another officer. "...once the tow truck driver pulled the vehicle out from underneath the semi truck it took away the orange paint so I wasn't able to correctly locate that." He made an estimate of the point using the scorch marks left by the car on the grassy median. He located what appeared to be a drivetrain part that had separated from the PT Cruiser at some point – a differential assembly, as another officer described it to him – and marked it on the diagram. He saw patches of fluid on the ground, including "a tremendous fluid mark at the beginning of the area of the impact all the way the entire route of the path of Vehicle #2," but didn't note these on the diagram because it was difficult to determine whether they were produced by one or the other of the crash vehicles, or by the fire-fighting effort, or were bodily fluids from one of the fatalities.

It was close to midnight before Deases and Schad finished their work and left the site. The remains of the PT Cruiser and the tractor-trailer had been towed away and put in storage. Traffic was again flowing in both directions on 101.

The next day Deases started to write his report, in which he would conclude, "Party #1 (Houck) caused this collision by making an unsafe turning movement to the left, crossing through the center divider, and colliding with a Big Rig. This is a violation of section 22107 Vehicle Code which states: No person shall turn a vehicle from a direct course or move right or left upon a roadway until such movement can be made with reasonable safety." He could not know what had caused Raechel Houck to make that unsafe, fatal turning movement.

4

THE PHONE CALL

AROUND NINE O'CLOCK on the evening of the crash, Cally Houck's phone rang. It was Caleb Stevens, Jacqueline's boyfriend, calling to say the sisters had not yet returned. He wondered where they might be. Cally assured him that "they probably just stopped to get something to eat." It would not be unusual, she knew, for the girls to stop at a restaurant or at one of the many beaches that line the coast along the route to Santa Cruz.

Just after one a.m. the next morning the phone rang again. Cally was asleep; her companion, Carl Nienaber, answered it. A California Highway Patrol officer was on the line. The CHP had contacted Caleb after determining that the sisters were living at his home. From Caleb they had learned Cally's phone number. The CHP officer told Carl he was calling to inform Mrs. Houck that her daughters had been killed in a car crash late the previous afternoon.

Before waking Cally, Carl phoned the home of Nancy and Glenn Mason, neighbors and long-time friends of the Houcks. It was Nancy Mason whom the Houck sisters had visited on arriving in Ojai the previous Monday.

Glenn answered the phone. Carl was "badly shaken – he was trying to tell me but he was just having a really hard time," Glenn recalled. Carl asked them to come to the house and be there to provide support for Cally when she woke up and learned of her daughters' deaths. Glenn told Nancy, and they then called two more of Cally's close friends who lived in Ojai, Kim Armstrong and Ann Whitten. The three women went to the Houck home. By the time they arrived, Cally was awake.

"At that point, when we walked through the door, Carl was trying to pretend that… it was just too hard, I don't know what we were trying to do," Nancy said later. "It was all a blur."

At first Cally couldn't believe what they were telling her. She knew that Raechel was "a very diligent and vigilant driver." It seemed inconceivable that her daughter could have been in a severe crash. But when she called the CHP officer, he confirmed that indeed, Raechel and Jacqueline had died the previous afternoon in a head-on collision with a semitrailer on their way back to Santa Cruz.

Soon afterwards, two police officers from nearby Ventura, one of them a chaplain, showed up at Cally's door to deliver the same grim information. Nancy and Kim stayed with Cally and Carl through the night, praying and "crying and walking in circles." It was "surreal, we were in denial," Carl remembered.

A call from Ann Whitten earlier in the evening had led to Chuck learning of his daughters' deaths. Ann had phoned her husband Blair, who was staying at a guest house on Chuck's property in Westlake Village. Blair often stayed there during the week; although he and Ann lived in Ojai, he worked at Calabasas Mercedes, where Chuck, a close friend, was sales manager. It was only a few miles from Westlake Village, so staying at Chuck's during the week saved him the long daily commute to and from Ojai, which was 60 miles north.

"You never want to get that call to have to tell your best friend that both his daughters are dead," Blair said later. "I had a hundred yards from the guest house to the main house to try and figure out what to tell Chuck…" Ann had said there'd been "a horrific crash. The girls were killed." But "being secondhand information, all this is going through my mind as I am racing to the house, what if it was just a horrific crash, what if the girls are still alive? "

He reached the house and banged on Chuck's door. There's been a terrible crash, he told Chuck, but he couldn't tell him the girls were dead. At some point after that, Chuck and Cally talked by phone. Then Chuck put in calls to the CHP and the Monterey County Sheriff Coroner's Division, where his daughters' deaths were confirmed.

It was three o'clock that morning before Chuck finished making phone calls to family, close friends and the authorities. The Monterey coroner's morgue in Salinas had informed him they were in possession of both bodies and that he needed to designate a mortuary to which the bodies could be released. The next morning he and Blair, "still in a state of shock," went to the Ted Mayr Funeral Home in Ventura and made the arrangements.

Starting the evening of the crash, reports of the Houck sisters' violent deaths began to appear in news outlets along the route between Santa Cruz and Ojai. The first report was a terse news item, headlined "One Killed in Highway Crash...," that appeared that evening on the website of KSBW Channel 8, the Hearst television outlet for California's Central Coast:

"At least one person was killed in Monterey County Thursday night after a big rig and a car crashed head-on. The crash happened on Highway 101, just south of King City near the Camp Roberts area. CHP officials said the big rig and a Chrysler PT Cruiser both caught on fire after the crash, and flames spread to the center divider, causing serious traffic delays."

An update appeared the following night:

"The names of two people killed in a car crash in south Monterey County Thursday evening have been released. According to authorities, the victims are 24-year-old Rachael Houck, who was driving, and 20-year-old Jacqueline Houck – both from Santa Cruz..."

Other coverage followed over the next weeks. The Salinas *Californian,* the *Monterey Herald,* the Santa Cruz *Sentinel* and the *Ojai Valley News* carried extensive reports of the crash, with a heavy emphasis on the shock being felt by the sisters' friends at their deaths and the deep affection in which they had been held. "When the sisters were together, they were just inseparable," Jacqueline's boyfriend Caleb Stevens told the Ojai paper. "They really touched a lot of people everywhere they went, all around the world. They had such high energy, no one could help but be involved in whatever they were doing."

Seeking an explanation for the deaths, a reporter for the Santa Cruz *Sentinal* interviewed a CPH spokesman, Daniel Wheeler.

"Accidents along that open stretch of Highway 101 are not uncommon," Wheeler told her. "There were six fatalities there last year and 13 fatal wrecks to far this year...

"'It's a very rural stretch and people can fall asleep or lose control easily or not pay attention,' Wheeler said.... 'And usually when they lose control, they'll try to overcompensate and swerve back, and that's when they either overturn or roll.'"

In the story, Wheeler was quoted as cautioning that that it was premature to determine what had caused the Houck collision. Nonetheless, the reporter pointedly concluded the article by recalling a crash a few months earlier on a nearby stretch of 101. In that crash, a young woman from Santa Cruz had been ejected and killed when the driver, her boyfriend, "closed his eyes for a moment and lost control of the car."

▲ ▲ ▲

Since graduating from the Denver Automotive and Diesel College in 1973, Chuck Houck had spent his entire career in the automotive service field working at dealerships, first as a mechanic and then as a service advisor and service manager. When his daughters were killed in the crash of a Chrysler PT Cruiser, he had been working as a service manager for some years at Calabasas Motor Cars, a Mercedes-Benz dealership in southern California. Mercedes-Benz's parent company, Daimler-Benz AG, had "merged" with Chrysler Corporation in 1998. (Some alleged the transaction was not a true merger but a *de facto* take-over of the cash-rich U.S. company by the German one. It would end nine years later with

Daimler-Benz's spinoff of Chrysler to Cerberus Capital Management, a giant equity investment firm.)

A few weeks after the crash, a service advisor showed Chuck a defect recall notice involving Chrysler PT Cruisers. The advisor, Art Simcox, had been given the notice by one of the service technicians, Norberto Morales.

"Norberto had two PT cruisers and he got recalls, I believe, on both of them," Chuck said later. "And he brought this to Art Simcox to give to me 'cause he thought that maybe that's what happened to the girls... sounded like what happened with the accident. And so that's when Art gave that to me." Morales had received the notices in the mail from Chrysler, which was required by law to notify all owners of the possibly defective PT Cruisers.

Chuck read the recall notice. Then, "I went on to the National Highway Traffic Safety Administration [web] site and read more about the thing. There were seven or eight accidents on the site" involving the PT Cruiser defect.

"What I remember about it is what it talked about, the power steering hose, I remember the picture, I can't remember the actual – whether there's a transaxle or what, where it wears a hole through the power steering hose, and that lets an atomized spray of oil come out onto the catalytic converter, and if it's warm enough, if it's hot enough, it will immediately ignite, causing a fire." He recalled that from reading the police report of the accident, it seemed that "the car, for no apparent reason, went to the left and hit a big rig truck head-on and burst into flames."

Enterprise maintained an office on the premises of Calabasas Motor Cars; the dealership's service personnel sometimes used the rental office to acquire loaner cars for customers whose cars were tied up in repair, including repair of defects that had triggered recalls. Chuck asked someone at the office for a copy of the contract covering his daughters' rental of the PT Cruiser. An Enterprise employee printed out a copy of the contract from Enterprise's central data system and gave it to Chuck.

From the contract, Chuck was able to retrieve the PT Cruiser's Vehicle Identification Number, or "VIN." Every car manufactured for sale in the United States is given a unique 17-character code designation containing numerals and letters which, when deciphered, provides basic information about the vehicle – its manufacturer, place of origin, date of manufacture, vehicle type, etc. The VIN appears on the vehicle's title and registration, and also is inscribed on parts of the vehicle itself, including the engine, instrument panel and door frame. VINs are critical to the effective conduct of defect recall campaigns; in every recall, the manufacturer indicates the range of VINs that may include vehicles potentially afflicted with the defect, and under law it must keep records indicating which of the vehicles have been brought into dealers for repair and which still remain on the road unrepaired.

Like every other new-car dealer, Calabasas Motor Cars had access to the database websites maintained by the manufacturers whose cars it sold, including detailed information about product recalls. With the VIN of the Enterprise car rented to his daughters in hand, Chuck went to the computer, opened the Chrysler defect database and searched for the answers to two questions: Was the car rented to his daughters by Enterprise one of the PT Cruisers involved in the recall? And if so, had it been repaired? The answer to the first question was Yes; to the second, No. Chrysler had sold Enterprise a dangerously defective vehicle, and knowingly or not, Enterprise had rented it to Raechel and Jacqueline Houck without repairing it.

Meanwhile, Cally Houck had separately learned that some PT Cruisers had been recalled for a safety defect. "Here's what I found," her friend Jessica Standley told her in an email in mid-October. Pasted in below this note was the text of the recall notice issued by Chrysler, including the warning, "Power steering fluid leakage in the presence of an ignition source can result in an under-hood fire."

It was time to consult an attorney.

5

GRASSINI AND WRINKLE

WHEN YOU SUSPECT that your daughters have been wrongfully killed in the crash of a defective car manufactured by one huge business entity and rented to them by another, what kind of lawyer should you be looking for?

In criminal law, the interchangeable terms *trial lawyer* and *defense attorney* have unambiguous meanings. Both describe a lawyer who defends people being prosecuted by government for the alleged commission of crimes. But other than under rare conditions, corporations aren't charged with crimes when their conduct kills people. The arena in which people such as the Houck parents must seek redress is that of civil law. If redress comes, it comes in the form of monetary damages assessed from defendants. Nobody goes to jail.

The term *trial lawyer*, while clear in criminal law, becomes less so in civil law. *Trial lawyer* in the civil court system often refers to an attorney who initiates litigation on behalf of a private plaintiff - but not always. A less equivocal term, *plaintiff's attorney*, is often applied to lawyers who represent claimants alleging physical harm caused by a corporate or private party. *Personal injury attorney* is sometimes used synonymously.

The American Association of Justice (AAJ), formerly called the Association of Trial Lawyers of America, says it is "the collective voice of the trial bar" and provides support to its "plaintiff trial lawyer" members, whose dues and contributions largely fund the organization. AAJ describes its members' mission as ensuring "that any person who is injured by the misconduct or negligence of others can obtain justice in America's courtrooms, even when taking on the most powerful interests." The association says its membership "promotes justice and fairness for injured persons, safeguards victims' rights – particularly the right to trial by jury – and strengthens the civil justice system through education and disclosure of information critical to public health and safety." Although it accepts membership from all lawyers, AAJ's most desirable member category – the only one that provides access to litigation strategy resources available from the association's member groups and document collections – is limited to individuals and firms who represent "plaintiff in civil litigation or defendant in criminal litigation for the most part, based on caseload and time." Members' names are public.

Supporters of so-called tort reform measures – proposals to restrict access to the civil courts by parties claiming harm from corporations – take a hostile view of the civil justice system. The American Tort Reform Association (ATRA) is a national-level organization funded heavily by large corporate members whose identities it does not disclose. It asserts that lawsuits brought against corporations for allegedly harming people are "bad for business; they are also bad for society." The right-wing Manhattan Institute's Center for Legal Policy, a vigorous tort reform advocate, asserts that "America's litigation system reduces innovation and investment, lowers safety and well-being, and erodes the risk-taking and personal responsibility essential to our free society." Enterprise Holdings, the parent of family-owned Enterprise Rent-A-Car, lobbies on behalf of federal tort-reform legislation.

Despite tort-reformer assertions that "aggressive" plaintiff's attorneys "systematically recruit clients" so they can "target certain professions, industries and individual companies" by suing them, it is actually not a simple matter for aggrieved victims of product-caused injuries or their survivors to find effective legal representation against a large corporation. To qualify, a plaintiff's law firm must meet a number of criteria. It must possess the dedication and financial wherewithal to pursue what may turn out to be a long and costly lawsuit; plaintiff's attorneys usually work under contingency fee arrangements in which the attorneys fund the case and the clients pay only if it is satisfactorily tried or settled. The firm must be willing to take on such a lawsuit, which may not be possible if the firm's workload is already at capacity. It must have a positive track record – a history of prevailing in cases against corporations with unlimited funds and legal resources for defending against injury litigation, and of resisting low-ball, easy-settlement offers from defendants along the way. And finally, it must, on the basis of little more than first impression, believe in the case – believe that it is meritorious and has a chance of succeeding at trial if it does not settle first.

In late 2004 the Houcks were referred by an attorney friend to a plaintiff's law firm in the Woodland Hills area of Greater Los Angeles that met these criteria. Grassini & Wrinkle was a small practice with an impressive history of successful cases and a singular make-up. Its two partners, Larry Grassini and Roland Wrinkle, had been together for four decades – a record in a profession where law firm partnerships often splinter after only a few years.

Although the two men collaborated throughout the course of every case handled by the firm, Grassini's emphasis was on arguing cases at trial, while Wrinkle's was on appellate matters – taking cases lost at the trial-court level to higher courts, and arguing against defense appeals, common in product liability litigation, aimed at overturning successful lower-court decisions. Grassini was a member of the prestigious Inner Circle of Advocates, a 100-member group of highly successful trial attorneys, and held in high regard not only by other plaintiff lawyers but by defense attorneys and judges as well. The firm rarely lost its cases, and never its appeals.

Over the years Grassini and Wrinkle had become close both personally and professionally, not only because they worked together but because of symmetries in their backgrounds and interests. Both men were religiously observant, Wrinkle as a Presbyterian who conducted Bible studies at his church, Grassini as a Catholic so devout that his mother had thought he might become a priest. The two families socialized and sometimes vacationed together. As lawyers, the two partners' respect for each other was almost palpable to an observer.

At first Cally Houck had reservations about going forward with a lawsuit. She recalled that unlike Chuck, she initially was indifferent to the idea of litigating. As an attorney and a mother, she believed that "justice would not be served by a lawsuit" – it would be about money, not the accountability of the defendants. Worse, she foresaw that DaimlerChrysler and Enterprise would do everything possible to avoid taking responsibility for her daughters' deaths by blaming them. "They would try to pin it on Raechel. 'Yes, we rented her a defective car but the defect didn't cause the accident.' That would be the whole case. I felt that coming and I knew there was going to be an attack on my daughter's character. They were going to make insinuations, ask whether she was on drugs, was an alcoholic, and start to kind of sway the whole thing toward driver error, because that's all they had."

"It was a very difficult meeting," Grassini said about the firm's first contact with the Houck parents. "They were distraught. They were brought in by a lawyer friend of theirs who brought them over to us because this is what we do." At that meeting, he recalled, the Houcks told the two lawyers what they had learned up to that point about the safety recall of the PT Cruiser in which their daughters had been killed. On that basis Grassini and Wrinkle decided to proceed with the case; their assessment was that Chrysler was the chief wrongdoer.

"All we knew is that the girls had had this terrible accident in which they were killed, and that they were driving a [recalled] Chrysler PT Cruiser, and we probably weren't thinking as much about the involvement of Enterprise as we were about the involvement of Chrysler," Grassini said. "As I remember, Enterprise was kind of a tail-end issue. They had rented the car from Enterprise but we had information about the defect and the recall. Our main thought was, here's the manufacturer of the car, they know they have a defect, they sent out the recall notice, maybe the recall notice didn't get there [to Enterprise] as soon as it should have, maybe they [Chrysler] should have realized they had a defect earlier."

"You start off as a strict products liability case for auto defect design," Wrinkle explained. "In California that's liability without fault if you can show there's a defect according to certain rules the Supreme Court has laid down, so naturally we gravitate towards that and say, we can do the best we can for these people on strict liability, so why look for a higher standard?" By recalling the car, Chrysler had admitted that it had a defect; strict liability was a perfect fit.

But then the firm learned that Enterprise had known about the defect *before* it rented the car to the Houck sisters – and had deliberately left it unrepaired. This was no longer just strict liability; it was negligence. Negligence in civil law requires a showing that the defendant knew its behavior might kill or injure someone. In a death case, it is akin to manslaughter in criminal law. At that point, "Everybody's hair started standing up on the back of their necks," Wrinkle said.

On June 28, 2005, in the California Superior Court in Hayward, Alameda County, Grassini filed a "Complaint for Wrongful Death – Strict Products Liability, Negligent Products Liability, Negligence" on behalf of Charles T. Houck and Cally S. Houck, "surviving heirs to Raechel and Jacqueline Marie Houck, Deceased," against DaimlerChrysler Corporation, three Enterprise Rent-A-Car entities, and the two Chrysler dealerships through whose hands the PT Cruiser had passed on its way from the manufacturer to Enterprise, its ultimate consumer. The complaint, leveling both strict liability and negligence charges against the defendants, was assigned case number HG05220018.

The strict liability charges relied on the known defective nature of the PT Cruiser to which DaimlerChrysler had admitted in its June 2004 notification to NHTSA. Once an auto manufacturer acknowledges the existence of a safety defect in any of its vehicles, it has closed the door on future attempts to downgrade or deny the existence of that defect.

Strict liability requires (1) that the product was in defective condition when it left the possession or control of the seller, (2) that it was unreasonably dangerous to the user or consumer, (3) that the defect was a cause – a "substantial factor" – of the plaintiff's injuries or damages, (4) that the seller engaged in the business of selling such product, and (5) that the product was one which the seller expected to, and did, reach the user or consumer without substantial change in the condition it was when he sold it. The PT Cruiser rented to the Houck sisters *prima facie* met all but one of those criteria even before the case was filed. The remaining criterion was causation. It would be up to the Houck attorneys to prove that the defect was what caused the deaths of the sisters.

But the Houck complaint's negligence charge went beyond this. It was aimed specifically at the three Enterprise entities. It stated that, "In or around June, 2004, defendant DaimlerChrysler Corporation conducted a safety recall of all Chrysler PT Cruiser vehicles for the years 2001-2005 which were equipped with naturally aspirated 2.4 liter engines and automatic transaxles which included the aforementioned 2004 PT Cruiser" rented to the Houck sisters. "On or about September 16, 2004, defendants Enterprise Rent-A-Car, Enterprise Rent-A-Car Company, and Enterprise Rent-A-Car of San Francisco... were issued a notification letter informing them of the aforementioned safety recall and the nature of the defect necessitating said recall."

After receiving the letter and up to the moment the car was rented to the Houcks, it asserted, the Enterprise companies "negligently, carelessly, recklessly and unlawfully failed to comply with the recall notification letter so as to cause the defect...to go without repair or remedy, thus remaining defective and unsafe, and thereby directly and legally causing the deaths of plaintiffs' decedents..."

"At bottom," says an informative learned treatise on the subject, "negligence law assesses human choices to engage in harmful conduct as proper or improper." It proscribes "failure to exercise the care toward others that a reasonable or prudent person would use in the same circumstances, or taking action that such a reasonable person would not, resulting in unintentional harm to another." So, because it was foresee-able to Enterprise that its failure to fix the defective PT Cruiser might result in harm to one of its customers, it could be deemed negligent for renting the car to the Houck sisters – if, that is, the defect was proved to be the cause of their deaths. Enterprise might argue that it wasn't cul-pable under strict liability because it was not the manufacturer or seller of the PT Cruiser, but it could not argue that it had not made a choice to "engage in harmful conduct" when it rented the car to the Houck sisters without repairing its defect.

The bottom-line challenge to Grassini and Wrinkle, then, was to prepare a case that would convince a jury that the steering hose defect, acknowledged by Chrysler and known to Enterprise, had triggered the fiery crash in which the Houck sisters were killed – that the defect was "a cause (a substantial factor) of the plaintiff's injuries or damages."

On August 24 DaimlerChrysler filed its answer to the complaint. Denying all the Houck charges, it blamed the sisters for causing the fatal crash "through their own negligence," "by the alteration and/or abnormal or improper use of the product," and for having "knowingly or intentionally altered, destroyed, destructively tested, discarded, failed to preserve or protect, sold and/or spoliated the subject vehicle..." On the same day Enterprise Rent-A-Car Company and Enterprise Rent-A-Car of San Francisco filed a joint answer similarly rejecting the Houck charges and similarly alleging that the sisters had died as a result of their own negligence and "unlawful conduct." Moreover, they alleged that the sisters had "actual knowledge of the particular danger" and an "understanding of the degree of risk involved in the activities surround-ing the accident," which had been caused by their "misuse, modifica-tion, alteration or change of the product..."

The answers, although couched in legal boilerplate, left little doubt that DaimlerChrysler and Enterprise intended to fight the Houcks all the way to trial.

6

CHRYSLER REDUX

THIS WAS NOT the first time Larry Grassini and Roland Wrinkle had sued Chrysler on behalf of parents for the wrongful deaths of their children in unsafe Chrysler vehicles. Ten years earlier, the two lawyers had taken the company to court in Los Angeles after three children – a 15-month-old, a 5-year-old and an 18-year-old – and an adult were thrown to their deaths when the rear tailgate door of a 1988 Dodge Caravan minivan opened in a moderate-speed crash. Another child, Iscela Ornelas, had been partially ejected and injured. Her mother, Beatriz Ornelas, was the ejected adult who died.

Unlike the Houck case, *Iscela Ornelas, etc., et al., vs. Chrysler Corporation, etc., et al.,* did not involve a recalled safety defect – at least not technically. The facts in *Ornelas,* however, were strikingly similar to those in *Houck,* and equally disturbing. In both cases, the evidence was clear that Chrysler had knowingly put a hazardous vehicle on the highways. In both cases, Chrysler would fiercely resist claims that its behavior had caused the deaths of someone's children.

On January 21, 1995, the Dodge Caravan, driven by Luisa Martinez and carrying 13 people, had been struck on its left rear side by a 1987 Toyota Corolla travelling at about 30 miles per hour. The crash occurred at a Los Angeles intersection. Many of the occupants were unbelted. The rear door latch failed, the door opened, and the four fatally-injured occupants were completely ejected from the back of the vehicle. "Each decedent was found lying near to or on the sidewalk in a pool of blood and in a 'spray' pattern, i.e., as if they were all shot out of the rear of the minivan at the same time," Wrinkle said in a court filing. The ejected occupants died of impacts with the pavement. The occupants who remained in the vehicle sustained only minor injuries, despite being unbelted.

Arguably the crash had been caused by driver errors in both vehicles – momentary inattention, perhaps – and arguably the occupants should all have been belted. But Wrinkle reminded the court that Chrysler's own chief engineer for auto safety, Roy Haeusler, had warned the company decades earlier that it was essential to distinguish between the causes of *accidents* and the causes of *injury*:

> The causes of motor vehicle accidents are many... In contrast, the causes of injury to car occupants, once the vehicle is involved in the accident, are much more limited and the vehicle plays a major role. In the typical accident the occupant has been injured because he has been thrown out, perhaps through an open door...

As early as 1955, Haeusler wrote, crash injury data had shown that "occupants who were thrown out of the car were much more apt to be severely injured or killed than those that stayed inside in similar accidents... occupants were thrown out of the car generally because one or more doors opened during the course of the accident." Improved door latches, he said, were successful in materially reducing the frequency with which doors came open, leading to "a significant reduction in serious and fatal injury."

It was common knowledge at Chrysler, which promoted its minivans with family-oriented safety claims, that children were often seated in the rear-facing seats of these vehicles, thus positioning them closest to the tailgate door. In other words, they required more protection, not less, than other occupants.

According to a skein of Chrysler internal documents, supplemented later by NHTSA investigative results, the minivan rear door latch – "by far the weakest on the market," Wrinkle told the court – had been known for many years by Chrysler's executives to be defective. "Long before this accident, the head of Chrysler's 'Minivan Safety Leadership Team' stood up and told Chrysler management that these were bad latches, that they were killing people, and that the latches must be replaced," he wrote.

On the basis of consumer complaints and accident reports, NHTSA had begun investigating the Chrysler door latch failure problem in January 1994, nearly a year before the *Ornelas* accident. Its investigation became a *cause celebre* in auto safety circles, and the subject of national press coverage. Chrysler was vigorously attacked by auto safety advocates for its failure to fix the rear door latches on some four million of its 1984-94 minivans – Dodge Caravan, Plymouth Voyager and Chrysler Town & Country models.

As the media increasingly focused on the battle between Chrysler, the regulators and the safety community over the seriousness of the minivan defect and how and when it should be fixed, the auto manufacturer found itself in the midst of a public relations debacle. "Safety has been a key selling point since Chrysler introduced the vehicles 10 years ago," the New York *Times* reported. "It is unhappy about the publicity created by its fight with regulators." Chrysler's attempts to burnish its safety image by such devices as creating a "Minivan Safety Leadership Team" were being badly tarnished by the tailgate door-latch controversy.

When NHTSA finally concluded its investigation in late 1995, months after the *Ornelas* crash, it did so in a way that appalled safety advocates. Despite reports that the agency had found 79 instances in which the tailgates of Chrysler's mini-vans popped open in accidents, resulting in 87 ejections, 60 injuries, and 29 deaths, NHTSA entered into what the *Times* called a "deal" in which the manufacturer would be permitted to recall the vehicles under an innocuous-sounding "service campaign" instead of a statutorily-required safety defect recall notification. This would exempt the latch replacement from inclusion in the list of federally-mandated recalls and relieve it of the onerous designation of "safety defect" correction.

Chrysler said it would send notification letters to van owners offering free replacement of the rear door latch, but not for "safety defect recall" purposes. "The letter, executives said, must walk a fine line between convincing owners that the repair is important and not panicking them," the *Times* reported. Chrysler, it said, hoped the "deal" would "support its assertion that the mini-vans do not have a safety defect and prevent the action from being used against the company in about 18 pending product liability lawsuits." One of those lawsuits was Grassini and Wrinkle's *Ornelas* case.

Safety advocates were already outraged at another NHTSA deal involving a serious vehicle hazard. The previous December the agency's parent, the U.S. Transportation Department, had forced it to back down from demanding a safety recall of six million General Motors 1973-87 C/K-model pickup trucks with side-saddle fuel tanks mounted on the outside of the vehicles – a design, NHTSA investigators had concluded, that made the tanks dangerously vulnerable to rupture and explosion in side impacts. The Center for Auto Safety had dubbed the trucks "firebombs"; the disparaging appellation found traction with the media, much to the manufacturer's chagrin. But instead of acknowledging the defect, GM had negotiated a voluntary settlement with DOT under which it would contribute $51 million to various unspecified research projects. There would be no safety defect recall of the "firebomb" pickup trucks and no fix for the vehicles' owners, despite NHTSA data showing that nearly 400 people had died in fire crashes involving the trucks up to then.

One of those critical of the GM-NHTSA firebomb settlement had been Ralph Hoar, an independent product safety consultant and former staffer at the esteemed Insurance Institute for Highway Safety. Commenting on internal documents showing that the company clearly knew the pickup truck fuel tanks were defective, he had said, "This is the legal equivalent of being caught with your pants down." Now, attacking the minivan rear door latch non-safety recall, he told the *Times,* "I don't know how you can convince people to bring in their vans to have the latch repaired at the same time telling them there is no hazard. I remain skeptical, and I have great concern for the future of the safety administration's enforcement authority."

Clarence Ditlow, head of the Center for Auto Safety and author of the "firebomb" label, had also chastised NHTSA for the GM pickup truck settlement, calling the fuel tank design "the worst auto crash fire defect in the history of the U.S. Department of Transportation" – worse, that is, than even the notorious Ford Pinto fuel tank design. Now, discussing the Chrysler minivan rear door latch deal in a letter to Center members, Ditlow called the Chrysler rear door latch hazard "the most lethal minivan defect… faulty tailgate latches which can pop open in low speed impacts." He accused Chrysler of having "stonewalled an NHTSA investigation, agreeing only to a service campaign" despite the high toll of ejection deaths, "many of them children."

Against this backdrop, the *Ornelas* case went to trial in March 1998. Grassini and Wrinkle intended to ask the jury not only to require Chrysler to compensate the families of the dead and injured children, but to penalize the company for its actions. "By clear and convincing evidence" they would "show that Chrysler's behavior was malicious, fraudulent, oppressive and despicable, i.e., 'conduct which is so vile, base, contemptible, miserable, wretched, or loathsome that it would be looked down upon and despised by ordinary decent people.'" In product liability litigation, compensatory damages redress specific losses – deaths and injuries – caused by a defendant's product or behavior. Punitive damages penalize defendants for causing such losses knowingly and maliciously. The *Ornelas* attorneys were demanding both.

Six months earlier, in South Carolina, Chrysler had lost one of the first tailgate latch cases to be tried when a jury awarded $262 million in compensatory and punitive damages to the family of six-year-old Sergio Jimenez, who had been thrown from the rear door of a 1985 Dodge Caravan when the latch failed during an accident. (The verdict was later partially reversed on appeal, after which the parties settled for an undisclosed sum.) A crucially important witness at the *Jimenez II v. DaimlerChrysler Corp.* trial had been Paul Sheridan, the former Chrysler executive who headed the manufacturer's "Minivan Safety Leadership Team" – the man, according to Wrinkle's brief to the *Ornelas* court, who had warned Chrysler's management that "these were bad latches, that they were killing people, and that the latches must be replaced." Chrysler had shut down the Safety Leadership Team and fired Sheridan after he went public with this information, and it now was suing the whistleblower for $82 million.

Sheridan was scheduled to be a witness at the *Ornelas* trial, where he was expected to repeat the testimony he had given in *Jimenez II* about Chrysler's knowledge of the latch defect and its refusal to correct it. "The jurors saw him as a key witness in what many of them said seemed to be some sort of corporate cover-up involving these latches," Grassini said later. But Sheridan was never called to the stand. Nor did the trial proceed to a verdict. While Sheridan waited outside the Los Angeles courtroom to be summoned to the witness stand, Chrysler and the *Ornelas* attorneys suddenly settled the case. Sheridan was convinced that the settlement was prompted by his presence as an insider witness who would testify that the minivan rear door latch was indeed defective despite Chrysler's assertions to the contrary. "Once Chrysler knew I was in the hallway, they settled," he told the Detroit *News*.

In *Houck*, of course, Grassini would not have to convince a jury that Chrysler's PT Cruiser was defective; the company had already admitted as much by recalling the vehicle. Instead, he would have to prove that the defect was what caused the crash that killed the Houck sisters. In trying to do so he would meet a barrage of resistance and counterclaims from Chrysler and Enterprise, along with a reprisal similar to Chrysler's firing of Paul Sheridan.

7

REPRISAL

ON FEBRUARY 6, 2006, seven months after Larry Grassini and Roland Wrinkle filed Cally and Chuck Houck's lawsuit against DaimlerChrysler and Enterprise for the wrongful deaths of their daughters Raechel and Jacqueline, Calabasas Motors fired Chuck. He had been the dealership's service and parts manager for ten years. His record was exemplary. The firing, he told Grassini and Wrinkle, came after he was warned by David Peterson, the dealership's owner, that if he did not drop the lawsuit he would be terminated.

Calabasas Motors was a Mercedes dealer. Daimler-Benz controlled both Mercedes and Chrysler. Further, the dealership had a close relationship with Enterprise Rent-A-Car, so close that Enterprise maintained a rental office on its premises. It was this office, ironically, that had helped Chuck track down his daughters' rental agreement for the defective PT Cruiser.

The two attorneys were appalled, and frustrated. "He was fired because the [expletive] who owned the dealership didn't like the fact that Chuck had sued his buddy Enterprise. The poor guy loses his two daughters to a company that's put out a vehicle that they now said was defective," Grassini said. "This is terrible!"

But the chances of a successful action against the dealership for wrongful termination were slender at best. Chuck was an "at-will" employee of the dealership; he had no employment contract. "The only way you could file a wrongful termination case is based on age, race, sex, disability or religion, or is a violation of public policy," Grassini recalled. "Roland researched it and said, 'It's an absolutely uphill fight. There are cases saying specifically you can't do it. Somebody fired you for filing a civil lawsuit? They can do that.'"

A leading California case that says "they can do that" is *Jersey v. John Muir Medical Center.* In 1997 Ester Jersey, a nurse at a Muir trauma facility, was assaulted by a patient and injured. She filed suit against the patient. The hospital directed her to withdraw the suit because it conflicted with hospital policy against suing trauma-impaired patients. When she did not withdraw the suit she was fired.

Jersey took Muir to court claiming that the termination was a "violation of public policy" in that it was meant to deny her access to the courts. But a lower court held that, "In general, there is no public policy that bars private party employers from reacting adversely to lawsuits filed by their employees" – exactly what Calabasas Motors had done to Chuck Houck. This interpretation of "public policy" in unlawful termination claims was upheld on appeal. The appellate court cited earlier cases holding that "the policy in question must involve a matter that affects society at large rather than a purely personal or proprietary interest of the plaintiff or employer; in addition, the policy must be 'fundamental,' 'substantial' and 'well established' at the time of the discharge." Ester Jersey's claim, it held, did not meet that standard.

Despite the odds against them, the two lawyers decided to go ahead with a wrongful-termination lawsuit on Chuck Houck's behalf against Calabasas and Peterson. Their decision was dictated by what Chuck Houck was going through. "He lost his two daughters in a fiery crash and he tried to vindicate his daughters, and he's lost his career," Wrinkle said. The lawsuit was going to be about "the incredible, unparalleled nastiness" of the firing; "they should have put their arm around the guy, not punched him in the mouth."

Precluded from citing age, race, gender, religion or disability as a cause of Houck's termination, Wrinkle decided that the only remaining option was to sue Calabasas and Peterson for wrongful termination in "violation of a fundamental public policy," Faced with *Jersey* it was a very long shot, and both lawyers knew it.

On October 11, 2007, while still in the preparation phase of the Houcks' case against Chrysler and Enterprise, Grassini and Wrinkle filed *Case No. BC378928, Charles T. Houck, Plaintiff, vs. Calabasas Motorcars, Inc.; David L. Petersen... Defendants, Complaint for Damages (Wrongful Termination in Violation of Public Policy)* in the Superior Court of California, County of Los Angeles. In it they sought to carve out definitions of "public policy" that would satisfy the criteria presented in *Jersey* – "affects society at large," "fundamental," "substantial" and "well established" – and thus allow Chuck's wrongful termination lawsuit to go forward. Citing numerous state and federal statutes, they asserted that:

- California public policy "is that rental car companies, such as Enterprise, shall not rent cars that are not mechanically sound and safe to operate."
- California public policy "is that automobile manufacturers, such as DaimlerChrysler, shall promptly notify all vehicle owners and lessees of safety recalls."
- Federal public policy "is to enforce motor vehicle safety standards, investigate safety-related defects, and ensure that the motoring public is not exposed to the dangers of safety-related motor vehicle defects."
- Federal public policy "is to issue vehicle safety standards and to require vehicle manufacturers to recall vehicles with safety-related defects in order to protect the motoring public from the dangers of safety-related motor vehicle defects."

- Federal public policy "is to reduce traffic accidents and deaths and injuries resulting from traffic accidents by, among other things, preventing safety-related automobile defects."

Chuck Houck's lawsuit against DaimlerChrysler and Enterprise, for which Calabasas had fired him, was intended to vindicate these public policies and "protect the motoring public from the dangers of such defects," the complaint asserted. It reminded the court that DaimlerChrysler had manufactured and distributed over 435,000 PT Cruiser automobiles with a defect which caused the vehicles to lose power steering control and/or start underhood fires. "As of March 2004, a substantial portion of such PT Cruisers were sold to Enterprise Rent-A-Car which regularly rented them to the general public."

Tying these facts to Chuck Houck's alleged role in furthering public policy, the complaint cited sections of the California Penal Code making it "illegal to induce another person to withhold true testimony" or "knowingly and maliciously prevent or dissuade any witness from attending or giving testimony at any trial, proceeding or inquiry authorized by law." It "was and is the public policy of the United States of America and the State of California that statutes and regulations, such as those described hereinabove, be enforced through the prosecution of tort damage actions, such as the action filed by plaintiff" against DaimlerChrysler and Enterprise. Calabasas Motors and Peterson had "knowingly, maliciously, wrongfully, illegally and tortuously" fired Chuck in retaliation for his "attempts to vindicate the various public policies described herein..." He was simply asking the court to award damages for the resulting harm to his livelihood and the emotional harm resulting from the firing.

Predictably, Calabasas Motors and Peterson responded with a demurrer moving for dismissal of the complaint on the basis of *Jersey* and similar cases. Even if the facts of Chuck's termination were as described in the complaint, they said, there was nothing in it that demonstrated that the termination was a "violation of a policy that is delineated in either constitutional or statutory provisions," such as age, gender, religion, disability or race. Nor, of course, were they admitting that the facts of the termination were as described by Chuck. (Amazingly, in a related filing with the court, they even disputed that Chuck "was ever terminated let alone terminated for pursuing a wrongful death action arising out of the tragic accident that took the lives of plaintiff's two daughters." It was a breathtaking claim – an assertion that Chuck Houck had lied to the court about being fired by Calabasas Motors – made even more distasteful by the pretense of commiseration in the word "tragic.")

After hearing oral argument by the two sides, the court dismissed the wrongful-termination complaint after finding an absence of "a violation of a policy that is delineated etc." It was not buying the argument that Chuck and Cally Houck's lawsuit against DaimlerChrysler and Enterprise for the wrongful death of their daughters served a public-policy purpose by supporting Federal and state auto safety statutes. Would an appellate court buy it?

Roland Wrinkle is one of California's outstanding appellate lawyers. U.S. News's listing of "America's Best Lawyers" credits him with "the largest punitive damage award affirmed on appeal in California," and has given the firm its highest national ranking, U.S. Tier One. Wrinkle's reputation for successful appeals was unparalleled. He knew that an appeal from the lower court decision against Chuck Houck would probably not succeed – *Jersey* presented difficult law to overcome. "We did a noble and righteous thing," Wrinkle recalled. They filed the appeal anyway. Written by Wrinkle, it was an impassioned plea for the justice they believed Chuck Houck deserved.

"A man loses both of his daughters in a fiery car crash caused by the defective power steering hose of a car that was rented, knowing that it was under a NHTSA recall, " the appellate brief said. "He files a lawsuit against Chrysler and Enterprise Rent-a-Car to vindicate various state and federal statutes and regulations governing the public safety aspects of the car manufacturing and rental industries. His boss (a car dealer) calls him in and orders him (inexplicably) to dismiss the lawsuit or get fired. Faced with the hideous decision of choosing between his livelihood (a service manager) and not allowing his daughters' deaths to be in vain (and to spare others from such cataclysms), he chooses to persevere against those responsible. The boss, true to his word, retaliates by terminating the father's employment.

"The question here: Is public policy sufficiently offended by such circumstances to offer a remedy? Does what the car dealer did (or is alleged to have done) violate our sense of fairness and decency...? Certainly – but that is not the question presented here. What is involved is a related but fundamentally different question: Did what the car dealer do violate California public policy?"

After enumerating the auto safety-related public policies that he contended were at issue in the firing of Chuck Houck, Wrinkle's brief turned to the defendants' assertion that they had violated no public policy and the termination suit should be dismissed. "If defendants' position were adopted as the blanket rule it purports to be," Wrinkle argued, "then the expressly 'important' public health and safety statutes and regulations alleged in the complaint, both state and federal, could be trampled and defeated by the establishment of an authoritarian regime whereby employers could dictate what public policy-based lawsuits employees are permitted to, or are prohibited from, pursuing. "

To support this sweeping claim in the face of the *Jersey* decision, the brief turned to decisions in other cases. One of these was *Green v. Ralee Engineering*, in which an aircraft parts manufacturer fired one of its parts inspectors after he reported that the company had shipped parts that were defective under federal safety regulations. In *Green*, a court had held that the firing violated public policies protecting employees from termination in retaliation for blowing the whistle on an employers' unlawful conduct. Wrinkle's brief sought to draw a parallel between that firing and Chuck Houck's. The facts of the two cases were "too close to allow for a different result.... What it comes down to is this: In California, should someone in Chuck Houck's position have to choose between his product liability rights against third parties and his ability to make a living?"

The brief concluded with an eloquent warning that a finding against Chuck Houck would have dire repercussions:

"So – now – here is the critical question: What is the next person who finds himself or herself in Chuck Houck's position going to do? Defendants hope their *in terrorem* approach will discourage any future would-be private litigator/vindicator of these automotive and rental safety statutes and regulations. 'Do you want to be the next Chuck Houck? And there's nothing you can do about it.'

"The 1578 handbook for inquisitors in Spain spelled out the purpose of inquisitorial penalties: '...*quoniam punitio non refertur primo & per se in correctionem & bonum eius qui punitur sed, in bonum publicum Ut alij terreantur & a malis committendis avocentur*' (i.e.,'... for punishment does not take place primarily and per se for the correction and good of the person punished, but for the public good in order that others may become terrified and weaned away from the evils they would commit.'). The methodology used by this car dealership is certainly rational and effective. But it is not moral... A father simply should not have to suffer the death of his daughters and then be forced to choose between his livelihood and the vindication of those deaths."

It was a valiant effort, and as Grassini and Wrinkle expected, it was doomed to failure. The appellate court decision upheld the lower court's dismissal of Houck's lawsuit, essentially on the grounds cited by the defendants, Calabasas Motors and its owner. As for Wrinkle's attempt to analogize the *Green* case with this one, the court concluded that Houck's lawsuit against DaimlerChrysler and Enterprise "does not constitute an act of whistle-blowing, for purposes of the public policy identified in Green... Houck's complaint contains no allegation that his action against DaimlerChrysler and Enterprise implicated misconduct within his own workplace. Moreover, he offers no authority that his lawsuit against third parties for violations of safety laws and regulations unrelated to his workplace amounts to whistle-blowing."

To Chuck Houck, Wrinkle recalled later, the decision was crushing. "He loses his daughters and he tries to do something about it and they

fire him and the court says, 'That's okay.' That's a very difficult thing."
DaimlerChrysler and Enterprise, it seemed, had successfully punished
Chuck Houck for challenging their roles in the deaths of his daughters, as Chrysler had punished Paul Sheridan ten years earlier for blowing the whistle on its knowledge of the lethal tailgate latch defect in its
minivans.

8

DEFENDING THE CORPORATIONS

O N THE MORNING of Tuesday, June 6, 2006, twenty months minus one day from the date of the crash in which their daughters were killed, Cally and Chuck Houck arrived at the offices of Grassini and Wrinkle to be deposed by lawyers for Enterprise Rent-A-Car and DaimlerChrysler Corp. The process of discovery in *Houck v. DaimlerChrysler et al* had begun.

Discovery allows each side in a civil lawsuit to interrogate the other side, through oral and written examination, for information bearing on the issues being litigated. In product liability cases, plaintiffs use discovery to probe the defense's actions, research, testing, policies, correspondence and anything else that might shed light on the allegedly defective nature of the product and its role in causing a death or injury. Defendants, for their part, seek to discover evidence in the plaintiffs' possession that offsets or negates the possibility that defendants' products or behavior caused harm to the plaintiffs – evidence such as some action by the injury victims that contributed to or entirely caused the resulting harm.

Today's depositions of Cally and Chuck Houck were an essential part of the discovery process – the defendants' first opportunity to probe for evidence supporting their assertions that the sisters' misconduct, not their own, had killed the two girls. The parents' testimony would be taken under oath; later the defense could introduce and read it to the jury at trial, just as though it were being given in the courtroom.

The defense lawyers today would focus particularly on Raechel's, the driver's, behavior in hopes it would turn out to be sufficiently suspect that a jury would blame her, not the admittedly defective PT Cruiser. They would also seek the names of other people who might have damaging information about the Houck sisters' condition on the day of the crash.

Deposing the Houcks would be two lawyers highly experienced in defending big corporations against injury lawsuits.

Dennis Raglin, an attorney with Sedgwick, Detert, Moran & Arnold, was appearing for DaimlerChrysler. Raglin was one of 300-plus attorneys with the San Francisco-based Sedgwick firm, a self-described heavy hitter in providing international litigation and business law services to "sophisticated corporate clients."

"Our clients include some of the world's largest corporations. Others talk. Sedgwick attorneys act," the firm proclaims in its marketing materials. Raglin was there today to act for such a client – Daimler-Benz Corporation, one of the world's leading motor vehicle manufacturers. The Daimler Benz-Chrysler Corporation merger had produced a corporate giant that ranked fifth worldwide in automotive production.

The Sedgwick firm's strategic approach to wrongful-death cases such as *Houck v. DaimlerChrysler et al* had been spelled out earlier in an article, "Shadow in the Courtroom," that appeared on the firm's website. Death, it said, "is perhaps the most potent weapon in the plaintiff's arsenal, evoking sympathy and an unconscious bias in the family's favor from the moment the word is uttered. And while death is a witness which cannot be cross-examined, planning and strategy can defuse it and, perhaps, even turn it to [the defendant's] advantage." What this called for was "legal jiu-jitsu" in which the defense would belittle as "of questionable value" any attempt by plaintiffs to "play the sympathy card."

Paul Stephan, an attorney with the law firm of Selman and Breitman, was representing Enterprise Rent-A-Car. Selman & Brietman's practice was confined to California, where its clients included small, medium and large companies. According to the firm's website, "We work to keep our clients out of court, but are prepared to bring our talent and resources to the courtroom when a client's business success depends on aggressive and result-oriented litigation." The firm claims "a long history of handling the worst-of-the-worst in catastrophic personal injury cases... Ultimately, if the case cannot be settled, we can and do try this type of case often, and we are not intimidated by the scope of the claim."

Stephan's client, Enterprise, was facing a claim not only of strict liability but of negligence, and a demand for nearly $50 million to compensate the Houcks for their daughters' deaths.

Cally had been apathetic about the lawsuit from the outset, and she didn't expect the depositions to alter this. Still benumbed by the loss of her daughters, living in what she later described as "a vacuum of grief," she wasn't too concerned that her deposition would be intolerable; "I just wanted to get it over with," she told me later.

Nor was she seeking sympathy. "I'm not fragile and I'm not a victim type." Essentially she wanted to "make sure my daughter's character and reputation were intact, because I wasn't going to let anybody make insinuations about her and I was closer to her than anyone."

After chatting briefly with Donald Liddy, the Grassini & Wrinkle attorney who would represent them during the depositions, the Houcks were shown into a conference room where Raglin, Stephan and a court reporter were waiting. Chuck was directed to a chair opposite the defense attorneys. Cally sat nearby. At 10:30 a.m. Chuck was sworn in by the court reporter and his deposition began, with Raglin doing the initial interrogation.

Raglin first asked whether Chuck had ever been deposed; he had, Chuck replied, in a suit filed against Calabasas Motors and Mercedes a few years earlier, during his time as service manager at the dealership. The suit had been brought against the manufacturer and the dealership under California's "lemon law" statute, which provides recourse for a new-car buyer whose vehicle fails to meet the manufacturer's express warranty despite multiple repair attempts.

RAGLIN: You were a plaintiff?
CHUCK: Yes, I was a witness.

Possibly out of nervousness, Chuck had given a confusing answer; clearly he could not have been a plaintiff in a case where he was giving evidence on behalf of the defendant. Liddy, responsible for protecting his clients' interests during their interrogations, interrupted:

LIDDY [TO CHUCK]: Hold on, hold on. You're talking a little too fast, he can ask questions quick, and if you give your answers too quick, then I'm about as useful as this potted plant... So let's just slow it down, 'cause he asked you if you were a plaintiff in that case and you said yes, you were a witness, so you can't be a plaintiff and a witness, I don't think... So let me just tell you, wait for him to ask his questions, then pause, give me a chance if I need to object, or do something.

Raglin spent the next half hour or so asking fact questions about Chuck's employment history and his experience as a service manager for Calabasas and other dealerships. Then, abruptly breaking off that line of questioning, he asked Chuck for his current address. Liddy jumped in again:

LIDDY: You mean you want his home address?
RAGLIN: Yes.
LIDDY: You can just use this [Grassini law firm] address to contact my client.
RAGLIN: Are you going to instruct him not to answer on home address?
LIDDY: Unless you have a good reason or some good cause that you should have the home address. That would violate privacy issues.

If Raglin wanted an answer, he would have to ask the court to compel it.

Denied Chuck's home address, the DaimlerChrysler attorney proceeded with a series of questions about his education, particularly automotive-related courses he had taken and professional certificates he had received, and his work as an auto mechanic prior to 1985.

> *Q. And then did you become a service manager or was there something else that you did?*
> *A. Service advisor.*
> *Q. And what is that?*
> *A. That's when you write the repair orders for the customers.*
> *Q. So your actual hands-on in the engine room or under the hood would have stopped at that point?*
> *A. Yes.*
> *Q. And that –*

Liddy jumped in again; something about this seemingly bland line of questioning didn't seem right to the Grassini attorney. Why was Raglin pursuing it?

> *LIDDY: Let me just inquire, if I might. There's no – obviously in a wrongful death case there's no lost earnings issues, so I'm not sure, and I know you're probably used to taking certain types of depositions, I'm not sure in this case what the employment background, other than generally speaking, has to do with any issue that might come up.*
> *RAGLIN: I think it has to do with this. We're talking about a vehicle and someone who's got vehicle experience.*
> *LIDDY: Okay, but how?*
> *RAGLIN: I would be asking questions later on that, talking about any knowledge he has that would be related to this type of an accident, this type of vehicle.*
> *LIDDY: I just don't see how he could have –*
> *RAGLIN: Well, we're almost done with this line of questioning anyway, so –*
> *LIDDY: Okay, or we can just move on. Let's not argue. To me, this is an exploration of what possible relevance there would be in a trial of my client's automotive abilities.*

RAGLIN: Your client is not the typical client. He has obviously a lot of vehicle knowledge.

LIDDY: So what does that have to do with this case?

RAGLIN: This case involves, obviously, a vehicle that caught fire, you have allegations of various problems with the vehicle.

LIDDY: Right.

RAGLIN: And I'm probing your client's knowledge of that. I'm getting the foundation right now of his experience. Either he does or he does not know or he won't have knowledge or it won't be relevant.

LIDDY: I don't see how it could be relevant in this case, but – you know. I'll let you go on a little bit more.

RAGLIN: And there's not much at all that's left, anyway, just a little bit more.

Wrapping up the "experience" line of questioning, Raglin asked Chuck to confirm that after becoming a service advisor and manager at dealerships, he had stopped doing hands-on vehicle maintenance and instead had concentrated on paperwork. Then, warning that "these are not going to be easy questions, and I apologize in advance," Raglin turned to the fatal crash itself, and to the possibility that something in the sisters' conditions might have contributed to it.

Q. Okay. How would you describe Jacqueline's health?

A. Excellent.

Q. Did she have any conditions such as cancer or diabetes, long-term chronic health problems?

A. No.

Q. Was she a smoker?

A. No.

Q. Do you know if she ever did illegal drugs?

A. No.

LIDDY (TO CHUCK): You don't have to answer that question.

RAGLIN: Why not?

LIDDY: What's the relevance?

RAGLIN: *If there's a question of substance abuse that could have contributed to the accident, that becomes relevant.*

LIDDY: *If there's a question of substance abuse that could have contributed to the accident, it may be relevant if she ever – well, what was your answer?*

CHUCK HOUCK: *No.*

RAGLIN: *The answer was no anyway, so –*

LIDDY: *I made my objection belatedly to the question. It's argumentative and it's not really calculated to lead to discoverable evidence.*

RAGLIN: *We were talking about Jacqueline and Raechel. Now –*

LIDDY: *We were talking about Jacqueline's – let's take a break.*

After a short recess Raglin continued his questions.

Q. Sir, before the break I think we were talking about, I was asking you some general questions about your daughters' health. I think we were talking about Jacqueline. As I understand your testimony, Jacqueline was in good health, correct?

A. Yes.

Q. Okay. Had she ever had any surgeries or hospitalizations?

A. Not that I can recall.

Q. Okay. Had she ever seen a psychologist or a therapist?

A. No.

LIDDY: *I'm going to object to that, it might be irrelevant, invasion of privacy. You can answer to the extent you know.*

CHUCK HOUCK: *Not that I can remember.*

RAGLIN: *Okay. Prior to her passing, had Jacqueline ever indicated to you thoughts of suicide or suicidal tendencies?*

A. No.

Q. You would describe her disposition as happy and positive?

A. Yes.

Q. Okay. Let's talk about Raechel. Prior to her passing, how would you describe her health?

A. Excellent.

Q. Okay. Had she ever had any hospitalizations or surgeries?

A. Not that I can recall.

Q. Had she ever taken any illegal drugs, to your knowledge?

A. Not that I'm aware of.

Q. Had she ever taken any prescription drugs, to your knowledge?

A. Antibiotics. Something to that effect.

Q. You believe she might have taken antibiotics of one kind –

A. Yes.

Q. But nothing long-term, as far as you know.

A. No.

If DaimlerChrysler and Enterprise were to learn the names of the girls' friends and physicians, they could subpoena and depose them about Jacqueline and Raechel's health and social habits, in hopes of producing evidence that somehow Raechel's driving had been impaired on the day of the crash. Raglin asked Chuck for the name of Jacqueline's doctor but Chuck was unable to recall it. He asked for the names of the sisters' friends, but Chuck couldn't remember them. Then he asked for another break; "I'm going to go through my notes and then I think we'll wrap up," he said. But there was more to come.

> *RAGLIN: We'll go back on the record. Sir, I only have a handful of questions and then I'll be able to wrap it up for you. Let me start with a general question. Why did you decide to sue DaimlerChrysler Corporation?*

To Liddy, it was the sort of question that should properly be put to attorneys, not to a plaintiff; it was attorneys who decided such matters. Obviously irate, he broke in and directed Chuck not to answer. But Raglin persisted: if Chuck had a basis for why he wanted to bring the suit, "I'm entitled to that."

> *LIDDY (TO RAGLIN): Go on, go on to something else.*
> *RAGLIN: Are you going to refuse to let him answer?*

DEFENDING THE CORPORATIONS

LIDDY: That question is ridiculous.
RAGLIN: The question is, are you going to refuse to let him answer?
LIDDY: There's no basis for that question. It's argumentative, calls for an opinion, and I'll instruct the witness not to answer that question.
BY RAGLIN (TO CHUCK): Okay. Your attorney has told you not to answer.
LIDDY: He's going to follow my advice. (TO CHUCK) You're going to follow my advice, so you don't need to answer the question.
THE WITNESS: Yes.
LIDDY: Okay. And that'll go for every time I advise you about a question, right?
THE WITNESS: Yes.

Raglin finished his questioning by asking about insurance on the rented PT Cruiser – whether there had been any and if so, what were the death benefits. Chuck replied that he had always urged his daughters to take out full insurance coverage when renting cars.

Raglin then wanted to know whether there had been death benefit payments to the Houcks after the crash. This would bring yet another objection from Liddy – the question violated the "collateral source" doctrine, which prohibits the admission of evidence showing that a wronged plaintiff's damages have been compensated by a source other than the culpable defendant.

RAGLIN: And did you receive a payment from Enterprise?
LIDDY: Let me just object to the collateral source. And if you would mark that part of the deposition, I would appreciate it. And you can answer.
CHUCK: Yes.
RAGLIN: Okay. How much was that?
CHUCK: I think it was –
LIDDY: Same objection.
CHUCK: I can't remember exactly.
RAGLIN: Do you have an estimate?

A. I think it was around – my mind's going blank right now, I'm sorry.
Q. I understand. Do you have a general – is it over $10,000?
A. Yes. I don't know, my mind just went blank. Fifty or a hundred thou-
sand, I can't remember exactly. I know it sounds foolish, but –
Q. That's all I am entitled to, is your best memory. Was this for both girls?
A. Yes.
Q. And since we're already on this line, did either girl have any life
insurance?
A. No.

Shortly after noon Raglin announced that he had no more questions. "I know this hasn't been easy, I can't imagine your loss, but I do appreciate your taking the time to be here," he told Chuck. His statement of commiseration was in keeping with his firm's defense-strategy article, which admonishes that a defense attorney must try to defuse sympathy for a plaintiff without offending the jury: "…the balance is a delicate one; the defense cannot appear callous."

Raglin was finished. Chuck wasn't.

Stephan, Enterprise's attorney, opened the second part of the deposition with a series of questions about Chuck's knowledge of the Chrysler notice recalling the defective PT Cruiser. He began by having Chuck describe how he had been shown the copy of the recall notice received by Norberto Morales, a technician at Calabasas Motors who owned two PT Cruisers.

Q. And when Mr. Morales showed you his recall, that came by U.S. Post
Office?
A. I would assume. I didn't see the envelope.
Q. Okay. Have you ever gotten a recall notice personally for any car
you've ever had?
A. I've had a recall, but not that I got on a document. Not mailed to me.

Q. You said a little while ago that you had gone onto another [internet web] page, and I think you said it was a DaimlerChrysler web page, and I think you said that the recall had not been done.

A. Yes.

Q. Okay. Now, for all of us that don't know the intricacies of this, what does that mean?

A. Well, I didn't either. I haven't, you know, done that before. What I did, and I can't remember exactly, it's been so long ago, but I just went on a general web page and I remember somewhere on there you could check your own car for recalls and you could plug in your VIN number and it would tell you if there's any recalls or things with that car. And that's where I found that it had not been done.

Q. And I presume –

A. It was open.

Q. And, I'm sorry, what does that mean?

A. Not done yet. I don't remember if "open" was the exact word.

Q. And just the last question was of this recall issue, I just want to make sure. You have no information suggesting that my client, which is Enterprise Rent-a-Car, actually in fact received a recall notice from DaimlerChrysler before the date of this accident for this VIN number, do you?

The question went to the heart of Enterprise's defense. If it hadn't received the recall notice, how could it be culpable for failing to have the car repaired? Liddy objected. Chuck could answer, he said, but only as to matters and documents that he hadn't learned about from his lawyers.

Raglin, Chrysler's attorney, objected as well, with no explanation. Perhaps he sensed an implication in the question that Chrysler may not have sent the notice to Enterprise in a timely fashion and therefore might be seen as the root cause of Enterprise's failure to remedy the defect – if so, a powerful weapon in Enterprise's defense arsenal.

LIDDY: That may call for speculation as to what the witness has gotten from his attorney, but you can answer it to the extent that it's something outside what was discussed with your lawyer.
RAGLIN: Join in the objection.
STEPHAN (TO CHUCK): I'm only looking for your knowledge.
A. I don't recall.
Q. You don't recall.
A. I really don't.

Raglin had asked Chuck for names of the sisters' friends but Chuck had been unable to recall any specific names. Stephan tried again:

Q. You were asked a little while ago about either daughter's closest – or friends of either daughter. And I'm just wondering, is there any one person that you could say, "This person, through the years, has been a friend for Raechel," or, "This person's been a friend for Jacqueline"? Just one.
A. There's a million of them. There's Suni, there's Nichole, there's – gosh, I can never remember. Jacqueline always used to call them the stable rats, there were six girls at the stable, they all hung out together, and sometimes when they were in front of me I could remember their names or not. There's the – oh, God. Dana. There's – who's the little –
LIDDY: Just –
THE WITNESS: I'm sorry. At any rate, if I'm involved in that, I can remember it more. Right now my head's just so fuzzy I can't tell you.

Stephan had at least gotten some first names to pursue. With that, he was nearly finished interrogating Chuck. He made one final effort to probe for evidence that Raechel's driving might have caused the crash:

Q. Now, my last question is obnoxious as heck, but do you know anything about the girls' medical history? The month before this accident,

*at all, do you know anything about any medical thing that was perhaps
bothering them the month before?*
A. Not to my knowledge.

Chuck's deposition had lasted two and a half hours. By now it was almost one o'clock. There would be a lunch break, after which Raglin and Stephan would depose Cally Houck. So far the two defense lawyers had elicited nothing remotely suggesting that something in the sisters' behavior, background or actions had been involved in causing the crash.

At ten minutes after two, the court reporter administered the oath to Cally. Raglin began his interrogation by having her review the events of the early morning of October 8, 2004 – the call from CHP taken by Carl Nienaber, her disbelief that her daughters had been killed, the visit from a local policeman and a chaplain, her call to Chuck. He followed this with a series of questions about her daughters' recent work and travel. Then:

*RAGLIN: In terms of, let's talk about the girls' health. I asked Mr.
Houck about that and I'll be asking you the same series of questions. For
Jacqueline, would you describe her health – how would you describe her
health?*
CALLY: Excellent. She – both of my daughters were athletes.
*Q. Did Jacqueline have a regular doctor, to your knowledge, at the time
of this accident in October of ' 04?*
A. No, I don't believe she did.
*Q. When you all four lived together prior to the separation, did the girls
have a regular doctor?*
A. Yes.
Q. And, okay. Who was that?
*A. It was a group. Mary Dial, Carl Gross, and I can't remember the
third.*
Q. And do you remember where this place was located?

A. In Ojai.

Q. And did it have a name?

A. I believe it was called Pirie Family Practice Group, but I may be wrong. P-i-r-i-e.

Q. And prior to the divorce, which I believe was 1999?

A. Yes.

Q. Prior to that time, as you sit here today, did either girl have any significant medical problems?

A. No. They were very healthy.

Q. Did either girl ever have any hospitalizations?

A. No.

Q. Did either girl have any surgeries?

A. No.

Q. After the divorce and until the time of this accident in October 2004, are you aware of any medical problems for either girl?

A. No.

Q. Okay. How would you describe – I think I already know the answer, but let me make sure I have a clear record. How would you describe Raechel's health?

A. Excellent. Athlete.

Q. Did either girl smoke cigarettes?

A. No.

Q. Are you aware of whether either girl used illegal drugs?

A. No, I'm not aware.

Q. As far as you know, did both girls have valid driver's licenses?

A. Yes.

Q. And in school, as I understand from Mr. Houck's testimony, both girls either graduated or got the equivalent of a high school diploma, correct?

A. Correct.

Raglin now asked the inevitable questions about the sisters' friends – their identities, relationships and whereabouts. He was "looking for people that you would consider very close to both girls," he told Cally.

She was able to recall a number of names. They included Chad Hogan, John Mora, Brenna Carlson and Nicole Pinto.

After that, the DaimlerChrysler lawyer turned to the hours before Raechel and Jacqueline had left Ojai on their fatal trip:

RAGLIN: And did the girls sleep at your house the night before the trip?
CALLY: Yes.
Q. And what time did they go to bed, roughly, do you remember?
A. Raechel and I went to bed early 'cause we were laying in my bed telling stories. And Jackie came to bed after that. [Cally inadvertently reversed the names. She and Jacqueline had gone to bed early; Raechel had arrived later.]
Q. Do you remember what time?
A. Twelve, 12:30, maybe.
Q. And do you recall what time you all woke up?
A. Yeah, the girls got up with me.
Q. What time is that?
A. I got up about 7:30.
Q. Okay. As far as you know, they slept the whole night through at your house?
A. I know they did.
Q. And did either of the girls have any alcohol the night before their trip?
A. No.
Q. Have you ever witnessed the girls drink any alcohol?
A. In Spain, or, I mean, in Italy, we had wine with meals, and yes, Raechel had wine with meals in Italy.
Q. As far as – I'm sorry.
A. Other than that, no.
Q. And as far as you know, did either girl ever have any drinking problem?
A. No.

Q. You said Italy. Was this a separate time from the one that you and I have talked about earlier, '02 to Europe?

A. Yes, Raechel lived alone in Italy in 2000 – see, she returned in December 2003 and remained there until late August of 2004. And I visited her in Italy.

Q. Gotcha. How was her health at the time?

A. Excellent.

▲ ▲ ▲

Q. All right. So as I understand what you're saying, the girls left for their trip back north, looks like about 12:30 from your office in Ojai intending to drive back to Santa Cruz?

A. Yes.

Q. Did they indicate to you that they were going to make any stops along the way?

A. Raechel was supposed to go by Brenda Carlson's and get fitted for a wedding dress, or a bridesmaid dress. She was in a wedding.

Q. Were they both going to drive to Brenda's?

A. No, Jackie sat with me in my office.

Q. So did Raechel actually leave and Jackie stayed with you?

A. Yeah, for – this was just around ten.

Q. Okay. How long did that take?

A. Raechel came back and picked up Jackie at about 12:30.

Q. And then did you walk the girls down to the car as they left or did they just leave?

A. Yes.

Q. And was it the PT Cruiser they were driving?

A. Yes.

Q. And who was driving it?

A. Raechel.

Q. And did you notice anything out of the ordinary with the car; smells, sounds?

A. No.

Q. Did either girl make any comment to you before they left that there were any problems with the vehicle?

A. No.

Q. So how long was Raechel gone with Brenda while Jacqueline waited with you?

A. Maybe an hour and a half, something like that.

Q. And do you know what Raechel did during that time?

A. She went and got fitted for her bridesmaid dress.

Q. And the friend, who was the friend she went with?

A. Brenda Carlson was the bride.

Q. And do you know where Brenda Carlson is?

A. Yes.

Q. Where?

A. She's in Ojai.

Q. And do you know the address?

A. No, I don't. She's married now. Has children.

Q. Is Carlson her married name?

A. No, it's the name she had, maiden name.

Q. Did she go to the same high school as Raechel?

A. Yes.

Q. As far as you know, did Raechel appear sober?

A. Yes.

Q. You didn't detect anything out of the ordinary with either girl?

A. No.

Q. Did either girl take any prescription medications?

A. No, not that I know of.

As he neared the end of his questioning, Raglin asked Cally why she and Chuck had decided after their daughters' deaths to "get attorneys involved."

CALLY: We believed that there was something wrong with the vehicle.
RAGLIN: And what brought you to that conclusion?

A. Well, Chuck gave me some information, I don't recall specifically what it was, but I also know Raechel was a very diligent and vigilant driver. And there was no explanation that I could come up with that could explain how she drove it into a truck.

Stephan, the Enterprise lawyer, had a few questions for Cally. Unsurprisingly, they were largely aimed at finding evidence supporting their clients' claim that the sisters, not the PT Cruiser, were to blame for the crash that killed them.

Q. Mrs. Houck, my name is Paul Stephan, I represent Enterprise Rent-a-Car. Did Jacqueline have a cell phone with her on the day of the accident?
A. I don't believe so.
Q. Do you know if she ever had a cell phone?
A. Yes.
Q. I think you said that – well, let me start over again. Who did you understand to be driving the car at the time of the accident?
A. Raechel was driving.
Q. Okay. And I think you told us that Raechel was a very diligent and vigilant driver.
A. Yes.
Q. Can you tell me how she received any training to drive an automobile? From what source or how?
A. In high school.
Q. Okay.
A. She got – she was in the Sunshine, I think it was called, Driving School, along with instruction by her father and me.
Q. And obviously I'm going to ask you the question, had she ever been in an accident before?
A. No.
Q. Did she have a European driver's license?
A. She may have, but I don't know.

Q. And if I might, you had told us a little bit about her travels the day of when she left. You had an expectation that she would be in Santa Cruz at a particular time?

A. Well, I knew that the girls, we had talked –

LIDDY: Wait, wait. The question, let's hear the question again.

CALLY: I thought she would be there by nine at the latest.

STEPHAN: I don't know if anybody asked this, but did you happen to look inside the vehicle when the girls got in to see if there was luggage in the back seat or things hanging up in the back or…

A. No, I didn't see anything like that.

Q. And, you know, I have to ask you this. Neither one of them have a –- one of those iPods or, you know, music device. Kids have them all…

CALLY: I don't know. No, I don't think so.

▲ ▲ ▲

Q. I don't think anybody asked you, but did Raechel wear any kind of glasses or sunglasses when she left your house, driving away at 12:30?

A. Well, she didn't. She had perfect eyesight, so I don't know if she had glasses on or not.

Q. Okay. I'm assuming by your answer that she wasn't wearing any corrective lenses, then?

A. No.

Q. How about sunglasses?

A. I don't remember. Probably.

At 3:20 p.m. the deposition ended. Like Chuck's earlier interrogation, it had produced no evidence supporting the "blame the victim" claims of Enterprise and DaimlerChrysler that somehow the sisters had been culpable in their own deaths. But in their search for such evidence, the defendants had hardly begun.

9

'BLAME THE VICTIM,' PART I

I F ENTERPRISE AND DaimlerChrysler could convince a jury that somehow the Houck sisters' behavior might have caused the crash that killed them, this would be a powerful counterweight to the contention that the PT Cruiser's fire-igniting defect was to blame. To succeed, the defendants would need to develop what has been called an "alternate cause case" – one that assumed a jury might not completely accept their "affirmative defense" claim that the defect played no part in the tragedy. As described by one attorney:

> In these scenarios, jurors often conclude that although the defendant company probably could have done more to make its product safer, the plaintiff was primarily to blame for the accident and injuries and that the plaintiff is therefore undeserving of any monetary award.

Jury experts have written volumes on the "blame the victim" approach taken by corporate defendants in civil personal-injury lawsuits. Is it effective, or too risky? Does it help or hinder in a product defect case? Can it backfire by creating more, rather than less, juror sympathy for the victims? One trial attorney who has studied scores of jury decisions in product liability cases has concluded that it depends on the severity of the injury and the extent of the victim's contribution to bringing it about. Juries, he believes, are "more likely to feel sympathy for the victim when the damage was severe and the victim was not to blame, sadness when the damage was severe and the victim bore relatively little blame, and anger at and disgust with the plaintiff when he or she was more blameworthy."

In a car crash case, the driver's susceptibility to blame can depend on a number of factors, most of them well known to the average juror. Young drivers are far more likely than older drivers to be involved in fatal crashes. Alcohol and drug use leads to an increased probability of loss-of-control collisions. Illness, chronic disability, lack of rest, distraction at the wheel, and even suicidal intentions may be involved. (Raglin, DaimlerChrysler's attorney, had pointedly asked Chuck Houck whether Jacqueline had ever indicated to him "thoughts of suicide or suicidal tendencies.")

Separately or in combination, these "blame the victim" factors can be exploited by the defense if there is evidence to suggest they may have been present in the crash. Whether they actually initiated the crash is another matter, of course; simply because a young driver is killed in a crash does not mean that the driver's youth was responsible for causing it.

A juror's determination of whom to hold responsible for a car-crash death may involve more than conscious consideration of these seemingly objective factors; deep-seated predispositions working at a subconscious level can be an even more powerful influence. Prominent researchers into the physical and psychological causes of accidents have long agreed that "blame the victim" thinking has deep roots in the teachings of religion. In the eyes of a wrathful deity, "People were responsible for their own safety, and the victim shared the guilt for his or her injury." Injured people thus may be held "partly or entirely responsible for the actions committed against them. In other words, the victims are held accountable for the maltreatment they have been subjected to." Those who employ "blame the victim" strategies do so "in order to have control and power."

Enterprise and DaimlerChrysler hardly lacked control and power in their own spheres. From its 1957 origin as a one-man business operating out of a basement in St. Louis, Missouri, Enterprise had grown into the nation's largest rental car company, with revenues exceeding $10 billion a year. Its founder and owner, Jack Taylor, was reputedly worth $14 billion; he ranked 37th among America's wealthiest individuals. DaimlerChrysler ranked fifth in size among the world's auto manufacturing giants.

From their depositions of Cally and Chuck Houck, the two defense lawyers had learned nothing that would help them construct a "blame the victim" scenario for the crash that killed the Houck sisters, but they at least had acquired the names of some of their daughters' closest friends – confidants, that is, who might possess damaging information about the sisters' habits and lifestyles.

Cally had identified Chad Hogan, John Mora, Brenna Carlson and Nicole Pinto as intimates of one or both of the girls. Thus armed, the defense attorneys issued subpoenas to depose each of the four. The depositions, held between September 2006 and July 2008, would probe the sisters' histories, focusing especially on Raechel, the driver, and the final two days of her life.

As the depositions unfolded, an outline of the events of those days took shape. Brenna Carlson recalled that on Wednesday, October 6, the day before the crash, Raechel drove from her mother's house in Oak View to Brenna's home in nearby Ojai, arriving at about 9 a.m. Brenna was getting married later that month and Raechel, whom she'd known since fourth grade, was to be a bridesmaid. Brenna wanted Raechel to try on her bridesmaid's dress – it turned out to be too big, so Brenna kept it to be altered. After the fitting the two friends chatted about Raechel's travels in Italy. She left between 10.30 and 11 a.m.

Chad Hogan had known Raechel since high school; he described their relationship as "best friends, attached at the hip." According to Hogan, that Wednesday morning he met Raechel and Jacqueline at their mother's house. They visited for a while, then he and Raechel picked up

Cally Houck at her office and the three of them had lunch at an Ojai restaurant. Jacqueline stayed at home.

Later that afternoon Chad and Raechel drove in his car to Nicole Pinto's house in Ventura, a drive of some 20 minutes. Nicole and Raechel had known each other since they were nine or ten years old, and Chad Hogan had gone to high school with both girls. Nicole recalled that at her house, the three of them sat around and talked, "basically just caught up."

Raechel and Chad met up with Nicole again that evening at Billy O's Restaurant & Saloon, a popular Ventura gathering place. Chad drove himself, Raechel and another friend, Kristen Kane. Arriving there between 9 and 10 p.m., they joined a larger group of people, including John Mora, another high-school classmate; his girlfriend Heather Gutierrez, and a third friend, Chelsea Castillo. They spent a few hours at Billy O's, leaving sometime around 11 p.m. or midnight. Mora and Heather gave Raechel a ride to her mother's house, which was on their way.

The next morning Raechel visited Brenna at her workplace in Ojai, arriving around 10 a.m. They spent a few hours together, mostly talking about Brenna's upcoming wedding. Raechel was "happy, she was excited about the wedding," Brenna recalled. From there Raechel drove to Ventura, where she had a brief visit with Nicole. They shared a breakfast burrito that Raechel had picked up on the way.

Raechel had left some CDs in Chad Hogan's car the day before, so she arranged to meet him at Chelsea Castillo's Ventura apartment and retrieve them. She and Jacqueline were there when Chad arrived with the CDs shortly before noon. They visited for less than hour in Castillo's apartment; then the girls headed back to Ojai to say goodbye to their mother and, with Raechel at the wheel, depart for Santa Cruz.

Was Raechel's driving en route to Santa Cruz impaired? Could it have caused the crash? What did her four best high-school friends know that would answer these questions, which were crucial to any "alternate cause case" that the defense might attempt to develop?

The first of the four to be deposed was Chad Hogan. On September 13, 2006, he spent nearly an hour answering questions put by Enterprise and DaimlerChrysler attorneys, most of them focused on drinking and drugs and many of them drawing a standard objection from Jon Holdaway, the Grassini firm's attorney – "Not reasonably calculated to lead to evidence admissible in trial. Vague. Ambiguous. Lacks foundation." If the case got to trial, a judge would rule on the objections at that time.

(BY DAIMLERCHRYSLER ATTORNEY CHRISTOPHER NEDEAU)
When you saw her, would you drink alcohol with her?
CHAD HOGAN: No, because I'm not a big drinker and I don't recall her ever after high school ever drinking unless we were at a bar.
Q. Did she use – did she use marijuana?
HOLDAWAY: Same objection. Same objection as previously.
HOGAN: Not in front of me.
NEDEAU: Well, do you have –
A. I don't know if she did.
Q. Do you believe that she did?
A. No, I have no reason to believe that.

▲ ▲ ▲

Q (BY NEDEAU): Prior to going to the bar in Ventura, had you had any alcoholic beverages that day?
A. No, sir.
Q. Had Raechel?
A. No, sir.

▲ ▲ ▲

Q. I think you testified that you were at Billy O's for a couple hours.
A. Yeah.
Q. You consumed alcohol there, I assume?

A. Let's see, yeah, a moderate amount.

Q. What were you drinking, if you remember?

A. Beer.

Q. What was Raechel drinking?

HOLDAWAY: Again, the same objections as previous.

HOGAN: That would be a guess on my part. I have no idea.

NEDEAU: Was it your custom when you would go to bars to buy a pitcher and share it or would you buy individual drinks?

A. No, it would have been an individual type of situation.

Q. What was Raechel's preference? Did she drink beer or did she drink mixed drinks, if you know?

A. She was more of a beer drinker to my recollection.

Q. So if you were – in your mind's eye, do you think that she was probably drinking beer that night?

A. In my mind's eye, she was only drinking beer.

▲ ▲ ▲

Q. Do you remember what was on [Raechel's] CDs that you had in your car?

A. I can only remember one because it's the only one she wanted to listen to.

Q. What was that?

A. Suicidal Tendencies.

Q. Is that a – is that the name of a song or a band?

A. No, it's a band, a great band.

▲ ▲ ▲

Q. Did you have an opportunity to observe the demeanor of Raechel and Jacqueline at your lunch break on October 7th?

A. Yes, I did.

Q. Had either of them, if you know, been drinking?

A. They hadn't, that I know.

Q. You didn't notice that?

A. No.

Q. Do you know if either of them had been using drugs?

A. No.

▲ ▲ ▲

Q. (BY ENTERPRISE ATTORNEY PAUL STEPHAN) Okay. Have you ever had occasion to talk to Raechel about – and again, this is an unfair question, about whether or not she ever used any drugs? Not prescription drugs and not over the counter, but I'm talking about drugs that are intoxicating at all.

HOLDAWAY: I'll object again. Not reasonably calculated to lead to evidence admissible in trial. Lack of foundation. Vague and ambiguous.

CHAD HOGAN: Okay. So the question is did we ever talk about her use –

Q. (BY STEPHAN): Drug use.

A. No, no.

Q. Never did?

A. No.

▲ ▲ ▲

Q. Okay. Now, I need to know this and I'm asking you this straightforward: Has there ever been a time when you ever have become aware that Raechel has used any of the drugs we just talked about and then driven an automobile afterwards?

A. No.

Q. How about alcohol, same question, have you ever known her to take – ingest alcohol and then drive a vehicle afterwards?

A. Absolutely not.

By the time the deposition was over, "alcohol," "beer," "drugs," "bar," "drink" and words with similar implications had occurred forty-five times in the question-and-answer exchange between the defense attorneys and Hogan.

The pattern would repeat itself in the depositions of Brenna Carlson, John Mora and Nicole Pinto. Carlson was questioned on September 13, right after Hogan. She hadn't been part of the gathering at Billy O's the night before the crash and couldn't answer questions about it; her deposition was brief – about 25 minutes. Nevertheless, alcohol and drug-related terms showed up nine times in the interrogation. DaimlerChrysler's attorney wanted to know whether Raechel was a "big drinker" who "drank alcohol frequently," whether the two girls went to bars together, and whether they had ever "used illegal drugs, meaning marijuana or methamphetamine." Brenna answered these questions in the negative.

John Mora's deposition, on November 2, 2006, lasted more than an hour, during which terms related to alcohol and drug use occurred more than seventy times. At one point the Enterprise lawyer, Stephan, perhaps frustrated that he was not getting the information he wanted, admonished Mora that he might be "called as a witness in a jury trial... in front of 12 people and the judge and the family and everybody else... " So it was important, he said, that Mora "give us the right answers here today." Despite this, Mora's responses, like those of Hogan and Carlson, made clear he was not aware that Raechel had any alcohol or drug problems.

Nicole Pinto's deposition took place nearly two years later, on July 17, 2008. Why Enterprise and DaimlerChrysler waited so long to interrogate Pinto isn't a matter of record, but it's conceivable they had realized that the depositions of Hogan, Carlson and Mora failed to provide the ammunition they needed to develop an "alternate cause case" blaming Raechel for the crash and taking the spotlight off the defective PT Cruiser. Pinto's deposition was their last chance before trial to question someone who'd been an intimate friend of Raechel's for nearly twenty years, who was born within two days of Raechel, who was "like a sister" to her.

The deposition lasted more than an hour; terms linked to alcohol and drug use occurred seventy-seven times. By now the pattern was well established. Had Nicole ever known Raechel to drink and drive? When had Raechel started drinking? Had she ever appeared intoxicated? Had Nicole and Raechel ever had an alcoholic beverage with meals? Had Raechel ever taken narcotics? Smoked marijuana? Been high? Had Nicole ever had to tell Raechel she shouldn't be driving because "you had too much to drink?" Did Raechel ever tell Nicole that in Italy she'd had "too much to drink or had a wild time or anything like that"? On the day of the crash, did Raechel say anything to Nicole about "feeling unwell"? Yet again, the answers contained no evidence that Raechel Houck had had an alcohol or drug abuse problem.

From the depositions of Raechel Houck's closest friends there emerged a profile of a healthy, alert young woman who had no history of drug or alcohol abuse or of drinking and driving. There was no basis to conclude she had been impaired in any way on the day of the crash. The barrage of accusatory questions had failed to elicit evidence that Raechel was other than extremely moderate in her alcohol intake, which was occasional and limited to small amounts of beer or wine. Nor had any of the four seen her use marijuana. On the evening before the crash she'd consumed no more than one beer at Billy O's, and then had been driven home by a friend, John Mora.

As for the crash itself, the coroner's report on the results of Raechel's autopsy was explicit in its toxicology findings: "ethanol, negative – drugs, negative." An additional note stated that neither of the sisters "was reported to be abusing drugs or alcohol. Neither was reported to be suicidal." On the CHP accident report form, check marks had been placed next to "cell phone not in use" and "none apparent" for inattention and "other associated factors."

If Enterprise and DaimlerChrysler still wanted to find a basis for blaming Raechel Houck for the fatal PT Cruiser crash, they would have to go elsewhere.

10

'BLAME THE VICTIM,' PART II

E NTERPRISE AND DAIMLERCHRYSLER now turned to a consulting firm well known for its willingness to testify on behalf of corporate defendants in product injury cases. Intent on blaming Raechel Houck for the crash that killed her and her sister, they retained Exponent, Inc., a company with a reputation for tailoring its testimony in product injury litigation to the needs of its corporate clients. Exponent assigned Douglas Young, a human factors specialist, to testify on behalf of the manufacturer and the rental car company in *Houck v. DaimlerChrysler et al.*

"By introducing a new way of thinking about an existing situation, we assist clients to overcome seemingly insurmountable obstacles," Exponent promises in its marketing literature. The defendants' "existing situation" in *Houck v. DaimlerChrysler et al.* was that so far it had been able to find no evidence on which to base its "blame the driver" assertions.

Exponent's helpfulness to corporations accused of causing human harm has been the subject of considerable documentation by public-health advocates, congressional investigators and the general press. Its experts craft positions favoring corporations under attack for causing human harm, whether the harm is to individuals in crashes of defective cars or through widespread assaults on public health and the environment. Exponent admits to depending on such work for its revenues. In its filings with the Securities and Exchange Commission, it states that laws, regulations and "other factors" that reduce the exposure of manufacturers to liability, such as regulations that discourage industry conduct which leads to harmful products and behaviors, could mean that corporate demand for Exponent's services would be "significantly reduced."

The consulting firm was founded in 1967 under the name "Failure Analysis Associates." It focused on investigating and analyzing accidents, principally on behalf of manufacturers being sued for injuries caused by product defects. In 1989 Failure Analysis formed a holding company and in 1990 it went public. In 1998, according to its marketing material, "we changed our name to Exponent, meaning 'one who expounds or interprets' - which is exactly what we are best at!" (The word "exponent" also means "a person or thing that is a representative, advocate... proponent, promoter." Some would maintain that this meaning better fits Exponent's work on behalf of corporations whose products or services are suspected of causing human harm.)

From its early incarnation as Failure Analysis, an important part of the consulting firm's revenues has come from testifying on behalf of motor vehicle manufacturers being sued in crash injury cases. Today more than half of its $220 million in annual revenues comes from litigation-related work; Exponent provides expert testimony in about 6,000 cases a year. It has armed itself with hundreds of professionals claiming credentials that qualify them as expert witnesses for motor vehicle manufacturers. Many have previously worked for or with car companies; Exponent boasts that of its 900 staff members, more than 200 have prior work experience with General Motors, Ford, or Chrysler.

Leon Robertson, a highly-regarded epidemiologist with vast research and teaching experience in injury causation and prevention, examined the role of Failure Analysis experts in motor vehicle injury litigation in his 2006 book, "The Expert Witness Scam." Robertson documented examples of testimony given on behalf of car companies by Exponent professionals in which, he found, data were skewed in order to show that despite its unsafe design, a vehicle's risk of causing injury was somehow "acceptable" or "not unreasonable," and therefore the vehicle's hazardous characteristic did not make it defective.

Cases in which Exponent witnesses slanted data, he wrote, involved cars, pickup trucks and SUVs with demonstrably defective proneness to crash fires, rollovers, and restraint system failures. An Exponent witness in a case involving fire-caused fatalities in General Motors C/K pickup trucks testified that overall fatality rates for C/Ks were "about the same" as for Ford and Chrysler pickups, even though the rates for the three were 1.514, 1.45 and 1.16, respectively. (Subsequently NHTSA, after looking at similar data, concluded that the C/K fuel tank design represented a safety defect.)

Another Exponent witness, in a case involving injuries caused by lack of a shoulder belt in the rear seat of a General Motors car, asserted that "lap and shoulder- belted occupants in back seats were no better off than those with lap belts only," Robertson wrote. Yet even General Motors' own researchers had concluded as early as the 1960s that "lap shoulder belts, when worn and worn properly, had the potential of providing more overall effectiveness than either unrestrained or lap belt only occupants," as a GM executive admitted in a similar case. According to Robertson the Exponent witness, Jeya Padmanaban, also failed to distinguish between minor and major injuries – a crucial distinction in assessing the nature of a vehicle defect such as absence of a shoulder belt, which can cause a lap-only belt to focus crash forces on the spinal column and abdomen rather than spreading them across the upper torso:

In a case where the injuries to lap/shoulder-belted front seat occupants were minor but the rear lap-belted occupant was a quadriplegic, the police officer had coded them all as the same injury. After dancing around the issue, Padmanaban finally admitted, "Well, as a nonmedical person, I can say quadriplegia is a little more severe than the injuries sustained by the front-seat occupant." Another new definition in statistics – inability to walk is only a "little more severe" than no permanent disability.

As Exponent's consulting activities have expanded beyond providing witnesses to car companies in crash injury cases, the firm has come under scrutiny for its work in other areas involving the impact of corporate products, policies and services on human health. "Doubt Is Their Product: How Industry's Assault on Science Threatens Your Health," is one result of such scrutiny. In the book, published in 2008, David Michaels, an esteemed epidemiologist whose public service includes senior positions in government and university-based research, places Exponent in the forefront of "the coterie of consulting firms that specialize in product defense":

> ...They profit by helping corporations minimize public health and environmental protection and fight claims of injury and illness. In field after field, year after year, this same handful of individuals and companies come up again and again.
>
> The range of their work is impressive. They have on their payrolls (or can bring in on a moment's notice) toxicologists, epidemiologists, biostatisticians, risk assessors, and any other professionally trained, media-savvy experts deemed necessary. They and the larger, wealthier industries for which they work go through the motions we expect of the scientific enterprise, salting the literature with their questionable reports and studies. Nevertheless, it is all a charade. The work has one overriding motivation: advocacy for the sponsor's position in civil court, the court of public opinion, and the regulatory arena. Often tailored to address issues that arise in litigation, they are more like legal pleadings than scientific papers.

"Doubt Is Their Product" gives numerous examples of such advocacy by Exponent, including the following:

- "MBTE is a gasoline additive 'so foul that a tiny amount makes water undrinkable.' It is also a possible human carcinogen and has been classified as such by California. Communities across the country have sued the major oil companies and the MTBE manufacturers for the costs of cleaning up their water supplies. In response, a firm that provides the methanol used for making MTBE hired Exponent to produce a series of studies that concluded, not surprisingly, that MTBE is unlikely to pose a public health hazard and has not significantly impacted California's drinking water."

- "An article in the Annals of Emergency Medicine suggested that the new generation of amusement park rides exposed thrill seekers to g-forces (a measure of acceleration) that exceed those experienced by astronauts and recommended that emergency physicians consider these rides as 'a possible cause of unexplained neurologic events in healthy patients.' Six Flags Theme Parks, Inc. immediately commissioned Exponent to produce an 'Investigation of Amusement Park Roller Coaster Injury Likelihood and Severity.' The press release on the report was headlined 'Roller Coasters, Theme Parks Extraordinarily Safe.'"

- "In 2005 an Exponent scientist conducted a study on behalf of the American Beverage Association that concluded that the number of beverages consumed from school vending machines 'does not appear to be excessive'" – a study helpful to soft-drink manufacturers being attacked for promoting childhood obesity. "In this case, however, the public just could not be convinced. The soft drink industry jettisoned these findings and in 2006 agreed to stop selling soda in schools."

- "Defense giant Lockheed Martin turned to Exponent when faced with the huge potential cost of cleaning up underground water sources contaminated with perchlorate, a rocket fuel component that according to the National Academy of Sciences causes thyroid disease in infants. Exponent's studies minimized the risk associated with perchlorate exposure."

- "When a study by consulting epidemiologists discovered a high rate of prostate cancer cases at a Syngenta plant that produced the pesticide atrazine, Exponent's scientists produced a study that found no relationship between the chemical and the disease."
- "After numerous studies that linked pesticide exposure and Parkinson's disease appeared in prestigious scientific journals, Exponent's scientists produced a literature review for CropLife America, the trade association of pesticide producers, whose conclusion maintained that 'the animal and epidemiologic data reviewed do not provide sufficient evidence to support a causal association between pesticide exposure and Parkinson's disease.'"
- "Exponent specializes in literature reviews that draw negative conclusions. The company's scientists have produced several reviews of the asbestos literature for use in litigation, all of which conclude that certain types of asbestos and certain types of asbestos exposure are far less dangerous than previously believed."

Others in the public health community who have questioned Exponent's impartiality in its work for corporate clients include Gerald Markowitz and David Rosner, leading public-health historians who co-authored the book "Deceit and Denial: The Deadly Politics of Industrial Pollution." In a 2003 paper in the Journal of Public Health Policy, they noted that Exponent's clients figured prominently in a 2002 Congressional investigative report by the staff of Rep. Edward Markey, "Turning Lead Into Gold: How the Bush Administration is Poisoning the Lead Advisory Committee at CDC." The report referenced Centers for Disease Control (CDC) estimates that 890,000 American children age 1-5 have elevated blood lead levels due to deteriorated paint in older housing, dust and soil contaminated by such point, and past emissions from leaded gasoline. It then warned that the Bush Administration was attempting to set back progress in reducing lead blood levels in children by changing the membership of CDC's Advisory Committee on Childhood Lead Poisoning Prevention, which had guided CDC policy in positive directions for more than a decade:

> This report reveals recent changes to the membership... that indicate that the nominations of renowned scientists with a long record in determining the health effects associated with childhood lead poisoning are being rejected, and that instead the vacancies are being filled by individuals who have direct ties to the lead industry, which has a financial interest in the policies adopted by the Advisory Committee. If the acceptable blood level limits are raised upwards, or if new scientific evidence indicating they should be revised further downwards is ignored, the health of many children in this country will be imperiled, and the corporate polluters will be allowed to trade the long-term health of children for short-term commercial gain.

More recently Exponent has been the subject of publicity for its role as a self-styled "independent" expert retained by Toyota Motors – more precisely, by the corporation's litigation defense law firm, Bowman & Brooke – to help fend off assertions that millions of Toyota vehicles may have defects in their electronic control systems that could lead to sudden unintended acceleration and, in some cases, crashes with severe injury consequences.

On February 18. 2010, the Los Angeles *Times* ran an article headlined, "Toyota Calls In Exponent Inc. as Hired Gun." The firm "is known for helping big corporations weather messy disputes" but "denies accusations that it skews results to benefit its clients," the article said. It quoted an Exponent executive, Mike Gaulke, as calling such criticism a "cheap shot":

> "Do we tell our clients a lot of what they don't want to hear? Absolutely," Gaulke said. He said the firm often comes up with

results that don't favor clients, although he couldn't provide specific examples.

Exponent told the *Times* it had performed tests demonstrating the absence of an electronic systems glitch which could trigger sudden acceleration. But according to the newspaper, "...the tests described by Exponent did not appear to duplicate the sophisticated methods that automotive engineers say are needed to ensure that electromagnetic interference does not cause failure of the hardware or software of engine controls. Indeed, Exponent did not say it placed any Toyota vehicle in a test chamber that automakers routinely use to bombard cars with high-powered electromagnetic signals known to disrupt automotive electronics."

The *Times* article also made reference to Exponent's work on behalf of cigarette manufacturers:

"If I were Toyota, I wouldn't have picked somebody like Exponent to do analysis," said Stanton Glantz, a cardiologist at UC San Francisco who runs a database on the tobacco industry that contains thousands of pages of Exponent research arguing, among other things, that secondhand smoke does not cause cancer. "I would have picked a firm with more of a reputation of neutrality."

On February 23, 2010, a Congressional investigative hearing, "Response by Toyota and NHTSA to Incidents of Sudden Unintended Acceleration," considered Exponent's role in the Toyota sudden acceleration matter. The hearing chairman opened the proceeding as follows:

In an attempt to quell concerns that sudden unintended acceleration occurs, Toyota attorneys commissioned a study titled, Testing and Analysis of Toyota and Lexus Vehicles and Components for Concerns Related to Unintended Acceleration by a company called Exponent. Toyota has presented this preliminary report to prove that the electronic system cannot cause sudden unintended acceleration.

However, this committee requested an independent expert assessment of the Exponent study; and these experts identified numerous shortcomings, including that the review did not follow sound scientific method; major categories of testing such as electromagnetic interference and radio frequency interference were not addressed; only one of the seven vehicles used in the study was on the recall list; and the study did not examine a single vehicle that had experienced sudden unintended acceleration.

It is clear that the flawed Exponent study is nowhere near adequate for a valid scientific review.

On May 20, 2010, as the Toyota sudden acceleration controversy grew more heated, *USA Today* weighed in with a lengthy article by Jayne O'Donnell, "Toyota Investigator Exponent Often Defends Automakers," that described the firm as "part of a thriving industry of firms that do research and scientific and engineering analysis for hire and provide expert testimony and reports for companies facing product disputes, government regulation and lawsuits." It said that "Exponent supplies a steady stream of experts and data to product-liability attorneys defending automakers, as well as reports that are used by automakers internally and in comments on NHTSA's regulatory docket."

Douglas Young was one such expert. Prior to his assignment to "assist clients" in the Houck case, Young had already appeared at least twice as a paid witness for DaimlerChrysler in litigation. For example, in *Guillot v. DaimlerChrysler Corp.*, a Louisiana jury found that a Jeep Cherokee's defective transmission slipped from park to reverse, allowing the vehicle to roll backward and pin a pregnant woman against a wall, injuring her unborn child so severely that it died shortly after birth. DaimlerChrysler, for whom Young testified, had maintained in the case that the Jeep's driver, who was the woman's husband, actually had left it in reverse when he briefly exited the vehicle. Evidence introduced at the trial showed that the manufacturer and NHTSA had knowledge of so-called park-to-reverse failures in similar Jeeps. The jury award against DaimlerChrysler was later upheld on appeal.

Young showed up at the Grassini law office midday February 3, 2009, to be deposed by Donald Liddy. Representing the defendants were attorneys Robert Hunter of the Pleasant Hill, California firm of Snyder and Hunter, and Troy Wiggins, of Wiggins, Richard & Romano, a San Francisco firm.

Young was prepared to testify that the PT Cruiser crash that killed the Houck sisters was caused by Raechel's "fatigue or inattention." In his opinion Raechel had "failed to maintain a proper lane position," which was "consistent with reduced perceptional processing, improper decision-making and/or some erroneous or inefficient movement behaviors"; her "steering behavior" was "consistent with a driver who is experiencing fatigue or inattention while operating the vehicle"; the vehicle's braking pattern was "not consistent with the general and typical types of emergency maneuvers drivers typically produce," and finally, any "loss of power steering" due to the defective power-steering fluid leak "would not have influenced her control of the vehicle during the event, at least initially."

The deposition began at 1:15 p.m. After getting Young's opinions on the record, Liddy asked him how many times he had testified at trial. "Probably about 25 or 30 times, I would estimate," Young said. How many of those had been auto crash injury cases? "Probably half." Was it usual for Young to get hired and then testify about the cause of the collision? "I've done that, yes." Had he ever testified that the cause was a defect in a vehicle? "No."

Liddy asked whether Exponent had a policy against providing expert witnesses in litigation where auto manufacturers were the defendants:

YOUNG: Well, we have a policy that involves a conflict system, so it's a situation in which if there are cases open against an auto manufacturer, then we're not allowed to go adverse to them, generally.

LIDDY: Have you ever – you've never testified against an auto manufacturer?

A. I've not.

Q. Do you know when the last time anyone at Exponent had testified against an auto manufacturer?

A. I don't.

Q. No recollection?

A. No.

Young had coauthored a paper which concluded that "the various designs in a [car] cockpit were not associated with unintended acceleration episodes." Was Young working on Toyota sudden acceleration cases? "Yes."

LIDDY: In the unintended acceleration article you place the blame on the drivers; correct?

YOUNG: Well, I don't know that we necessarily are placing the blame on anyone, but simply making the research, evaluate possible factors that could be causally related in those.

Q. Were any – did you conclude that any of the factors were caused by a defect in the vehicles?

A. No.

Q. So if there's no defect in the vehicles, the cause of unintended accelerations, in your opinion, was blamed on the driver; correct? Because it couldn't be blamed on anything else other than the vehicle or the driver, unless I'm missing something.

A. Certainly the driver is the primary factor in those, yes.

Young had already reached an opinion in one of the Toyota sudden acceleration cases he was working on:

LIDDY: And in that case you blamed the driver?

YOUNG: The driver made a pedal misapplication, yes.

Liddy asked Young about a paper he had written entitled "Human Factors and Product Recall Planning." What was the paper's conclusion?

> *YOUNG: Oh, essentially that during the [recall] process one should consider various human factors that are involved in a recall, so how owners may or may not, as an example, comply with a recall.*
>
> *LIDDY: Having looked into human factors and the role they play in product recall planning, did you reach any opinions concerning whether a recalled car such as this PT Cruiser should have been rented to the Houck girls?*
>
> *A. No.*
>
> *Q. Why not?*
>
> *A. I'm not giving any opinions about the business practices or recall in this particular matter.*
>
> *Q. Well, let me ask you: What is your opinion? Do you believe Enterprise should have rented this car to the Houck girls?*

Liddy's question brought a flurry of objections from the defense attorneys, but finally Young had to answer.

> *YOUNG: I don't have an opinion.*
>
> *LIDDY: Why not?*
>
> *A. I haven't evaluated it to generate an opinion.*

Liddy wanted to know whether Young was "interested in how to make the business operations of the clients that hire you safer." Young replied that he wasn't; it was "beyond the scope of my engagement." Why, then, had Young chosen the field of human factors for his work? Did he have "any interest in making the world a safer place?

> *YOUNG: Would be great if we had a safer world, absolutely.*
>
> *LIDDY: And did you do anything in this case to help the defendant who hired you to run their operations more safely?*

[More objections from defense counsel].
YOUNG: No.

Liddy made Young go over his opinions in detail. Did Young believe Raechel was asleep at the wheel? "I don't know that I can state she was asleep." When Young said that driver "fatigue or inattention" were the "most probable underlying causes" of the crash, did he state this as "a 51 percent likelihood or a hundred percent likelihood in your mind or somewhere in between?" Young was unable to narrow it down any further. As between fatigue and inattention, which did Young think would have more likely caused the crash? "I don't think we'll ever know exactly... I don't really know that I can separate them out."

Liddy questioned Young closely about the presence of smoke and possibly flame in the PT Cruiser's occupant compartment. Could this have influenced Raechel's driving behavior? If so, how?

Young said he was relying on a database of North Carolina crashes in which drivers had reported the presence of smoke and sometimes fire inside the moving vehicle prior to a crash. The implication was that since the drivers had made the reports, they had been able to control their vehicles sufficiently to avoid fatal crashes.

LIDDY: And if a driver is killed due to an accident caused by smoke coming inside the vehicle, they wouldn't be there to tell the officers what happened, would they?
YOUNG: They wouldn't be alive, correct. But accident reports are filled – completed for fatalities as well.
Q. Yes, accident reports are completed for fatalities, but they don't get to hear from the driver, do they, when the driver's dead?
A. Correct.

As the deposition was winding down, one of the defense attorneys asked for a break. When the deposition resumed, Young unexpectedly raised a new issue. He told Liddy he had also formed an opinion about Carlos

Wood, the driver of the truck involved in the fatal head-on collision with the Houck vehicle. Wood's recollection of seeing smoke coming from the PT Cruiser before the crash, Young now said, reflected faulty "memory reconstruction" rather than actual eyewitness memory. Wood had undependably "reconstructed" the event based on questions put to him later by the police and attorneys in the Houck case.

What had prompted Young's last-minute attempt to impugn Wood's eyewitness account of the PT Cruiser's condition in the split-second before the crash?

> *LIDDY: So did the attorneys for Enterprise remind you of this testimony on the break?*
> *YOUNG: No. No, they indicated that I'd forgotten to provide some of the bases [for my opinion].*
> *Q. And what's the difference between reminding you and indicating that you had forgotten?*
> *A. Well, they said, "Did you give all of your bases? And I said, "I think so." And they said, "I don't think so," basically. So as we had discussed yesterday in our meeting, I had told them of that and obviously had forgotten today.*

Liddy had no further questions. The deposition concluded at 3:08 p.m.; it had taken less than two hours. It was hard to see how Young's attempt to "blame the driver" in *Houck v. DaimlerChrysler et al.* had lived up to Exponent's promise to "assist clients to overcome seemingly insurmountable obstacles."

11

SETTLEMENT SNARES

THE USUAL ROUTE from Ojai to San Francisco takes the traveler north on Route 101, along the Pacific coast and past the site where the Houck sisters were killed in the crash of the defective PT Cruiser rented to them by Enterprise. On the rare occasions since the crash when she needed to drive to San Francisco, Cally Houck had avoided the 101 and instead taken a slightly longer inland route – the I-5, which connects to I-580 and enters the city via the Golden Gate Bridge.

Joined by her friend Nancy Mason, who had been with her the night she learned of her daughter's deaths, Cally drove to San Francisco on Tuesday, June 27, 2008. Nancy's sister JoAnn Ferns, a schoolteacher who lived in nearby Santa Barbara, came with them. At the request of Larry Grassini's office, Cally and Chuck Houck were to be available the following day for a court-ordered pretrial settlement conference in *Houck v. DaimlerChrysler et al.* at the San Francisco offices of Dennis Raglin's firm, Sedgwick Detert, which was representing Chrysler. (Although the defendant's name on the court docket remained unchanged, the DaimlerChrysler merger had come unglued a year earlier and the financially crippled survivor, Chrysler, had been taken over by Cerberus, a private equity firm.) Nancy was there to provide moral support for Cally

The first image the word "litigation" brings to mind for many people is a courtroom, complete with judge and jury. Yet the majority of civil cases never reach a jury. Although trial is "the focal event in American civil litigation," as the Oxford Companion to American Law notes, more civil cases end in settlement than go to trial. Depending on how the parties view their chances of prevailing before a jury, trial "can be either a specter that facilitates or an enticement that blocks settlement." One of the court's purposes in ordering a settlement conference is to encourage the parties to resolve their differences short of a trial, which entails high costs in time and money.

Cally contemplated the settlement conference with subdued expectations. Thus far her journey through life had taught her to put intellect and reason above emotion – to take things as they came, whether painful or otherwise.

The daughter of a Los Angeles deputy sheriff whose family had originated in Quebec, then migrated to Manchester, New Hampshire in the 1920s, Cally Houck remembered a childhood punctuated by contrasts, some of them jarring. When she was in first grade, her mother had a serious nervous breakdown and was treated with frequent doses of electroshock therapy. She recalled witnessing her mother's "terrifying meltdowns" during that period. That was when she "developed her Teflon," as she put it in describing her resilience in the face of misfortune.

The biggest influences in her childhood life had been her father and her maternal grandmother. Armand Spenard was a workaholic, a decorated full-time deputy sheriff who also ran a one-man business supplying bait to recreational fisherman at Lake Sherwood, north of Los Angeles. Cally often went with him on his bait-delivery trips. She remembered herself as a tomboy – the son her father never had – and him as "a man's man, liked the ladies, great sense of humor, great story teller, beloved by everyone." He was a Goldwater conservative but as she became increasingly liberal he encouraged her to express her own views even as they argued politics. Above all, she felt, he was devoted to social justice and compassion. "You're going to be a lawyer someday," he told her, and she never forgot that.

Her maternal grandmother, Florence Capri, was a first-generation American of German descent whose husband had come from an Italian immigrant family. They had moved to California from New Hampshire. Like her father, her grandmother had a strong sense of justice and fairness, and compassion for those who were less fortunate. She lived with her grandmother on and off during her mother's illnesses and her father's absences due to work.

Unlike her grandmother, her older twin sisters and her mother, who were practicing Seventh Day Adventists, and her father, a nonobservant but believing Catholic, Cally questioned the dogma of organized religion. She attended Seventh Day Adventist schools for much of her childhood and, like her siblings, did volunteer work at a church-run hospital, but looked to Eastern thought for insights into the meaning of things.

Early on she discovered the writings of J. Krishnamurti, the Indian-born teacher known for declaring that "truth is a pathless land" not reachable by "any religion, any sect... No organization can lead man to spirituality." She found his "profound reasoning" to be far more valuable than the doctrines of any church.

Right after high school Cally began to assert her independence with a series of moves away from home that took her, over time, to jobs in Laguna Beach, the Brian Head ski resort in Utah, and Las Vegas, and involved her in a number of relationships, including one that led to a brief unsuccessful marriage. At her father's urging she eventually enrolled at Southern Utah State College (now University) in Cedar City and studied for an undergraduate degree.

After she and Chuck Houck married, they moved to Ventura, California, where Cally took up commercial photography. She soon became pregnant with Raechel, and a few years later Jacqueline was born. She discovered that motherhood was her calling. "That was all I wanted to do, to have my children thrive, have huge open minds. I became a real hands-on mom, fascinated by my children."

So that she could be near her daughters all the time, the couple rented a house in Ventura big enough to accommodate Cally's photography studio, where she did portraiture and other assignments. Unlike most of the area's commercial photographers, she did her own film processing, in which she developed techniques that introduced intriguing tones of light and shadow into the final product. It worked out well; she was able to be with her children almost all the time while still earning an income.

When she became pregnant with Greg, her youngest child, the family moved to Ojai, inland from Ventura. There she continued to do freelance photography as a source of income while keeping her main focus on her children. When they were old enough, she enrolled in night classes at Ventura School of Law. She passed the bar in 1995 and opened a solo practice in the Meiners Oaks neighborhood of Ojai, near her home. On October 4, 2004, Raechel and Jacqueline Houck, eager to see their mother, had made that office their first stop on arrival from Santa Cruz in the PT Cruiser rented from Enterprise.

Cally's expectations for the settlement conference were low. The defendants were still acting as though they believed they could convince a jury that Raechel, not the defective PT Cruiser, had caused the Houck sisters' deaths. This made the likelihood of a settlement, reasonable or otherwise, slim at best. But Cally believed that Larry Grassini and Roland Wrinkle were "capable and tenacious and wanted to win this," with or without a settlement. So far a firm trial date hadn't been set – the plaintiffs wanted one but the defendants had been resisting. As a lawyer, Cally knew that under California's procedural rules a trial was required to be held within five years of June 28, 2005, when the case had been filed. The longer DaimlerChrysler and Enterprise could delay a trial until the last moment, the more it would add to the expense and stress imposed on the Houcks and their lawyers, and this appeared to be the strategy the two huge corporations, with their seemingly bottomless resources to spend on defense lawyers and experts, were pursuing.

Cally, Nancy Mason and JoAnn Ferns reached San Francisco late that Tuesday afternoon after a six-hour drive from Ojai. They checked into the Adante on Geary Street, one of many small, lower-priced hotels in the Union Square neighborhood, and walked to a nearby Chinese restaurant for dinner. The weather was clear, cool and breezy. Despite the somber purpose of the trip, Cally recalled that it had some bright spots.

The Adante was one of them; there were "seaside murals all over the hotel. Rooms were vintage with deep seated windows that would open. Fire escapes at the front of the building... It was lovely."

The next morning the three women took the California Street cable car down to the Embarcadero district. Sedgwick Detert's offices were on the upper floor of a building at One Market Plaza, a business complex in the Embarcadero. On entering the lobby Cally was struck by "a huge poster displayed on a window outside one of the ground-floor offices. The poster was of an enormous butterfly, and I remember I believed it a good omen, because butterflies were frequently used symbolically in the writings and art of Raechel and Jacqueline, and thus symbolic to me."

While Nancy and JoAnn waited downstairs, Cally went up to the Detert offices and talked briefly with Grassini and Wrinkle. She and Chuck were asked to stay nearby so they could be called into the conference in case the defendants made a realistic settlement offer. David Garcia, a retired California Superior Court judge who had become a professional mediator, presided.

As it turned out, Cally and Chuck were never called in; there was no settlement offer. Larry Grassini recalled that the defendants wanted to show animations supporting their crash causation claims; he refused to see them. It was clear to Grassini and Wrinkle that Chrysler and Enterprise were running out the clock to avoid trial for as long as possible and keep the pressure on the Houck parents by making them "sit there and suffer," as Wrinkle put it, and perhaps even despair to the point of abandoning the litigation. First Chuck had been fired for bringing the lawsuit, Wrinkle recalled, and then "we can't get inside a courtroom – that was indescribably frustrating for both of them. It was so difficult... One of the most frustrating things in handling the whole Enterprise case was how we couldn't get a trial date. Everything keys off of the trial date. If you don't have a trial date, the defendants don't get serious about the case."

After the conference Cally met with Grassini and Wrinkle and had what she remembered as her first extended conversation with the two attorneys. "Larry and Roland were discussing that the whole issue was going to be causation, and I knew from my profession that meant protracted litigation, and I also knew that causation is a tool that defense counsel uses all the time in a war of attrition. They want to run up the expenses for the other side." In her own practice Cally had "seen a lot of unscrupulous attorneys"; it had taken her awhile to warm to Grassini and Wrinkle. But at this meeting she felt an "instant rapport" with the two men. They were clearly committed to the case; as Wrinkle described it later, in the face of the defendants' run-up-the-costs stonewalling tactics his and Grassini's attitude was, "We're going to beat 'em, we're going to do this."

Reinforcing Cally's sense of connection to the attorneys was her recent knowledge that eighteen months earlier, Larry Grassini's 26-year-old son Leo, an emergency medical technician and hospital volunteer, had died suddenly. "Anybody's who's lost a child feels an instant bond," she said.

Nothing had been accomplished at the settlement conference. The parties were "so far apart on damages, so far apart on liability, on causation... no numbers were ever discussed with us," Cally recalled. The disheartening outcome of the conference made her especially grateful that Nancy Mason and her sister had come with her to San Francisco. "Those girls really helped me out, they kept me focused."

June 28 was also JoAnn Fern's birthday. To celebrate and put that day's unproductive settlement conference behind them, Cally, Nancy Mason and JoAnn went for dinner to Magnolia, a popular brew pub in the Haight-Ashbury district. As they were leaving, Cally heard someone calling her name. It was one of Raechel's high school friends, Laura Laszlo. They stood outside the restaurant and talked for a while. The young woman told Cally that she'd been living in France for a few years and now was home visiting her mother, who lived in Haight-Ashbury. She had heard about the sisters' deaths and wanted, Cally remembered, to "express her sadness... It was surreal that, out of all the people in the city, she was the one we'd run into."

The possibility of settlement now seemed remote to Cally; "I hunkered down for the long haul." But then, eight months later, she learned from Grassini and Wrinkle that a Chrysler settlement offer might be in the works.

"We'd been told that Chrysler counsel wanted to settle from as early as February 2009. We also knew the settlement amount would not exceed one million dollars," she recalled. Chuck and I had discussed this with Grassini and Wrinkle and we decided we'd put whatever was received, or at least a sizable portion, toward the costs of the suit, as they were quite high after four years and Grassini and Wrinkle hadn't received any fees at all during the litigation." The two lawyers, however, were planning to turn all the funds over to the Houcks.

Settlement discussions with Chrysler became more serious as the likelihood of the ailing corporation's bankruptcy increased. Bankruptcy would relieve the corporation of its debts, including funds owed to plaintiffs in auto-defect death and injury cases, and would remove it as a defendant in the Houck litigation. Larry Grassini recalled that "when they were getting ready to go into bankruptcy, the lawyer for Chrysler called me up and he said, 'On certain righteous claims, Chrysler wants to do the right thing, and they want to pay some money. So they'll pay the Houcks a million dollars right now'... I brought the Houcks in and talked to them. I said, 'Here's the situation. It looks like they're going to go into bankruptcy where you're not going to get anything. At least, this would get something from them.'"

On April 23, 2009, the Houcks, their attorneys, and the attorneys for Chrysler finalized the settlement agreement. On April 30, the court issued an order validating the settlement. On the same day, Chrysler filed for bankruptcy. Grassini called the Chrysler lawyer. "I said, 'I want to be sure this thing doesn't go sour.' The lawyer said to me, 'I'll tell you how I'm going to do it. I'll have Chrysler put the check into my trust account, the defense lawyer's trust account, and I'll call you when I have that check, and once the check is in my trust account you can have [the Houcks] fill out the release and send it out.' Calls me up and says, 'I've got it, check's in my trust account. We bring them in, have them sign the release, send it off.' Then I get another phone call from the guy, he says, 'You won't believe this. They stopped payment on the check.' Chrysler stopped payment on the check! So now we've got to call up the Houcks and say, No check."

The Houck attorneys were outraged but helpless. "It was in the lawyer's trust account, can you imagine that?" Wrinkle said. "They stopped payment on the check they promised their lawyer, that he put in his trust account so he could pay one of the many, as he put it, 'righteous claims'." Larry and Roland had been told that despite the bankruptcy, "that would not happen, they weren't in bankruptcy at the time of the settlement... We had thought we were going to get the money, that they were protecting us. 'Yeah, we're going to do it this way'... The Chrysler bankruptcy reached out and took the money back from Chrysler's lawyers!"

What had seemed to be a slight step forward for the plaintiffs in *Houck v. DaimlerChrysler et al.* had turned out to be yet another turn for the worse for the Houcks, whose travails in the case Wrinkle thought were of biblical proportions. "The system just seemed to be absolutely against them. Now it's the locusts!"

12

PIERCING THE ENTERPRISE VEIL

WITH CHRYSLER NO longer a defendant, the Houck litigation would focus entirely on Enterprise. What had the giant rental-car company done, or failed to do, that resulted in the Houck sisters' deaths? Had it been negligent in renting the recalled PT Cruiser to Raechel and Jacqueline? And even if it had been negligent, was the PT Cruiser's admitted defect, and therefore Enterprise's negligence, the cause of the fatal crash?

And what, after all, was this thing called "Enterprise"? There was the national company, the "parent company," known as Enterprise Rent-A-Car Company, with headquarters in St. Louis, Missouri. There was Enterprise Rent-A-Car of San Francisco, an "operating subsidiary" of the parent company. There were so-called "regionalized subsidiaries" of Enterprise Rent-A-Car of San Francisco, and there were branches of the regionalized subsidiaries – also known as offices, dealerships, agencies or "locations" – such as the one in Santa Cruz from which the PT Cruiser had been rented by the Houck sisters.

To further complicate the Enterprise structure, a privately-owned holding company, "Enterprise Holdings," was created in 2009 by the family of Jack Taylor, who founded the rental car business in 1958, as an umbrella to control Enterprise Rent-A-Car, National Car Rental,

Alamo Rent-A-Car and other Enterprise-owned properties. Despite its byzantine complexity, the Enterprise Rent-A-Car kingdom had remained under the private control of the Taylor family, who made all policy decisions affecting its operations – presumably including the decision to defend itself so aggressively in the *Houck* case. Roland Wrinkle assumed that as the litigation progressed, Enterprise "had some very significant involvement in what was going on… their reputation was at stake so I would guess they had a very strong influence if not just absolute control."

Corporate defense attorneys are adept at getting product-liability cases against their clients thrown out of court by asserting that the business entity named by the plaintiffs as a defendant, although part of the client's corporate universe, is technically not the one responsible for the injury that triggered the lawsuit. Enterprise's labyrinthine organizational structure lent itself to this kind of argument. Wrinkle's research had suggested that this indeed might be a problem in *Houck*; in the past, the parent company had been able to avoid being targeted as a defendant in most liability cases because of the "corporate wall" between Enterprise St. Louis and the local renting agency. The headquarters company would claim that it could not be held liable for harm involving Enterprise rental vehicles because those vehicles were "owned and operated" by the subsidiaries, not the parent. It would make this claim while simultaneously boasting in its marketing materials that it "owns and operates more than 1.2 million cars and trucks, making it the largest car rental company in the world."

As the plaintiffs' discovery against Enterprise proceeded with depositions and interviews of executives and employees, the Gordian knot into which the mammoth auto rental empire had fashioned itself gradually loosened, revealing a policy of indifference or worse toward the urgency of fixing safety defects in recalled vehicles before they were placed into the hands of its customers. Proof began to take shape that it was the negligence of Enterprise of St. Louis – "headquarters" – and not of some lower-level entity.

In cases such as *Houck,* the plaintiffs' attorneys begin the discovery process by giving notice of their intent to depose "the person most knowledgeable" (PMK) about a specified aspect of the company's conduct, organization, policies, etc. The defendant then must designate that person, usually from within the company's staff, and ensure that he or she "is educated on all topics for which he or she is designated." The PMK must then be produced, with relevant documents, for deposition by one of the plaintiffs' attorneys.

Grassini and Wrinkle's first PMK discovery demand called for designation by Enterprise Rent-A-Car of San Francisco, the regional entity to which the Santa Cruz rental office belonged, of a PMK witness who could testify about "ensuring that vehicles subject to recall are not rented to the public; why the subject vehicle was rented to the plaintiffs daughter after the recall notice was issued; your policies and procedures for processing recall notices issued on vehicles you rent to the public, and the means used to repair the PT Cruisers subject to [NHTSA] recall No 04V-268." On Wednesday, May 16, 2007, at its lawyers' offices in San Francisco, Enterprise produced for deposition its designated PMK – a man named Thomas Moulton, whose title at Enterprise Rent-A-Car of San Francisco was "group vehicle repair manager" – and some documents related to his designation. Donald Liddy of the Grassini firm was the deposing attorney. The proceeding began at 2 p.m., with Troy Wiggins again representing Enterprise of San Francisco and a new attorney, James Green of the Tulsa law firm Conner & Winters, appearing for Enterprise of St. Louis.

Within minutes it became clear that Moulton, despite having worked for Enterprise for more than nine years, either did not know or would not disclose the information described in the "most knowledgeable person" designation:

LIDDY: Are you the person most knowledgeable regarding the processing
of recall notices?
MOULTON: Yes.
Q. And can you explain to me what your job is in that regard?

A. My job is to monitor the process, to speak to my original people to try to get them to follow up with branches and be as compliant as we can to get recalls performed.

Q. Is there any paperwork or documents which instruct you on how to process a recall notice that you receive?

A. No

Q. How do you know that?

A. None that I've seen.

Q. Have you asked anyone about those documents?

A. The – I guess, can you rephrase that?

Q. Well, let me ask you a different question. Did you receive any training on how to process a recall notice?

A. I honestly cannot recall. I mean, if I did, it would have been – I don't remember how I received the knowledge.

Turning to the 2004 recall of the defective PT Cruiser, Liddy wanted to know when Moulton had found out about it and what, if anything, he had done in his capacity as the "person most knowledgeable" about recall matters at Enterprise of San Francisco. Moulton said he couldn't recall ever seeing the PT Cruiser defect notice.

LIDDY: When did Enterprise receive the recall notice?

MOULTON: Well, when did Enterprise receive that particular recall notice?

WIGGINS: When you say Enterprise here, are we speaking about Enterprise Rent-A-Car Company of San Francisco?

LIDDY: Any Enterprise entity that he has any knowledge of.

WIGGINS: That's all right.

MOULTON: It would be September 9th.

Q. How do you know that Enterprise – or some Enterprise entity received the recall notice on September 9th?

A. In the documents that I just – we were given.

Q. When did you find out that Enterprise received a recall in September 9th, 2004?

A. Probably – well, exactly when I received those documents was when I found those dates out.

Q. When was that?

A. [To Wiggins] Would be – was it Tuesday that I received that?

WIGGINS: You need to answer.

MOULTON: Yeah, it would be Tuesday.

LIDDY: When you say Tuesday, do you mean yesterday?

MOULTON: Yes.

Q. Why was it that you just found out yesterday when the recall notice came in?

A. That was when I received the information.

Q. Did you wonder why you just found out yesterday when the recall notice came in?

A. I never had any thoughts on why or when.

Q. Have you had any thoughts on why the vehicle was rented to the Houcks after the recall notice was received?

A. No.

Q. Have you asked anybody at Enterprise about why Enterprise was renting cars after recall notices were received?

A. No.

Q. As you sit here today, do you have any interest in that topic?

Wiggins instructed Moulton not to answer the question, calling it "argumentative...an attempt to cast his testimony in a bad light." Liddy rephrased it:

LIDDY: Did you ever consider the possibility that Enterprise should not rent cars to the public after they've received recall notices from the manufacturer?

MOULTON: No.

Q. So you have no knowledge why the PT Cruiser rented by the Houck girls was rented to them after the recall was received?
A. No.
Q. Does anyone at Enterprise have knowledge why that car was rented after the recall was received?
A. I have no idea.
Q. Have you made any attempt to find out if anyone at Enterprise has the knowledge of why that car was rented after the recall was received?
A. I personally have not.

Wiggins broke in again, this time to assure Liddy that "there is nobody who is more knowledgeable on those topics than Mr. Moulton, at least that we've been able to find." Did that mean, Liddy asked, that "no one at Enterprise is responsible for getting cars off line when they receive a recall notice?" Moulton answered that he was "the one responsible to ensure that we perform the recalls in a timely manner," which he defined as "when we can get them done."

At Liddy's prompting Moulton then proceeded to describe the system by which, he said, Enterprise tried to keep track of defect recalls and have the recalled vehicles repaired. When a defect notice from a manufacturer was received by the headquarters company, it was supposed to be added to the computerized "unit history" of each vehicle covered by the notice. Liddy wanted to know how an employee renting a car to a customer would find out from the "unit history" whether it was under recall.

MOULTON: We'd have a database where they could plug in the actual unit number into — enter in. The history would come up for it. They would hit maintenance history, and then that history would be involved in that. It would say — stating needing a recall, if that were the case.
LIDDY: And is there any requirement that the Enterprise employee pull up the unit history before they rent the car to a customer?
MOULTON: No.

Liddy asked whether, at the time that the PT Cruiser was rented to the Houck girls, the recall was "part of the unit history of that vehicle."

> *MOULTON: I'm not sure. I would definitely say from the information we received, I'm not sure if it has or not. I can't state either way.*

If Moulton – the "person most knowledgeable" – didn't know, who did? Liddy asked him who within the Enterprise organization was "responsible for looking at the recall notice to determine if it's something that's dangerous," like "the car catching fire."

> *MOULTON: I don't know.*
> *LIDDY: Did you make that determination, that the recall in this case involved something that was a danger to the public?*
> *A. I'm not sure.*
> *Q. And you don't know if anyone at Enterprise did that?*
> *A. It's – not to my knowledge. I'm not sure how that process determines what "danger" is, is there; however typically we will get more information from the manufacturer in those cases.*
> *Q. Who determines if after a recall is issued and received, whether cars continue to be rented to the public?*
> *A. Well, that would be at the branch level.*
> *Q. Who at the branch level makes that determination?*
> *A. I'm not sure who made those determinations.*

Liddy asked Moulton to describe the activities of the parent company, Enterprise of St. Louis. He couldn't or wouldn't. In that case, Liddy asked, what were the activities of Enterprise of San Francisco, Moulton's employer?

> *MOULTON: Rent cars, fleets, and we rent – we do daily rental, fleet services, truck rental, ride share.*
> *Q. Do you sell cars?*

A. Yes.

Q. Do you sell cars to the public that have been subject to a recall without doing the recall fix?

A. I have no idea.

At the outset of his deposition Moulton had admitted he didn't see or know about the PT Cruiser's defect or its recall until the day before being deposed. He had found out, he said, from a document that the Enterprise lawyers had shown him one day earlier, after being forced to disclose it to the plaintiffs in discovery – the email notification of the defect received by Bob Agnew, a staff person at Enterprise headquarters. Signed by an executive at DaimlerChrysler National Fleet Service named Greg Burke, it had been sent at 12:41 p.m. on September 9, 2004, nearly one month before Enterprise rented the PT Cruiser to the Houck sisters. Moulton identified the recipient, Agnew, as a "service operations manager" who reported to Thomas Gieseking, the assistant vice president of service operations at Enterprise headquarters.

It now had become indisputable that Enterprise Rent-A-Car knew about the PT Cruiser fire-hazard defect prior to October 4, 2004. Why hadn't the defect been remedied before the vehicle was rented to the Houck sisters? Of the multiplicity of Enterprise entities controlled by the St. Louis company, which one or ones were ultimately responsible for having rented the unrepaired vehicle to the sisters?

Moulton had implied that the buck stopped at the branches. He'd been asked who determined whether cars continue to get rented to the public after a recall is received. His answer: "Well, that would be at the branch level." Were Enterprise headquarters and Enterprise Rent-A-Car of San Francisco trying to avoid accountability by passing it off on the tiny Santa Cruz office?

Moulton's reference to Thomas Gieseking's role at Enterprise Rent-A-Car of St. Louis suggested that Gieseking might be responsible for the headquarters company's defect-recall policies. Shortly after Moulton's deposition, Grassini and Wrinkle served notice that it intended to depose Gieseking as the "person most knowledgeable" at the headquarter company on the issues for which Moulton had been questioned: "...ensuring that vehicles subject to recall are not rented to the public; why the subject vehicle was rented to the plaintiffs daughter after the recall notice was issued; your policies and procedures for processing recall notices issued on vehicles you rent to the public, and the means used to repair the PT Cruisers subject to [NHTSA] recall No 04V-268."

The deposition was scheduled for August 16 at a court reporter's office in St. Louis; on August 14, Enterprise's lawyers filed a thirteen-page set of wide-ranging objections to its intended scope. Over and over again, the objections repeated what would become the mantra for the headquarters company's assertion that it wasn't responsible for renting the defective vehicle to the Houck sisters:

> "Enterprise Rent-A-Car Company does not own vehicles or rent vehicles to the public. Each of Enterprise Rent-A-Car Company's independent operating subsidiary corporations, such as Enterprise Rent-A-Car Company of San Francisco, which do own and rent vehicles to the public, develop their own procedures for handling manufacturer's [sic] recalls on their vehicles."

It was clear from the objections that no matter what the Grassini lawyer might ask him, Gieseking's answers would be confined to information about the headquarters company's electronic system for logging defect recall information into the "unit histories" of vehicles "owned and operated by the subsidiaries." Any suggestion that Gieseking could answer questions about the NHTSA recall of the PT Cruiser would be resisted, because even though the headquarters company admittedly had received the DaimlerChrysler email notice, it "did not receive" a copy of the NHTSA notice. (This was a misleading argument; owners of a recalled defective vehicle typically receive notice from the manufacturer, not NHTSA.)

The deposition began at 10:20 a.m. August 16 at a law office in St. Louis. James Green was there to represent Enterprise Rent-A-Car Company of St. Louis. Troy Wiggins was there for Enterprise of San Francisco. Don Liddy was again representing the *Houck* case plaintiffs.

Within minutes of Gieseking taking the oath, Green was challenging Liddy's questions in an aggressive proactive attempt to block anything suggesting that the "parent" Enterprise company had a responsibility for the renting of a recalled defective car to the Houck sisters.

LIDDY: And are you the most knowledgeable person at the parent company concerning the recall of vehicles that Enterprise rents?

GIESEKING: Considering the electronic communications of recalls, yes, from the manufacturers to the subsidiaries.

GREEN: Counsel, we have, as you know, filed – or served on you responses and objections to each of these categories. If you would like, I can read that response into the record or we can make these as an exhibit to the deposition.

The thirteen pages of objections were made part of the record. Liddy attempted to move forward with his interrogation of Gieseking:

LIDDY: Is there somebody at Enterprise who sets the policies for how vehicles that are recalled are not rented to the public?

GREEN: Objection to the form of the question. We need to determine which Enterprise entity you're talking about, Counsel. Enterprise Rent-A-Car Company, as this witness is the representative?

LIDDY: Are there different policies for each Enterprise entity for ensuring that recalled vehicles are not rented to the public?

GIESEKING: Enterprise Rent-A-Car, the parent corporation, which does not own or operate vehicles, does not set the policies for its subsidiary. Each subsidiary independently is responsible for setting their policies.

Q. Why is that? Why is it that each subsidiary sets their own policy for making sure that recalled vehicles are not rented to the public?
A. Because we do not own and operate those vehicle.

In that case, Liddy asked, what was the parent company's relationship to the subsidiaries? "We act as consultant and will assist the subsidiaries when called upon," Gieseking told him.

LIDDY: So does the parent company have any policy with respect to ensuring that recalled vehicles are not rented to the public?
A. No.
Q. How, if you know, do the subsidiaries establish their policies for ensuring that recalled vehicles are not rented to the public?
A. Sir, I don't know. Varies by subsidiary, which is their – which is their call.

Had anyone at Enterprise expressed "any interest in determining whether recalled vehicles are rented to the public?" Liddy asked Gieseking. Green immediately objected, calling it an "improper question" that "calls for speculation on his part."

Liddy had the witness confirm what was already on the record from Moulton's deposition – that someone named Bob Agnew at Enterprise headquarters had received the PT Cruiser recall notice from DaimlerChrysler on September 8, 2004. Then he walked him through a series of questions, often drawing further objections from Green, about Enterprise headquarters' process for alerting the subsidiaries to safety recalls and recalls for non-safety issues. How did headquarters differentiate between the two types recall?

GIESEKING: We follow the manufacturer's designation.
LIDDY: And how was this recall designated?
A. This recall was designated as a safety recall.

Q. And when you get a recall that's designated as a safety issue, do you treat that recall any differently than a non-safety recall?

If the policy of Enterprise headquarters required that the subsidiaries and branches should treat safety recalls differently from non-safety recalls, this might suggest a degree of headquarters involvement in the process that Green and Geiseking were attempting to disown.

Geiseking gave a lengthy description of the sophisticated electronic system by which headquarters alerted the subsidiaries to safety recalls, which he said were called "priority" by headquarters and were distinguished from "non-safety recalls." Unlike "priority" recalls, he said, headquarters left it "up to the discretion of the subsidiary" whether to enter "non-safety recalls" into their information systems or not. From the standpoint of the headquarters company's claimed lack of responsibility for fixing safety defects in recalled vehicles, the fact that the headquarters "alert" system even made such a distinction seemed puzzling.

LIDDY: Did this – did this [PT Cruiser] recall have a priority level?
GIESEKING: This was a safety recall.
Q. Is there a priority level within Enterprise for recalls?
A. It is – it is whatever the manufacturer dictates is safety or not. So if you see priority, yes. Priority, nonpriority. Priority equals safety. If the manufacturer dictates that it is a recall, then Enterprise translates that to a priority recall.
Q. So you just have two levels, priority or not?
A. Priority and not priority, correct.
Q. What does priority mean?
A. Priority means safety recall.
Q. And when a recall is given priority, what does that mean?
A. Well, that the – the subsidiary interprets that as being a safety-related recall.

Why hadn't the system created by Enterprise headquarters worked to prevent rental of the defective PT Cruiser to the Houck sisters?

LIDDY: Do you have an understanding of why this vehicle was rented to these customers after the recall was entered in the system?

GIESEKING: No, I don't.

Q. And as we sit here today, do you know whether vehicles that are subject to a safety recall at the present time are still being rented to Enterprise customers?

A. I do not know.

Q. And have you – have you talked to anybody at Enterprise about not renting recalled vehicles to the public?

A. Enterprise the parent as we've spoken?

Q. Right.

A. No, sir.

Q. Have you talked to the Enterprise subsidiaries about whether it's a good idea to rent recalled vehicles to the public?

WIGGINS: Objection, overbroad.

A. No, each subsidiary is responsible for their own policies.

LIDDY: Is the parent company not responsible for its subsidiaries?

GREEN: Objection to the form of the question. It's vague and ambiguous and calls for a legal conclusion on the part of the witness that's not designated to give a legal conclusion.

LIDDY: Is that your understanding?

GIESEKING: Yes.

Liddy asked Gieseking whether anyone at Enterprise was responsible for "making sure vehicles are safe when they're rented to the public." Not to his knowledge, the witness replied. When Liddy attempted to press for more information about responsibility within the Enterprise system for vehicle safety matters, he drew a storm of objections from Green, who argued that because the PMK notice had not specifically used the word "safety," Gieseking shouldn't be asked such questions. When Gieseking finally responded, it was to repeat yet again that, "Enterprise Rent-A-Car, the parent, does not own or operate cars. The subsidiaries make those decisions. Enterprise Rent-A-Car of San Francisco makes their own policies."

LIDDY: But the parent company does own the subsidiaries, doesn't it?
GIESEKING: Correct.

The deposition lasted for two hours, with the witness, Gieseking, and the Enterprise lawyer, Green, hewing to the position that it was the branches, not headquarters or the subsidiaries, that were ultimately responsible for seeing to it that recalled vehicles were fixed before being rented out. And like Moulton in his deposition three months earlier, they could not explain why the Houck vehicle had been rented out with an unrepaired safety defect – or they did not want to.

13

BLAMING THE BRANCHES

WHETHER THE COURT would accept the Enterprise parent company's contention that it did not "own or operate cars" and therefore had no responsibility for the rental of a recalled defective car to Raechel and Jacqueline – or, for that matter, to any customer – was crucial to whether the plaintiffs could prevail in *Houck*. Policies and procedures governing rentals of recalled vehicles were solely the province of the local branches, the defense argument went. If it held up, the likelihood that the court would allow the case to go forward against "headquarters," or that a jury would find for the Houcks, would plummet.

It was a curious argument; Enterprise's own extensive promotional materials seemed to give the lie to it. One of the company's many website self-encomiums proclaimed, "With annual revenues of $16.4 billion and more than 78,000 employees, Enterprise Holdings and its affiliates own and operate almost 1.4 million cars and trucks." Another declared, "Our parent company and executive management team set the tone for the way we do business, from our values and culture to our commitment to diversity, local communities and corporate citizenship." Enterprise headquarters seemed to be claiming that the rental of recalled defective cars was somehow exempt from the tone-setting.

To test that claim, it was essential to learn how Enterprise's branch-level managers and employees handled safety recalls, and to what extent "headquarters" and the regional offices influenced the process.

Documents produced by Enterprise headquarters and disclosed to the plaintiffs at the Moulton and Gieseking depositions had included computer records of a "rental unit history" and an "open recall history" for the defective PT Cruiser. These revealed that the vehicle had been rented out not once but four times subsequent to Enterprise receiving the recall notice – the fourth time to Raechel Houck.

All the rentals had been made from the Santa Cruz branch office. All the customers lived in or near Santa Cruz. According to the rental unit history, Karen Maddox had rented the car on September 11, 2004, two days after Enterprise received the recall notice from DaimlerChrysler. Maddox returned it on September 27. It was immediately rented to Cathy Temme, who returned it on September 29. That day it was again rented, to Karen Cummings, who returned it on October 2. Two days later that it was rented to Raechel Houck.

The "rental unit history" ended with a notation showing that the car had been "totaled" October 7; "last location unknown." Nowhere on the vehicle's rental or maintenance history logs was the September 9 recall made note of, other than in a terse entry in the latter made on October 13, six days after the crash: "Incomplete-Recall Cmpgn-D18."

The unsafe PT Cruiser thus had been driven continuously by rental-car customers from virtually the day Enterprise learned about the power steering hose defect until the crash on October 7. The three renters prior to the Houck sisters had put nearly 900 miles on the vehicle; like the sisters, they were unaware that it had a defect which could cause a fire. Meanwhile, as they unsuspectingly drove the recalled car, its power steering hose was being further abraded, eventually producing the fire-igniting leak of flammable power steering fluid that led, Grassini and Wrinkle contended, to the Houck sisters' deaths.

According to notations at the top of each rental agreement, either "Ali" or "Ian" had handled the transaction for Enterprise. Alisha Jensen and Ian Burnham were two of the three Santa Cruz branch office employees involved in renting the car to Raechel Houck; the third was Andrea Avecilla, the on-site manager.

To pursue its inquiries into Enterprise branch-office handling of defect recalls, Grassini and Wrinkle retained an investigative firm, Batza and Associates, that it had used in many previous cases. The firm, with offices throughout California, worked only for attorneys seeking information for ongoing litigation.

One of the Batza firm's first assignments was to determine whether Enterprise trained its employees in the handling of defect recalls. Tracy Hasper, an attorney who worked for the firm as a senior investigator, obtained a set of Enterprise employee training materials. On June 18, 2008, she sent them to the Grassini and Wrinkle with the following description:

> [Enclosed is] the 2004 Enterprise New Hire Employee Handbook, which was provided to all new employees during their five-day training session… This is the handbook which would have been in effect when the PT Cruiser was rented to Raechel and Jacqueline Houck in October 2004.
>
> We reviewed the entire handbook and noted no references to vehicle recall procedures. There is a sample 'unit history' report…; however, it only identifies 'maintenance history' as part of the report, and again, there is no reference to vehicle recall procedures, or how staff should handle a vehicle which is recalled.

On August 7, 2008, Jennifer Conta, another attorney-investigator with the Batza firm, interviewed Ian Burnham by telephone about his recollection of the Houck rental. Burnham confirmed he had been a manager-in-training at the Enterprise office in Santa Cruz on October 4, 2004. "I rented them the car, or my co-worker did," he told Conta. At the time he'd had no knowledge that the vehicle being rented to the Houcks had been recalled. When Conta told him about it he was taken aback: "I didn't even know there was a recall on the PT Cruiser, until today. If our office would have known about that recall, especially it being a safety recall, we would never have rented out that car."

Burnham described the Enterprise procedures by which, he said, the recall should have been brought to the Santa Cruz office's attention, such as by being documented in the vehicle's unit history, and how it then would have been handled. "The protocol is that as soon as we hear of a recall, the physical keys are tagged, and we take the keys from where they are hanging, and hang them on the 'do not rent' side." But that hadn't happened with the PT Cruiser recall; Burnham said he was "not aware of the PT Cruiser recall status via any of these resources, and surmised again that the most likely reason was that his office location did not receive the recall information from regional headquarters in a timely fashion," Conta wrote.

"If I were to guess at the blame" for the Houck rental, "I would really blame it on the corporate side, from the area manager on up," Burnham told Conta. "As far as our office, we wouldn't do anything intentional like that. That would expose huge liability. We do put our cars on the road to make money, but it wouldn't be done if it was a safety issue. But on the corporate side, they are all about making money, wanting to be better than Hertz, growing to beat other areas within Enterprise. I wouldn't be surprised if they thought the [PT Cruiser] recall was no big deal, and just didn't get around to handling the recall right away."

But, he added, it could have been simply a mistake. "Nothing would surprise me if something was overlooked, though. It could have been an error. It could have been an employee who accidentally deactivated the recall and forgot to ensure the keys were tagged and the car was pulled. I just can't say for sure."

The next day Conta interviewed Alicia Jensen by phone. Jensen, like Burnham, had been a manager-in-training at the Santa Cruz office at the time of the Houck rental. And like Burnham, she'd had no knowledge of the recall until Conta told her about it.

Jensen said that on the morning of the rental the PT Cruiser had been at an off-site maintenance yard for routine servicing. She had picked it up and then picked up Burnham at the office and gone to Raechel Houck's residence. They had driven Raechel to the office and Jensen had proceeded to execute the rental contract. There was a delay because Raechel wasn't financially qualified, but the branch manager, Andrea Avecilla, had approved her anyway, "I think because she was such a nice girl, she lived locally, and seemed trustworthy," Jensen said.

Raechel had asked for a small car but the PT Cruiser "was the only car we had left on the lot... that was the smallest we had," Jensen told Conta. "It was also an upgrade, but we gave her the upgrade for free, since we had no other choices... She was all excited. The car was really clean, and she liked it."

Jensen told Conta there was "no indication" that the vehicle had been recalled, and that she "would have never rented that vehicle" to Raechel Houck if there had been. "I feel awful about that. I wish I would have known."

According to Jensen, the office regularly received reports when vehicles in its fleet were recalled. But, she told Conta, she'd "never noticed" the PT Cruiser listed in any of the reports. Nor did she recollect Andrea Avecilla, the branch manager, ever discussing a PT Cruiser recall in her weekly meetings with the staff. "Sounds to me like the recall hadn't gone through yet. Regional headquarters must not have activated the recall yet, or else we would have known about it," she said.

The Santa Cruz office staff was "devastated" to learn of the crash, Jensen told Conta. "It was about 3 or 4 days after we rented her the car when we found out what happened. Our Area Manager, Mark Matias, was standing in our office, and he got off the phone, and said, 'Hey, do you remember that girl you rented to a couple days ago? She was killed in a car accident.' I was like, 'What? Oh my gosh.' But that was it. We didn't talk about anything else, definitely nothing about a recall. I really don't think any of us knew about that."

On August 22, Conta interviewed Andrea Avecilla, the Santa Cruz branch manager at the time of the Houck rental. Avecilla told Conta she did not remember anything "amiss" concerning the rental; "I didn't see those keys tagged as a recall, and the car was not grounded." Her office, she said, "would never have rented her that car if we knew it was a priority recall." She herself "wouldn't have known about the recall unless someone directly told me about it, or we pulled up the recall warning on the computer, when we closed out a contract. I don't recall hearing anything about it at all."

Might Jensen or Burnham have rented the PT Cruiser to Raechel Houck knowing it was under recall? "That was the best team I ever worked with," Avecilla told Conta. "They followed the rules, and did what they were told. I don't believe they missed any recall warnings."

The senior-most person whose name had come up in Conta's interviews was Mark Matias. Matias had spent eleven years as an employee of Enterprise of San Francisco. He was a seasoned Enterprise executive, an Area Manager in charge of the operations of seven Northern California rental branches, including Santa Cruz, known as Region W. Jensen had recalled learning about the Houck crash from Matias when he came to her branch a few days after it happened.

Conta contacted Matias, who no longer worked for Enterprise, and asked him about the Houck tragedy and the rental-car company's handling of defect recalls. His answer, in the form of a sworn declaration admissible at trial, raised troubling questions about Enterprise's claim that it had no responsibility for the rental of unrepaired recalled vehicles to its customers.

In the declaration, signed on August 27, 2008, Matias said he had been "contacted by a legal representative, on behalf of Enterprise, regarding this matter, and was asked not to speak to anyone about this case. But it is important to me to tell the truth."

He had not known about the PT Cruiser recall prior to the Houck crash, he said. But he did know that "Enterprise Branch Managers, within Region W, authorized the rental of recalled vehicles, even with safety recalls. Safety recalls are referred to as priority recalls. When the fleet was short, and there was demand for vehicles, these recalled vehicles would be rented to the public."

"As an Area Manager, I knew how operations were handled. When demand called, we rented out recalled vehicles. It happened; I won't lie. If the only vehicle left on the lot was a recalled vehicle, the branch would rent that vehicle to the customer." He said he also knew of "instances where employees knowingly rented recalled vehicles to customers without a manager's approval, when there was a shortage of vehicles on the lot.

"To my knowledge, the managers and/or employees who knowingly rented recalled vehicles were never reprimanded by Enterprise executives; however, I am not sure whether corporate headquarters had knowledge of these instances."

At the corporate level, Matias said, Enterprise "pressed the local offices to run a tight operation. Their philosophy was, 'You've got to keep booking, because you don't know when you are going to get a car back.' But then of course, you run short on vehicles, and if all have are recalled vehicles on the lot, you rent them out. It was a given. The whole company did it. Enterprise's corporate offices looked the other way regarding this fact."

There were other problems, he said. "Many times the recall warning attached to a vehicle's unit number on the computer screen, did not say safety recall or priority recall. Only when that vehicle was taken into the dealership, and the dealership ran the VIN number, would specific information about the recall become available."

Matias was critical of Enterprise's recall-handling procedures. "When a recall warning does come up on the screen that says priority recall, the respective employee is required to take the key of that vehicle and place that key in an area for non-rentals; however, here is where the procedure is too loose, and mistakes can happen. An employee is only required to write the word 'recall' on a post-it note, which is placed on the keys. There is nothing in place that keeps an employee from renting that car. The computer system doesn't lock up. There is nothing to prevent an employee from taking those keys, and renting that vehicle to the next customers." Nor was a specific policy in place requiring that recall information – unit histories, maintenance histories, and daily reports – be printed out and distributed to employees and management.

On August 28 Conta interviewed Mike Fortino, who had been Vehicle Maintenance Manager for Enterprise Rental Car of San Francisco from 1999 to 2006. He had been responsible for maintenance-related vehicle issues at the Region W branches, including Santa Cruz. He essentially corroborated Matias's criticism of the company's handling of recalls.

"Did we rent out vehicles with safety recalls? Can I say that never happened? I'm sure it did. Was it policy? Not really. It was not something that was really addressed by corporate," he told Conta. "If the recall was in our [computer] system, is it possible that the [PT Cruiser] vehicle was rented out? Yes. Unless things have changed since I left (in 2006), that would be the most probable scenario... We operate on high utilization. We overbook, and there are not a lot of vehicles on our lots. As a result, you rent out whatever you have. If all you have is a recalled vehicle, or a vehicle that needs an oil change, you rent it out."

Fortino had worked for other car rental companies in the past, where, he said, the computer system "physically locked up," preventing an employee from renting a recalled vehicle. But at Enterprise there was nothing to prevent an employee from renting out a recalled vehicle; "the computer system does not lock up, and the recalled vehicle is still operational," he told Conta.

Grassini and Wrinkle retained two experts to assess Enterprise's policies and practices on the handling of safety recalls. Lloyd Rae had owned and operated a rental car business for twenty years before becoming a consultant on rental car matters. In *Houck* he was retained as "an expert in the standard and practice in the car rental industry, including, but not limited to, the procedures to be followed in the event of a recall" and "the conduct of the defense with regard to recall." Robert Cunitz was a human-factors expert who had frequently testified in court concerning the adequacy of product-hazard warnings and instructions, the behavior of corporations regarding customer safety, and the extent of user-behavior contribution to injuries caused by unsafe products.

Rae was deposed by Hunter, representing Enterprise "headquarters," and Wiggins, representing Enterprise of San Francisco, for nearly four hours on the afternoon of December 8, 2009. Liddy represented the plaintiffs. Rae had reviewed the depositions of Moulton, Gieseking and the former Enterprise employees interviewed by Conta; based on these and on his own experience in the rental car industry, he had reached the conclusion that Enterprise's recall handling policies and procedures fell far short of the industry's "standard of care."

"Nobody has shown me [an Enterprise] policy and procedure on how to deal with a recalled vehicle," Rae said angrily at one point in the deposition. "So I don't see one. There is talk of it, no policy. So that's one thing. Enterprise has a dangerous, reckless, and unconscionable attitude by putting profits before safety. They rented this vehicle to the two young [women] that had a safety recall on it. If Enterprise Rent-A-Car did not rent that vehicle to them, we probably wouldn't be here today. These two young girls would probably have families in the works, and these parents were probably getting ready to play with their grandchildren." That wasn't happening, he said, "simply because Enterprise Rent-A-Car wanted to put their profits before safety by renting this vehicle and getting their money on it, instead of letting it sit in a lot and getting it to a dealer" for repair.

Hunter wanted to know what basis Rae had for expressing this harsh conclusion.

HUNTER: Do you have an opinion that it's Enterprise policy to put profits before safety?
RAE: Yes, sir.
Q. Have you seen a policy to that effect?
A. I've seen actions that speak louder than a policy.
Q. You have not seen a policy to that effect?

A. I have not seen a policy on anything especially on handling of safety recalls.

Q. So what you have is the actions of some branch employees; is that right?

A. Managers and employees, yes.

Q. What did Mr. Gieseking do that was an action that put profits before safety?

A. They didn't have a procedure. They don't have a procedure. They don't have a computer department, even though they have 1,000 IT employees, to build a computer system that would notify a rental agent before they rent the vehicle that it has a safety recall on it. They have done nothing.

Q. Do they have a procedure that brings the recall information up when the vehicle is checked back in for rental?

A. They say they do, but the documents do not support that. There's vehicle histories there that it didn't show up when the vehicle was returned, because the vehicle was rented three or four times after the recall notice went out and it never showed up on the history reports.

▲ ▲ ▲

Q. In your opinion, the industry standard requires the recall notice to appear on whatever screen the rental agent is looking at before the rental; is that correct?

A. That would be one way of doing it.

Q. What's another way?

A. Another way is to have a procedure in place that when a recall notice comes in, any car in the lot, they can check to pull any car in the lot, that they can go to the contracts that are on rent and notify the renter that the vehicle has been recalled, may we exchange your vehicle or may you go into another one of our other locations so we can put you into a safe vehicle.

Hunter asked Rae what he knew about Enterprise's employee training practices and materials. Wasn't there formal training at the local level?

RAE: I believe there was a rental agreement training and incremental sales training. I think it was five days, if I recall correctly. But I've never seen the training manual that has anything in it about recalls, discussing recalls. You can have training day in and day out, but if there is nothing dealing with recalls and safety – the public and safety, the training is really not beneficial unless you're just going out to make the bucks.
HUNTER: So in order for the training to be effective it has to be in writing, it has to be a manual?
A. No. Just show me something. Just show me something. It helps, because if you're relying on a manager, assistant manager to do on-the-job training and they have no format to follow, it's too easy, as you can see in these documents, to overlook discussing that with a rental agent. They don't know what they forgot. They have nothing to go back and refer to.

As the deposition wound down, Liddy, over strenuous objections from Hunter and Wiggins, directed a series of questions to Rae which were clearly intended to further bolster the plaintiff's contention that Enterprise had been negligent in renting the defective PT Cruiser to the Houck sisters.

As a rental car expert and former agency owner, Liddy asked, what did Rae think it would have cost Enterprise to "put this PT Cruiser in the back of the lot, lock it up and take away the keys so that is wouldn't be rented to these girls."

RAE: Basically, it wouldn't cost them anything unless they want to say, well, I missed out on a rental for a couple of days. And basically, the way to recoup that loss is, the following year, when we negotiate with the manufacturer to buy those vehicles, we would show them a report of our out-of-service vehicles, how many days and how long they were out of service. And we'd negotiate a better price for the vehicles or we'd get an extra free car out of it. So in the short term, it would have cost them the price of a rental. In the long term, it wouldn't have cost them anything.

Liddy asked Rae to explain the benefit to Enterprise, if any, of renting recalled vehicles to its customers.

> *RAE: By renting a vehicle that normally shouldn't be rented, it's an extra vehicle on the road making money. And if you have 20-30,000 of those vehicles, it's a lot of money to be made by renting recalled vehicles to the public.*

In all his years in the rental car business, had Rae ever "heard of a company that would rent a vehicle that had a safety recall on it to the general public?"

> *RAE: Never in 30 years. Never deliberately, no.*

Two months later, on January 5, 2010, Cunitz was deposed for four hours, again by Hunter and Wiggins, with Liddy present for the plaintiffs. Asked by Hunter to describe his work in the case, Cunitz said he had developed opinions in two areas: the corporate behavior of Enterprise and the "human factors issues associated with the occupants of the vehicle in response to an emergency – serious emergency – such as smoke and fire."

Enterprise, he said, had received "sufficient warning" about the PT Cruiser defect from Chrysler; "Enterprise's response or lack of response to that was a major, substantial cause of the tragedy and loss of lives of these two women." It had rented the vehicle to them "knowing that there was a hazard associated with its use and knowing that by renting the vehicle out with the hazard uncorrected and unprotected, that its customers would be unreasonably exposed to the danger of fire and the consequence thereof."

Enterprise "had no policy in effect to effectively ground or prevent the rental of vehicles subject to recall" Cunitz said. "My professional opinion is that Enterprise, at the highest level, did not put into effect the controls, policies, procedures necessary to prevent such a thing happening. And that's the real root cause of this tragedy."

Cunitz next addressed Raechel's probable response to a fire breaking out under the hood of the vehicle. He assumed, he said, that the
fire "broke out in five to ten seconds prior to the collision, that the passenger compartment began to fill with smoke, and the toxic fumes that
are generated in such a fire, that this constituted a sudden, unexpected
emergency situation for Raechel Houck who was driving the vehicle, and
for her sister." Raechel had responded appropriately, he said, by "getting
off the highway into a place where conceivably she could stop the vehicle
and escape from the smoke."

He then proceeded to paint a detailed picture of what he believed
might have taken place in the PT Cruiser during the seconds before it
crashed:

*At the time this all occurred, three things were going on. They were very
dangerous. First, was the unexpected nature of having a fire and smoke
coming into the passenger compartment, which clearly is going to be horribly frightening to anybody. And I would expect any human being to
respond with substantial concern, agitation, be quite upset. "Frightened"
is the right term for that kind of thing.*

*The second thing that's going on is, visibility is going to be reduced.
The third thing is the toxic nature of the fumes generated by the fire. The
components of the smoke, the products of combustion are well-known to
cause all kinds of very unpleasant consequences like disorientation. And
among other things, hydrogen cyanide, I read and have learned, is capable of killing you in a few seconds at high enough dosages. Certainly,
one would expect some interference with the ability to drive a car successfully in the face of toxic fumes.*

*So those three factors, the suddenness and frightening nature of the
incident in the first place, the – whatever reduction of visibility occurred
as a result of the smoke coming in the passenger compartment, and the
consequence of exposure to toxic fumes all made it very difficult for somebody to successfully avoid and recover from the situation, which leads
me to the conclusion and opinion that Raechel Houck acted reasonably*

given her circumstances. And the tragedy was unavoidable once the fire got going.

Cunitz noted that there had been "some discussion" by the defense "about the potential of Raechel having fallen asleep, and that's what set this all off. And I think that's highly unlikely that two women – there were two of them in the car – both fell asleep at the same time, and all this happened as a result of that kind of activity. It seems very far-fetched, and there was no – there was nothing to support that."

Hunter challenged Cunitz to state "what effects that smoke had on Raechel Houck." How could Cunitz know what those effects were, he asked, without knowing the exact toxic components of the smoke at the time it entered the passenger compartment?

> *CUNITZ: The only thing you can know is it wasn't good for her. You can know that. How bad it was, I don't know. But it wasn't good... There were three things that weren't good. One was the suddenness of this appearance, the alarm it would produce behaviorally and psychologically. The second is the toxic effects of smoke, as there is some limitation on visibility.*
>
> *How bad any of those were and how they all combined, we know in the end how – what resulted. The vehicle was not maintained in a safe area of the median, but rather crossed onto oncoming traffic. We know that happened. Just which of those three components was the overriding one, I don't know. Or whether it was a combination of all three of them, which is more likely...*

Assuming there had been no fire or smoke in the PT Cruiser, Hunter asked, were Raechel's actions "consistent with a driver response to momentary inattention?" They were not, Cunitz replied.

Was it important to Cunitz, Hunter asked, that the vehicle had been characterized as an "upgrade" when it was rented to the Houck sisters?

CUNITZ: Yeah. I think so. It's kind of – how do I put this? It's kind of an inherent fraud in terms of what was done here. They were told that they're getting a better – a better vehicle, an upgraded vehicle when, in fact, they were getting one that was actually not anywhere near as good as they thought it was or as the original was, whatever it was they were supposed to get. There's a big disparity there. And something just doesn't sound right about it.

Three hours into the deposition, Hunter returned to Cunitz's initial opinion that "the real root cause of this tragedy" was Enterprise's failure to have policies and procedures in place to prevent the rental of unrepaired recalled vehicles. He asked Cunitz which Enterprise entity he believed had been responsible for renting the PT Cruiser to Raechel Houck. What had led Cunitz to conclude, he wanted to know, that "the Enterprise entity in Saint Louis had control over the vehicle" despite its ownership by Enterprise of San Francisco?

CUNITZ: My understanding – and I don't have a thorough understanding of all of the corporate relationship – [is] that the various local activities were controlled to some extent in terms of policy, procedures, computer systems, records and all the like by the national headquarters... I'm not, to be fair to you, distinguishing particularly between the two clients that you gentlemen represent.
As far as I'm concerned, they work together. That the corporate relationships are, at least, as far as the public [is] concerned, of no particular interest.
I think if you believe and can convince a jury that somehow the national level Enterprise Rental Car activity has no responsibility for what's going on at the local level, then, you know, have at it. But I think the public does not distinguish. And, in any case, it seems pretty clear that information is transmitted from the national level down to some of the local operations and offices. That certainly suggests some level of control and influence over that. If the national level was totally uninterested in

what was going on and had no control over it, it wouldn't bother sending anything out.

I don't buy it, but maybe you could sell it to a jury. I don't think you will, but you can give it a try, I suppose. It would seem to me that it's all one and the same. As far as [the] public's concerned, as far as I'm concerned as a safety expert, the Enterprise name is on it. The Enterprise owners who control the corporate headquarters and the rest of the operation have knowledge of the danger because they were warned effectively by Chrysler. And they had the ability to make sure there's a corporate policy that no Enterprise office would rent out a car that was subject to recall where safety was clearly at stake.

Enterprise's contention that "headquarters" was not to blame for renting unrepaired recalled cars to its customers seemed to be thoroughly discredited by testimony from its own management and employees and by the expert opinions of Rae and Cunitz. But even so, if it could convince a jury that the PT Cruiser's power steering hose defect was not what had triggered the Houck sisters' catastrophic crash, Enterprise still could avoid a civil-court judgment that its negligence had killed the two women.

14

RECONSTRUCTING THE CRASH

As 2009 CAME to a close, it was clear that the trial in the *Houck v. Enterprise* could not be put off much longer, even by the defense's delaying tactics. California civil procedure required that "an action shall be brought to trial within five years after the action is commenced against defendant"; the five-year anniversary of the case's filing date of June 28, 2005 was a mere six months away. Courts have discretion in enforcing the rule, of course, but generally it is followed unless all parties and the court agree to a further delay. In *Houck* the plaintiffs, if not Enterprise, were eager to have the case tried. But still to be deposed were expert witnesses on whose testimony the outcome of the case would most likely hinge.

Both sides had retained accident reconstruction specialists to render opinions concerning the movement of the PT Cruiser during the moments leading up to the crash, and from those movements reach conclusions bearing on Raechel's behind-the-wheel behavior. The reconstructionists were highly experienced in giving courtroom testimony in auto-injury court cases – and in having that testimony aggressively disputed by lawyers for the opposing party.

How the conclusions of these experts contradicted each other would be repeatedly demonstrated as they underwent depositions during the final pretrial days of the *Houck* litigation. So would the observation, of-fered in a 2010 paper in the American Journal of Forensic Psychology, that depositions and cross-examinations of an opposing party's expert witnesses are characterized by "intense questions that may seem to be a form of harassment, are repetitive, or difficult to answer with 'yes' or 'no'." The deeply adversarial nature of the U.S. civil justice system com-pels parties in lawsuits such as *Houck* to pit expert witnesses against one another. In contrast, some court systems, such as the U.K.'s, provide for the court itself to retain independent experts who, it is hoped, will ren-der impartial opinions slanted toward neither party.

The reconstruction experts – Gregory Stephens for Enterprise, Andrew Irwin for the Houcks – were deposed early in 2010. From the same base of evidence, including skid marks at the accident site, they had made sharply divergent findings. At trial, it would the jury's job to determine which were credible, which not.

Stephens, initially retained by DaimlerChrysler and now testifying for the rental car company, travelled from his office in Gig Harbor, a suburb of Tacoma, to attorney Troy Wiggins's office in San Francisco on January 19. There he reviewed some documents, including portions of the other side's reconstruction. His deposition, by Don Liddy, started at 11 a.m. the following day.

After determining that Stephens had carried out the usual work under-taken by a reconstructionist in car crash cases – visiting the crash site, map-ping it in detail for evidence, running sophisticated computer programs to analyze the results – Liddy dove in with a terse demand for Stephens's opinions and a clear readiness to contest them:

Q. Tell me all your opinions as to why the PT Cruiser went off the road.
A. Well, my understanding based on my reconstruction analysis is that we had a PT Cruiser that was traveling in the No. 1 lane at approxi-mately 75 to 80 miles an hour, drifted off the road or drifted out of the lane of travel at least and made a couple of steer inputs, corrective and over-corrective type of steer inputs, which eventually led into a trajectory

and a side slide across the median and ultimately into the opposing lanes of travel where it met up with a Freightliner tractor/trailer going the opposite direction at about 60 miles an hour.

Q. Have you now told me all your opinions as to – well, strike that. Do you have an opinion as to what caused the PT Cruiser to leave the roadway?

A. My opinion based on the work that we've done and the fact that the PT Cruiser would be going off to the left side would be something similar to an inattentiveness or a falling asleep type of accident and then reacting to that accordingly.

The opinion resonated with Enterprise's "alternate cause" strategy, which depended on a showing that Raechel's behavior, not the PT Cruiser's defect, had somehow been the cause of the crash. Liddy wasn't about to leave it unquestioned. He demanded that Stephens list each and every piece of physical evidence that would support his "inattentiveness or a falling asleep" opinion.

In response, Stephens identified skid marks left by the Houck vehicle when it left the road, along with the degree to which the vehicle had drifted from its path as it left the roadway and crossed the median, as the principal bases for his conclusion. So far he had made no reference to the possibility that the PT Cruiser's passenger compartment was filled with smoke from burning power-steering fluid. Liddy wanted to know whether the witness had ever reconstructed an accident in which there had been smoke in the passenger compartment.

STEPHENS: What I've looked at in the past is driver reactions in terms of inattentiveness and all kinds of things, factors, leading up accidents, and some of that may have included smoke or fires. But I couldn't tell you specifically.

LIDDY: As you sit here today, can you point to any study or any experience that you have concerning the way drivers react to smoke or fire?

A. Nothing specific, no, sir.

Q. Did you look for any research on that issue?
A. No, sir.
Q. So before you ruled out smoke or fire causing the driver to leave the roadway, do you think it would have been a good idea to research that issue before you were going to testify under oath in this case?
A. Again, not based on my experience. My experience has told me that with regard to these types of an event, you would expect braking and pulling off the road and essentially getting out of the vehicle as a more appropriate and typical type of reaction, I would think. And the production of physical evidence that we have in this case is much like ones that I've reconstructed many times in the past, that is, steering an evasive type of maneuver, reacting to potentially going off the road or drifting or inattentiveness.

Too many words. Liddy wanted a straightforward response.

Q. Can you answer that question yes or no?
A. I believe I did, which is no, I didn't feel that it was necessary based on the previous answer.

Liddy proceeded to ask a series of questions about Stephens's analytical work in support of his conclusions concerning the movement of the Houck vehicle leading up to the crash, as well as his criticisms, if any, of other witnesses' conclusions. Then he returned to the defense claim that Raechel Houck may have caused the crash by falling asleep, phrasing his questioning so aggressively that it brought repeated rebukes from the Enterprise lawyers.

Q. Is it your opinion that both of the Houck girls fell asleep before the crash?
A. I have no opinion on that.
Q. You have no idea?
A. With regard to specifically falling asleep, no, I have no opinion on that.

Q. Do you have no idea? Is it true to say you have no idea whether they both fell asleep or not?

WIGGINS: Object to the form of the question.

STEPHENS: Again, with regard –

LIDDY: Not "again." That's the first time I've asked that question. Is it true that you have no idea whether both girls fell asleep or not? True or false?

WIGGINS: Same objection.

STEPHENS: I apologize for interrupting, but I thought you had asked me before whether or not I had any evidence that the driver fell asleep, and that's the only reason why I was asking or telling you again. I apologize. But having said that, with regard to the driver's actions, we have what we have in terms of the physical evidence and what I feel is necessary to produce that. With regard to the passenger, I really don't have any evidence one way or another on that.

LIDDY: So do you think it's more likely than not that the driver of the PT Cruiser fell asleep before the crash?

A. Again, all I have –

Q. Yes, no, or I don't know?

HUNTER: Objection. Argumentative and burdensome and oppressive. Let him finish his answers.

STEPHENS: I apologize. I was just answering a question that you had asked earlier, which is my opinion of the production of this physical evidence based on the reconstruction.

LIDDY: Do you have an opinion whether the driver of the PT Cruiser fell asleep? Yes or no?

A. Specifically, no.

Liddy continued to bore in:

Q. How was Raechel feeling?

A. The driver? Is that the driver?

Q. Do you know who was driving the car?

A. Yes, sir. I can look that up.

Q. Who? As you sit here today, without looking it up, do you know who was driving the car?

A. It indicates on the police report – sorry – that Raechel Houck was driving.

Q. Do you know how she was feeling before the crash?

A. Not specifically. I have the indication in the police report of the 24-hour profile that is reported on in the police report.

Q. Do you have any opinion as to whether Raechel Houck was not physically fit to drive the vehicle at the time of the crash?

A. I haven't studied that.

Q. So your opinion is no?

A. No.

Stephens had earlier made reference to the "inattentive type of maneuvers" that might be cause crashes. Liddy zeroed in on the term, asking the witness to identify those maneuvers.

Q. You don't know if it was falling asleep; right?

A. What I've described to you is that it's an inattentive type of maneuver. So there are many different types of inattentive type of maneuvers. Falling asleep is one. Alcohol impairment is another; dropping something on the floor and trying to pick it up is another; changing radio stations and drawing your attention off of the road for any significant amount of time is another. These are all inattentive type of maneuvers that could lead to an accident such as this. I'm not saying that the girls were specifically doing any one of those. It's just an inattentive type of maneuver.

Q. Okay. Let's start with falling asleep.

A. Yes, sir.

Q. You don't know whether the girls fell asleep or not, do you?

A. No, I don't.

Q. You don't have an opinion as to whether it's likely that they did, do you?

A. In terms of specifically falling asleep, no.

Q. And do you have any evidence that alcohol had anything to do with this crash?

A. I don't have any evidence of that.

Q. Why did you bring it up?

A. I was bringing it up in response to your question of or explaining inattentive type of maneuvers.

Q. And do you have any evidence that dropping something was a cause of this crash?

A. Not specifically, no.

Q. Do you have any evidence that changing radio stations was a cause of this crash?

A. Again, not specifically, no.

Liddy returned to the issue of smoke in the occupant compartment as a possible cause of the crash. Did Stephens have any knowledge of how people "generally react to smoke and fire in their vehicles while driving?"

A. I would generally think that they put on the brakes.

LIDDY: That wasn't my question. I didn't ask you what you thought or what your speculation was. Let's have the question back.

(Record read as follows: "Q. Do you have any knowledge of how people generally react to smoke and fire in their vehicles while driving?")

THE WITNESS: Yes.

LIDDY: Tell me the basis and source of that knowledge.

A. My background, training and experience.

Q. Let's be specific. You had a case where steam came up from a vehicle once; correct?

A. That I recall, yes.

Q. And you had a case where someone dropped a cigarette?

A. I believe that that was an example of inattentive, yes.

Q. Right now we're talking about smoke and fire, your experience with smoke and fire. Was there smoke and fire as a result of the cigarette being dropped?

A. I don't know.

Q. Was there smoke and fire as a result of the steam coming up from the vehicle?

A. I would expect no on the fire part.

Q. Okay. So what is the sum total of your experience with smoke and fire as it pertains to the reaction of drivers?

A. Again, looking at accidents and going – being a part or part of presentations and seminars that talk about how accidents are produced.

Q. You've never reconstructed an accident in which smoke or fire was a cause of a crash; true?

A. I don't know that.

Q. Well, who would know other than you?

A. Well, again, based on my memory as I sit here, there may have been reactions to other smoke and fire type of things that produced an accident.

Q. Is it true that you have no memory of any accident that you reconstructed in which smoke or fire was a factor in causing the crash?

A. Again, not without looking at all of my cases that I've reconstructed over the years. I don't have any memory of specifically smoke and fire.

Q. And you have no memory of any paper –

A. I'm – sorry. And I'm assuming you mean within the occupant compartment as opposed to outside the occupant compartment.

Q. Smoke or fire anywhere affecting the driver. Smoke or fire anywhere inside or outside the vehicle.

A. Not as I sit here, not without going through all my cases.

Q. And you can't remember a single paper that you read concerning the reactions of drivers or passengers to smoke in the vehicle?

A. That's correct.

Q. All right. So my question is then, where does this opinion concerning how drivers react to smoke or fire come from other than from thin air?

Liddy wanted to further nail down Stephens's opinions, or lack of them, concerning Raechel's alleged "inattention" as a possible cause of the crash.

> *LIDDY: What else do you think might have caused the inattention that you believe was a cause of the accident other than what you've already told me?*
>
> *A. There's many different possibilities is all I can say.*
>
> *Q. This is the time to tell us.*
>
> *A. Perhaps looking out at the scenery to the left or right of her.*
>
> *Q. Anything else?*
>
> *A. Perhaps trying to retrieve something from inside the occupant compartment that would divert her attention away from the roadway.*
>
> *Q. Anything else?*
>
> *A. I believe that's all I can think of as I sit here.*
>
> *Q. How is retrieving things different from dropping things in your mind?*
>
> *A. I don't know that they're terribly different in – I don't think any of these are terribly different in that they produce an inattention to the road in front of you.*
>
> *Q. I didn't ask you whether it's terribly different. In your mind, when you said dropping things and then you added retrieving things, was there a difference between those two acts?*
>
> *A. One may be accidental and the other one may be purposeful.*
>
> *Q. And do you have any evidence that the driver was retrieving something just before the crash that caused the accident?*
>
> *A. Again not beyond what I've already talked about...*

Liddy proceeded to interrogate Stephens about the skid marks produced when the Houck vehicle's movement off the road and into the median began. Stephens had testified that the marks supported his opinion that steering movements produced by "driver inattention" were at fault. Liddy asked whether the witness had "an opinion as to whether the – any of the steering movements that you've described are a result of a driver being frightened."

A. I would defer to others on that, but it certainly seems that these are evasive type of maneuvers, which sometimes can be related to a driver being frightened or reacting to something.

Q. So do you have an opinion in this case whether the steering input before the vehicle left the roadway was a result of the driver being frightened?

A. Not with any more specificity of what I talked about.

Q. Is that yes or no?

A. Again, my previous answer was that it certainly can be consistent with a driver being frightened because somebody was going off of the road or the rumble strips caught their attention and then reacting accordingly. That could be a frightening type of thing.

Q. Do you think smoke or fire coming out of a car is a frightening event?

A. I would defer to others on that, but it could be a frightening event. I don't know that it would necessarily produce this type of reaction, but I think we've talked about that.

After three and a half hours of intense questioning, Liddy was done with Stephens.

Like Stephens, the Houck's reconstruction expert, Andrew Irwin, had considerable experience as a witness in car crash litigation. Irwin travelled from his office in Dallas and arrived at the Grissini and Wrinkle law firm's office on January 13, 2010, to be deposed by Wiggins and Hunter. The deposition began at 11:14 a.m.

Irwin had visited the crash site, made detailed diagrams, maps and notes concerning evidence he found there, reviewed police and other photos and charts made at the time of the crash, and analyzed his data with a number of specialized computer programs. He brought with him a large diagram of the scene showing the trajectory of the PT Cruiser as it moved from the highway, across the median, and into the front of the eighteen-wheeler. Wiggins asked for a detailed explanation of Irwin's diagram and conclusions, which the witness provided, adding.

With respect to whether there was a fire or not, I don't know if there was a fire or not on the vehicle, nor do I know if the power steering hose failed. I am of the opinion, however, if that – the defect identified by Chrysler and NHTSA manifested itself on this vehicle, that it would be the precipitating event and would have caused this crash. I'm of the opinion that the loss of power assist would not necessarily or inevitably result in a loss of control. But I think the combination of circumstances that could have existed, given how the defect is described, can create a situation that I think can perceived – can be perceived by a driver as dangerous enough to explain what happens.

At trial, Irwin said, he would explain to the jury the vehicle dynamics involved in the crash. Wiggin asked him to define that term:

I would describe it as the – the vehicle movements that are necessary to satisfy the physical evidence in the case. So I wouldn't necessarily get into the handling qualities of a PT Cruiser per se, but I would say, "Folks, here's how the vehicle needed to move to leave the marks on the road or in the median; here's the steering wheel inputs that I discovered needed to take place, at least for the range I was able to determine to explain those marks, and then of course the braking." So I think vehicle dynamics would deal with how the car needed to be operated and what path it needed to follow and what speeds it needed to follow to satisfy what I know happened...

Wiggins wanted to know whether Irwin's reconstruction had considered the possibility that the crash was caused by Raechel's falling asleep:

Q. How about the scenario involving falling asleep, is there anything inconsistent in this data with the driver of the PT Cruiser falling asleep? A. There is in my mind.

Q. Please tell me what – what you see is inconsistent with that potential scenario?

A. Well, I don't have a shallow exit [of the PT Cruiser] from the roadway, for starters. So when this vehicle leaves the roadway, it's under a more dramatic heading angle with enough steering input to indicate the driver is making control inputs to the car. So at least starting at position A, I know that the driver is not asleep. [Note: "Position A," also marked as "point A" on Irwin's map of the crash scene, indicated the point at which the vehicle left the road and entered the median.] *So I think the question might be, is there anything to indicate that the driver fell asleep prior to point A that resulted in the physical evidence that begins there? There isn't any evidence to indicate that that was the case. I don't have the [investigating officer's report] telling me he found marks that showed that she drifted off the road one way or the other and correspondingly reacted by ending up in position A, doing the things I've already told you I think she did. And I don't have a witness that tells me that. So I don't have anything that I think is consistent with the falling asleep scenario.*

Why, then, Wiggins asked, did Irwin think Raechel had driven off the highway and into the median? Irwin said his "general opinion...is that she's reacting to something, that there is something that has occurred within the confines of her driving environment that she perceived as threatening and she dealt with it."

Wiggins revisited the power steering issue and the impact that loss of power steering would have had on Raechel's control of the PT Cruiser. Irwin responded that while "a power steering loss by itself doesn't inevitably result in a crash," it "creates a situation that's potentially unsafe. If you combine it with a vehicle fire and take that next step to his new hypothetical, then that sounds like a dangerous enough set of conditions that it can cause this accident."

Wiggins and Hunter then took Irwin through a detailed description of the calculations, computer programs, and assumptions he had used in reconstructing the crash sequence from just before the PT Cruiser left the road. He described these as the scientific basis for his conclusions, which he said had yielded a set of results that seemed to match the testimony of the crash-scene eyewitnesses.

The deposition was finished in less than two hours. In contrast to the deposition of Stephens, the defense reconstructionist, it had been largely non-confrontational, with the Enterprise attorneys offering little in the way of challenge to Irwin's conclusions.

Top: The crash of the defective Enterprise rental car
in which the Houck sisters were killed
Bottom: Racheal and Jacqueline Houck

Racheal and Jacqueline Houck

Carol "Cally" Houck, mother of Raechel and Jaqueline

Top: Larry Grassini and Roland Wrinkle, attorneys for the Houcks
Bottom: Cally Houck testifying in the Senate on the
rental car safety bill named for her daughters

15

GUENTHER AND BANTA

O F THE TWO prongs of Enterprise's defense against the Houck lawsuit, one appeared to be increasingly flimsy. Its lawyers had been able to find no convincing evidence that Raechel's driving behavior had caused the crash; on the contrary, the testimony of the girls' friends, coupled with that of the plaintiffs' reconstruction and human factors experts, compelled the conclusion that the Houck sisters had done nothing whatsoever to contribute to their deaths.

The rental car giant now would have to depend heavily on the viability of the second prong – its assertion that even though it had knowingly rented the sisters a PT Cruiser under U.S. government recall for a safety defect that could cause a fire to break out in the vehicle, that defect had not led to the crash. It brought in two experts to help bolster this position.

Dennis Guenther and Robert Banta were seasoned engineering experts with long track records of testifying for car companies in injury litigation. Banta, whose specialty was the analysis of vehicle fires, had worked for Chrysler Corporation from 1967 to 2006, after which he became a consultant and expert witness in litigation for Chrysler and other automotive clients. Guenther wore two hats; he was an engineering professor at Ohio State University as well a professional expert witness in injury lawsuits, principally on behalf of auto companies.

Banta and Guenther had collaborated in a series of tests purporting to show that the PT Cruiser defect had not been responsible for the Houck sisters' crash. Enterprise was relying on their presentation of the tests to the Houck trial jury. Predictably, the two men would face tough questioning at their depositions.

Banta's deposition was held at Wiggins's San Francisco office on October 28, 2009. The witness showed up with a large volume of documents, CDs and DVDs describing the tests he and Guenther had conducted. He would be prepared, the Enterprise lawyers had stated, to "respond to the allegations of defect raised by the plaintiffs and their experts." The deposition began at 11:10 a.m. Again Don Liddy was doing the questioning of the Enterprise witness.

Noting that Banta had been a Chrysler employee at the time of the PT Cruiser recall, Liddy wanted to know about Banta's involvement in the recall, if any. Banta said he had helped conduct surveys of PT Cruiser owners who had reported fires caused by the power steering fluid leak, had assisted in "analysis of fire input records," and had participated in "answering the federal inquiry and establishing the corrective action in the plant, then in the field." Clearly he had been a major player in the company's defect-management activity. That being so, Liddy asked, had Banta asked the Enterprise lawyers why their client had not complied with the recall notice?

> *BANTA. No. I know that the recall was not performed on this vehicle at the time of the incident. And I knew that before I – I did the first inspection. And – but I do not know what Enterprise's business practices are internally. I just don't know.*

Did Banta have an opinion whether, in the Houck case, "Enterprise unreasonably endangered its customers" by renting out a recalled car that hadn't been repaired?

A. No, I do not. I honestly have not given that consideration. I don't know the effectivity [sic] of Enterprise's notice and I don't know their reaction to the notice. I simply don't know.

When the defect had been discovered at Chrysler, Banta said, he had become "very concerned" at its appearance on PT Cruisers being driven by company employees. Liddy wanted to know why.

A. I was concerned because the appearance of abrasion on the 10 to 15 vehicles indicates that there was a potential for wearing through the pressure hose and in some circumstances it was possible for a leak to occur, and should that happen, in still some additional circumstances, it was possible for a fire to occur. And fires are not an acceptable consequence of a manufacturing defect.

Prompted by Liddy, Banta disclosed that once the abrasion defect had been discovered in cars operated by Chrysler employees, those cars were taken out of service and the employees were not permitted to drive them again until the defect had been repaired.

LIDDY: And you did that because you were concerned about danger to your Chrysler employees; isn't that correct?
BANTA: Well, at some level, yes. More importantly, we just did not want it to fail.
Q. Your answer is, yes, you were concerned about danger – at least somebody was at Chrysler – concerned about danger to the Chrysler employees?
WIGGINS: Objection. Misstates his former testimony.
HUNTER: Joined.
THE WITNESS: Yes.

Based on the tests he and Guenther had conducted and on his "experiential knowledge" of vehicle fires, Banta told Liddy he had concluded that the power steering hose on the PT Cruiser rented to the Houcks "was not leaking on the day of the accident." So did this mean, Liddy asked, that the car was not defective? Since DaimlerChrysler had admitted in its 2004 recall notice that the car was defective, the question put the witness between a rock and a hard place.

> *BANTA: I don't know. I – I didn't say it was not. I said I don't – I just don't know.*
> *LIDDY: So you have – you're not sure whether the PT Cruiser rented to the Houck girls on the day of the crash was defective?*
> *A. I don't know the degree to which contact existed on that vehicle, if it existed at all. It's unlikely that it did statistically. And the evidence indicates that it did not have contact and did not proceed to failure.*
> *Q. Was the PT Cruiser that was rented to the Houck girls on the day of the crash – strike that. Was the PT Cruiser that was rented to the Houck girls dangerous?*
> *A. Not necessarily.*

Liddy was not about to let Banta off the hook. Would the vehicle fire expert, "knowing what you know about this safety defect," have accepted the Houck PT Cruiser as a rental vehicle for his own family? The question drew objections from the Enterprise attorneys but Banta had to answer it.

> *BANTA: Knowing the history [of the] vehicle? I – well, I'm familiar with this issue. It wouldn't have troubled me. I – I would prefer not to have that car but it wouldn't trouble me if I did.*
> *LIDDY: Q. Do you have children?*
> *A. I do, yeah.*
> *Q. How many children?*
> *A. Two.*
> *Q. Boys or girls?*
> *A. One of each.*
> *Q. Would you have wanted your daughter or your son to have rented this particular vehicle from Enterprise and driven it down the coast just like the Houck girls did?*

WIGGINS: Calls for speculation. Incomplete hypothetical.
HUNTER: Joined.
THE WITNESS: Knowing the background of the recall condition, prob-
ably not.
LIDDY: And that's because there was a potential danger to customers that
were given this vehicle to drive before the recall work was done, correct?
A. Yeah, there was a suspect condition in that population.

Banta had more opinions about the likelihood of the "suspect condition" having resulted in the Houck vehicle crash. He believed that "a fire could not occur at 60 or 70 miles an hour road speed" or for that matter at any speed above 20 miles an hour; that there was "no evidence" at the crash site of "a preexisting fire" in the vehicle, and that smoke could not "enter the cabin at road speed and smoke will not be visible to the driver at road speed..."

LIDDY: So you've never seen or heard of a case in which a fire started
in the engine compartment when the vehicle was traveling more than 20
miles per hour, correct?
A. Oh, I've – I've heard of claims of that but the claims are – are not
valid.
Q. So any customer who has claimed that a fire started at speeds greater
than 20 miles per hour in the engine compartment has either been wrong
or untruthful in your opinion?
A. Yeah. Generally – yes, that's right. Yeah, they're either mistaken or
they're just not telling the truth. I mean, you can't fool science. And people
say these things, but when you question them further focusing on speed
and incident, they will admit to you that they're not sure that it didn't
start, you know, two blocks back when they were stopped at a traffic light
or something.
Q. Was that part of your job at Chrysler, to question people who made
claims that fires had occurred in vehicles and you believed those claims
were – were dubious?
A. Oh, sure. That's – that's not uncommon.

Banta said that over his years with Chrysler he had interviewed "hundreds" of customers who reported fires in their cars. But he couldn't estimate how many of them believed their car was travelling faster than 20 miles per hour when the fire started.

To support his opinion that smoke could not have been visible to eyewitnesses of the Houck crash nor have entered the occupant compartment of the Houck vehicle, Banta produced DVD's of tests that he and Guenther had run. In the tests, PT Cruisers were driven on a test track at 60-70 miles per hour. While they were underway, power steering fluid, released from a shunt attached to the power steering fluid hose, dripped onto hot engine surfaces. But there was a problem; in one of the videos, smoke began to appear outside the vehicle, which was being driven by Banta, but then the vehicle abruptly disappeared from the scene. Liddy wanted to know why.

> *BANTA: There's a chase car in front of me and I pulled off to the skid pad to do some low-speed circle maneuvers and the chase car didn't realize I was doing that so he lost me in his camera.*
>
> *Q. Do you show the smoke in some other view on here?*
>
> *A. Those are the three takes we have on the cameras.*
>
> *Q. Do you have – do you have any other film showing the smoke that comes from the PT Cruiser?*
>
> *A. No. Those are the only views we have.*
>
> *Q. So it's – it's your testimony it was just coincidence that you turned out of the view of the camera at the time the smoke began?*
>
> *A. Yeah, the chase vehicle lost me.*
>
> *Q. Your answer is "yes"?*
>
> *A. Yes.*

Was there "another camera or any view that shows the smoke coming from the vehicle when the power steering is released?" Liddy asked. No, Banta answered.

Liddy wanted to know what tests Banta and Guenther had run to show that smoke could not have entered the occupant compartment of the Houck vehicle prior to the crash. Banta described tests in which a flare-like "smoke candle" had been activated in the engine compartment, producing "copious amounts of smoke." Then the vehicle had been driven at 60-70 miles per hour, with Banta at the wheel.

> *BANTA: I – as a driver in the vehicle, I would see nothing. There's no smoke coming out of the hood. There's no smoke coming out of the front end. It's not coming into the interior space. It's going out the underbody of the car and out the back.*

Liddy asked what that proved.

> *BANTA: Well, the – premise is that the smoke is being produced yet we see nothing, absolutely nothing.*
> *LIDDY: Is the air conditioning on?*
> *A. It's on recirc, yes.*
> *Q. And did you try it if it's on fresh air?*
> *A. No, I tried it on recirc.*

It was a critically important revelation. The recirculation setting for automobile HVAC systems – "Heating, Ventilating and Air Conditioning" – severely limits the amount of outside, fresh air that can enter the occupant compartment. Its use is intended to be only temporary, such as when the driver needs to cool the car down quickly after starting it up on a very hot day. Leaving the system in "recirc" for an extended period of time can lead to an undesirable build-up of carbon dioxide in the compartment, as well as to general staleness of interior air. As the 2004 PT Cruiser owner's manual directed:

> *"Only use the re-circulate mode to temporarily block out any outside odors, **smoke**, or dust and to cool the interior rapidly upon initial startup in very hot or humid weather."* (emphasis added.)

Virtually every new-car owner's manual includes a similar directive. Why hadn't Banta run his tests with the car's air conditioning system set to allow unimpeded outside air to enter the occupant compartment, including air infused with smoke in the event of an engine fire?

> *BANTA: Because on the day of this incident, it was 90 degrees out on the freeway and I'm confident that these girls would have had the air conditioning max AC recirc.*
>
> *Q. And are you as confident about that opinion as you are about all your other opinions?*
>
> *A. Yes.*
>
> *Q. Ninety-nine percent sure?*
>
> *A. I can't say 99 for that point, no. It is more likely that it was on recirc than fresh air.*
>
> *Q. But if you're truly using the scientific method, what reason would you have for not putting the air conditioning on fresh air?*
>
> *A. Because there was no smoke coming out of the hood, so it wouldn't matter. In our test we had already determined that smoke did not come out of the hood, and if I have it on the fresh air side, it – it will not come in because it doesn't come out of the hood.*
>
> *Q. So if you have fresh air, you don't believe smoke would enter the cabin either?*
>
> *A. That's right…*

Although Enterprise had retained Banta as an expert on vehicle fires, toward the conclusion of his deposition – which by now had run in excess of five hours – he began to express opinions about the behavior of the Houck sisters in the moments leading up to the crash.

> *BANTA: My opinion is that a fire in the engine compartment while traveling down the highway cannot occur – cannot and did not occur in this case. So whatever Raechel was reacting to, it was not a fire.*

LIDDY: Move to strike as nonresponsive. My question is, do you have an opinion as to how – well, why don't you tell me all your opinions that concern the reaction to the presence of fire in this case.

A. The reaction to fire is that should it occur while driving at extreme low speeds, below those numbers that we talked about earlier in this deposition, that a driver will simply pull to the side of the road, step out of the car, and walk away or attempt to combat the fire, but they will not drive off the highway and into a median.

Q. And do you have any scientific literature that you base that opinion on?

A. No, I have my 25 years –

Q. That wasn't my question. My question was, do you have any scientific literature that you base that on? Yes or no?

A. No, I do not. No.

Q. Have you bothered to look in the literature to see if there's any scientific writings that support your hypothesis?

A. I have, yes.

Q. You have. And what did you find?

A. Nothing.

Liddy deposed Guenther, the final expert to be offered by Enterprise, on December 18, 2009, also in Wiggins's San Francisco office. The deposition ran only about two hours, in contrast to Banta's five-hour-plus interrogation two months earlier.

There was a reason. The Enterprise lawyers had indicated that Guenther, like Banta, would offer opinions supporting Enterprise's arguments - he would be prepared to "respond to the allegations of defect raised by the plaintiffs and their experts" – but Liddy's opening exchange with Guenther seemed to reveal otherwise.

LIDDY: What were you asked to do in this case?

GUENTHER: Set up a test program for Mr. Banta.

Q. Have you formed any opinions concerning causation?

A. No.

Guenther had obtained a PT Cruiser for Banta's test program, assisted in the videoed demonstrations that Banta had shown at his earlier deposition, and "that was it," he said. So, Liddy asked, did Guenther intend to offer opinions of any kind at the *Houck* trial? Yes, he would tell the jury "how a PT Cruiser steering system operates," what happens if "fluid is discharged from a hole at highway speeds," and what "that can or cannot do relative to any smoke production or fire initiation." Liddy asked again:

> Q. *So you have no opinion as to what caused the Enterprise vehicle to go off the road.*
> A. *I wasn't asked to do that. That's correct.*

As the deposition proceeded, however, it became apparent that although Guenther had not "formed any opinions concerning causation," he was prepared to discuss in detail his conclusions as to what *didn't* cause the crash – conclusions that agreed with Enterprise's position that the crash could not have resulted from the PT Cruiser's power steering hose defect.

> GUENTHER: *The first opinion is that in normal driving without putting in steering efforts, driving 101, but possibly for a lane change maneuver, there's hardly any need to have power assist, and therefore there's actually no fluid coming out. If you do a lane change at these speeds and you want to do it quick enough, then that can cause fluid to come out.*
> *If the fluid comes out, I'm of the following opinion, that it does not cause a fire. It can generate smoke. That smoke cannot be seen by the driver or the passenger. Smoke cannot enter the engine compartment.*

Guenther elaborated at length on these conclusions, frequently citing the tests he and Banta had run to bolster them. Was this a "crash causation" opinion, or not? Liddy asked again:

LIDDY: And you have no idea what caused the crash.
GUENTHER: I didn't reconstruct. I wasn't asked. I'm not saying I can't
do that, but I have no opinions. I wasn't asked to do that. I'm simply here
as a test engineer.
Q. You have no idea what caused the crash, correct?
A. I have no opinions.

Was Guenther saying, Liddy asked, that "a failure of the power steering
or power brakes on a vehicle cannot cause an accident?"

GUENTHER: I would never say anything about that.

The deposition turned to a discussion of testimony that the plaintiffs' expert witnesses might offer as to the cause of the crash. Gerald
Rosenbluth and Joseph Romig were the two automotive engineering
experts retained by Grassini and Wrinkle as their automotive engineering experts – the *Houck* lawyers' counterparts to Banta and Guenther.
Romig had been deposed a year earlier; Rosenbluth's deposition was set
to be taken early in 2010, at which time Enterprise would have an opportunity to learn the full extent of his test results and the conclusions
he drew from them – and, of course, to attack them.

In the transcript of Romig's deposition, Guenther had read that
some of Rosenbluth's work for plaintiffs would involve bench testing –
recreating, in a laboratory setting, real-world conditions that appeared
to have caused the fire and smoke that precipitated the Houck vehicle's
crash. Although Rosenbluth had not yet been deposed, Guenther was
prepared to criticize that testing, he told Liddy. He had "no problem
with the testing... and what they wanted to do," he said, "but to make the
next leap, in my opinion, to say some of those observations or his opinions, Dr. Romig can then take to a vehicle traveling at 60 miles an hour
on the highway, I do have some – I do have some opinions on that, that
I don't think you can do a one-to-one correlation because of the highly
turbulent unsteady flow that you have within the engine compartment."

To support his criticism he quoted from a Society of Automotive Engineers technical paper in which the "highly turbulent and often unsteady nature of the flows resulting from the complexity of the engine compartment geometry" was briefly mentioned.

LIDDY: Anything else in that paper that is relevant to this case?
GUENTHER: No. It just supports the fact of the unsteady turbulent flow in an engine compartment.
Q. Isn't this telling us there's not sufficient data on which to conclude? I mean it's not saying that – it's not saying that – it's saying that. Strike that. It's saying there's not enough data to draw conclusions. Is that what your understanding is?
A. Correct, because it's turbulent unsteady flow. You can't do it.
Q. And this paper was published when?
A. '91. It still holds today.
Q. And my understanding is you have no disagreement with the testing that Mr. Rosenbluth did, but you do have a problem with taking that data and drawing conclusions about the cause of the fire.
A. That may be a little broader, but yes, I would say that is true, particularly in conclusions of bench testing to then apply that to this PT Cruiser driving down the 101 at about 60 miles an hour, yes, I have a problem with that.
Q. So is it your opinion that it's difficult to test, or impossible to test, or something else?
WIGGINS: I'll object. It's overbroad.
HUNTER: Join.
GUENTHER: It's not impossible, because you can, but the word is difficult to test, but then the real question is, can you take bench testing to the next level and put it to roadway highway speeds? That's what I'm critical of.
LIDDY: And it is your testimony that power steering fluid never causes fire at highway speeds?
A. I'm of the opinion that at highway – well, in this accident, I see no evidence that power steering fluid would ignite at highway speeds.

*Q. Now let's take it generally. What is your opinion with regard to igni-
tion of power steering fluids at highway speeds generally?*
WIGGINS: Overbroad.
HUNTER: Join. Vague and ambiguous.
*GUENTHER: The location of the hose is under the body. You're dealing
with shear forces of the air contact between – ground effect is what you
have occurring on the bottom of the PT Cruiser and the ground. You will
not have a fire occur.*
*LIDDY: Are you aware of fires caused in vehicles by ignition of power
steering fluid while the vehicle is underway?*
A. No.
Q. You never heard of it.
A. I haven't.
*Q. And how many fires were there on the subject PT Cruiser model that
was recalled?*
A. I have no idea.
Q. So you haven't looked at any of the recall data.
*A. I have some – I have – they gave them to me, but again, it's not my
area. I know there was a recall. I have no problem with that.*
Q. So you haven't looked at any of the recall data.
A. That's correct.
Q. And you don't know how many fires there were on PT Cruisers.
A. That's correct.
Q. No idea.
A. That's correct.
Q. And the reason you didn't look at that data is what?
A. It wasn't my area.

Enterprise had now laid out its entire case via its expert witnesses. Would
a jury accept the testimony of those witnesses at trial – testimony that
aimed to blame the Houck sisters for their deadly crash while exoner-
ating Enterprise? In part that would depend on the jury's assignment
of credibility, or lack of it, to the opinions of the rental car company's

experts. But it would also pivot on the testimony of the causation experts retained by Grassini and Wrinkle. The essential question remained: Had the PT Cruiser's defective power steering hose caused the crash? If it had, and Enterprise had knowingly failed to fix it, the rental car giant's responsibility for killing the Houck sisters would be extremely difficult to question.

16

ROSENBLUTH AND ROMIG

O N JANUARY 12, 2010, California Superior Court Judge Richard Keller, to whom *Houck* had been assigned, issued an "Order re: Case Management & Trial Setting" in the litigation. The four-page single-spaced document spelled out in detail the schedule and conditions that would govern the upcoming jury trial to determine whether Enterprise was or was not liable for the deaths of the Houck sisters.

Keller's order set the trial for June 1 at the Fremont Hall of Justice in Alameda County. It stated that prior to the trial, on May 18, the judge would hold a "Pre-Trial Readiness and Status Conference" with attorneys for the parties. In preparation for that conference, both sides were directed to provide the court clerk with exhibits they intended to use at trial, lists of the witnesses they intended to call, and other materials – motions, briefs, etc. – related to the conduct of the trial.

Grassini and Wrinkle's principal causation expert, Gerald Rosenbluth, an automotive engineering consultant from Tempe, Arizona, was scheduled to be deposed in April. Rosenbluth had been a frequent witness on behalf of plaintiffs in injury causation cases against motor vehicle manufacturers. According to his CV, he also was a consultant to the Center for Auto Safety, a non-profit advocacy organization founded by Ralph Nader, and to the Arizona Attorney General's Office.

The Houck attorneys' other causation expert, Joseph Romig, also from Tempe, had been deposed by the Enterprise attorneys on October 20, 2008, early in the discovery process. He had inspected the crash site in January, 2007 and subsequently had inspected the wrecked PT Cruiser's remains at a storage center in California.

Romig had found "physical fire damage that indicates a fire prior to the collision... The damage is associated with the coolant overflow. The bottom portion of the overflow [container] is burned out."

This referred to a plastic container which collected overflow from the car's radiator. Relying on California Highway Patrol photos taken after the crash, Romig had said in his deposition that although the container was shown lying flat next to the wreckage, from which it might have been torn during the impact, he believed that the burn-out pattern on the container's bottom "indicates a fire when the vehicle was still vertical," i.e., before its head-on impact with Carlos Woods's 18-wheeler. On that basis Romig had concluded that a fire started in the PT Cruiser's engine compartment before the car's impact with the truck.

At the time, Rosenbluth was in the process of conducting extensive tests to duplicate the condition of the PT Cruiser prior to the crash. Those tests, and the evidence from the crash site and the PT Cruiser's remains, led Romig to develop four opinions, he had told the Enterprise lawyers:

- "There was a vehicle compartment or engine compartment fire while the PT Cruiser was proceeding northbound on the highway."
- "...smoke could enter the passenger compartment."
- The "most likely fuel for the fire... was power steering fluid. Most likely release would be in the chafing region [of the defective power steering hose]."
- "The most likely ignition source would be the header... the exhaust system immediately upstream of the catalytic converter, coming off the manifold."

Seeking to cast doubt on the validity of those opinions, the Enterprise lawyers had questioned Romig for more than six hours, but ended up suspending the deposition until they could interrogate Rosenbluth.

They got their chance on April 15, 2010, just six weeks before the trial date.

The deposition was set to be held at Rosenbluth's office and laboratory in Tempe. Green, representing Enterprise Rent-A-Car Company – "headquarters" – and Wiggins, representing Enterprise of San Francisco, would do the interrogating. A new attorney, James Yukevich, from Los Angeles, was also scheduled to participate. Like Wiggins, he would represent Enterprise of San Francisco. Unlike Wiggins and Green, he would participate by telephone and ask no questions during the entire eight-hour deposition. His role in the case would become clear, however, as the June 1 trial date neared.

The deposition began at 10 a.m. in Rosenbluth's conference room. From that room Rosenbluth's laboratory could be viewed through a large plate-glass window. Rosenbluth and the lawyers moved to the lab where, as the deposition got underway, he began to describe the impressive array of exhibits he intended to show the jury at trial to demonstrate his conclusion that the PT Cruiser's defective power steering hose had triggered the vehicle's crash. The first exhibit was a cutaway section of a PT Cruiser mounted on a buck.

GREEN: Can you explain what this exhibit was prepared for, exactly what it is and what features you think are most salient for this case?
ROSENBLUTH: The buck that we're talking about is mounted on a fixture that rotates. The only reason for the rotation is to be able to see the undercarriage. It's the – roughly, the front half or slightly more of a 2004 PT Cruiser... it's strictly observational. And the points are the high pressure hose for the power steering system, which runs from this point at the pump, down around the engine and transaxle and down to, eventually, the steering rack and pinion gear hat.

Q. So what we're seeing is a view as if one was laying on their back, look-
ing up at the bottom of the vehicle; is that correct?
A. That's correct.

At trial, Rosenbluth said, the "specific [PT Cruiser] components that
we're going to refer to are in the same position that they would be in a
vehicle driving down the road pre-fire condition." The spatial relationship of the components is "exactly as it would be in a production vehicle." Green pointed to a piece of yellow tape on one of the components
of the cutaway PT Cruiser.

GREEN: What is the significance of placing that tape on the differential
cover at that point?
ROSENBLUTH: Where that tape is, is where you would have the chaf-
ing of the hose.
Q. And are you talking about the chafing of the hose in a situation in
which the vehicle is one that was described in Chrysler Recall D18?
A. Correct.
Q. Of course, in Chrysler Recall D18, it was set out that only a small por-
tion of the vehicles that were subject to the recall would, in fact, have that
condition; is that what you recall, your memory?
LIDDY: Let me object to the characterization as argumentative and
vague.
ROSENBLUTH: They – actually, in the recall, they say a small portion,
but they have no idea that it's going to be a small portion or a large por-
tion. I believe Mr. Banta in his deposition talks about checking these
cars in the[DaimlerChrysler] parking lot and finding, at least, 30 to 40
percent of them – whatever it was – that had chafing.

Green continued to inquire about the significance of the differential
cover to Rosenbluth's opinions.

ROSENBLUTH: If you run your finger very gently across this differential cover – and you have to run it on a bias, don't run it longitudinally – you'll feel just how sharp it is.

GREEN: Are you saying that – that if there was a hole in the power steering hose on the subject PT Cruiser in this case, that the hole would have been rubbed by contact with the differential cover on that vehicle in the area that you've designated with yellow tape?

A. Yes.

Q. So the hole, then, would be as it would have existed on the power steering hose, if there was a hole in the power steering hose, on the subject vehicle, directly opposite to this edge of the differential cover that's marked with yellow tape, correct?

A. Correct.

Q. So that it would be –

A. It would be a breach, not necessarily just a hole –

Q. A breach.

A. – a big, round hole.

DaimlerChrysler could have provided a better design for the power steering hose, Rosenbluth said; he had developed such a design, which used an additional clamp to hold the hose in place. But he "really had no issue with Chrysler. They saw the problem, they addressed the problem, they issued the D18 recall. But when that's done, the people who own the vehicle have a responsibility to have that recall performed." Meaning, in this case, Enterprise.

Rosenbluth turned to a second buck in the lab, also made from a 2004 PT Cruiser. This one, he said, was used for "exemplar vehicle smoke testing."

Unlike Banta and Guenther, Rosenbluth had run his tests of PT Cruisers without setting the air conditioning system to "recirc," thus allowing more outside air to enter the occupant compartment.

ROSENBLUTH: We have a smoke generator, which generates 2,500 CFM, cubic feet per minute, of smoke. And the smoke on the HVAC, without recirc, will then enter into the cowl area, which is the area of fresh air intake. And it enters where we have all of these arrows. It also would enter where we have a drain. So it enters the cowl area and the fresh air intake area.
GREEN: Are you saying that this mockup that you have here is exactly as the subject vehicle would have been?
A. Exactly as it was intended to come out of the factory.

Banta and Guenther had testified that grommets in the firewall would have prevented smoke from entering the passenger area of the Houck car. Green questioned Rosenbluth about the effectiveness of grommets – rubber seals intended to prevent engine odors from seeping into the occupant compartment through areas in the vehicle's firewall "where certain things such as wiring and other things go from the engine compartment to the – say, to the instrument panel."

ROSENBLUTH: To the occupant compartment.
Q. Right. And –
A. It's not only wiring, it's steering, it's HVAC – it's all kinds of things.
Q. And every one of those has a rubber or plastic grommet around it to seal off, to keep fumes from going into the passenger compartment, correct?
A. It's designed to do that under normal driving conditions.
Q. All right. And –
A. They're not designed to be fireproof, if that's your point.

Rosenbluth had prepared a set of "break-apart" exhibits to show the location of engine components, grommets in the firewall, and the path of an engine-compartment fire in proximity to those parts. He described these in detail, pointing to their features as he talked.

ROSENBLUTH: There are three exhibits. We have the exhaust. And now we can see the exhaust manifold, which is cast iron, without the shields. And we can see the tabs, where the heat shields would be attached. There's an upper and lower heat shield. Then we can see the catalytic converter. In between those two, we have the header.

So now we can see the relationship. If we have a fire and the fire emanates from the header area, the heat would go directly up along the firewall towards the bottom. The heat would also be distributed to each of these little grommets – grommet, grommet, grommet, grommet. And this is your steering. So this probably will take a little bit longer, because that's not a soft material. It's a hard material.

GREEN: Well, show me the grommet that you think would take the least amount of time to melt or burn and allow – sufficiently to allow smoke to come through the hole.

A. You're probably talking about this HVAC condensator [sic].

Q. And do you have –

A. Only because it's the lowest. It's on the side with the most fuel, and it's the softest grommet.

Q. And do you have an opinion as to how long after the fire started it would take for that grommet to melt or burn sufficient to allow smoke to go through this hole, into the passenger area of the vehicle?

A. I would just estimate between one and two minutes, if that.

Q. And now –

A. With a hot fire.

But, Rosenbluth stressed, "none of these grommets would have to fail in order to get smoke and odor inside the occupant compartment" because smoke from the fire would already be entering the compartment through the air conditioning vents.

Green asked Rosenbluth to list the kinds of on-road testing he done in the case. "Dynamic brake testing, dynamic exhaust temperature testing, dynamic fluid distribution and broadcast pattern testing, dynamic smoke pattern testing, dynamic steering force testing and dynamic wind velocity testing" using an exemplar of the PT Cruiser in which the Houck sisters had been travelling, Rosenbluth said. He displayed power steering hoses he had used in the tests, along with various types of power steering and brake fluid.

As the deposition wore on, it became contentious and argumentative. When Green asked Rosenbluth for his Social Security number, Liddy interrupted:

LIDDY: Objection. You don't have to give him your Social Security number.

GREEN: You're directing him not to answer?

LIDDY [TO GREEN]: You know, why don't you get to something that has to do with this case. All of these questions you're asking are a matter of record. We'll give you a reasonable amount of time for the deposition. But these questions are simply a matter of record, and I would suggest not a good way to spend all of our time in this case at this point.

GREEN: Well, I appreciate your suggestions, but it's my deposition and I'll ask the questions that I feel are appropriate whether you like them or not, counsel.

Green wanted Rosenbluth to identify any of his previous cases that had involved under-hood fires in cars – but only those that involved "a contention that there was an under-hood fire at highway speeds between 65 and 75 miles per hour as a result of power steering fluid."

A. That's not necessarily the case.

Q. What do you mean it's not necessarily the case?

A. I just answered your question.

Q. Are you saying that you've never worked on a case like that before?

A. No.

Q. Are you saying that you have?

A. I think there's a distinct probability that I have.

Q. Okay. Tell me each and every case that you've previously worked on that has those characteristics.

A. And I'm telling you that without doing the research into each case and without guessing about my recollection of each case, I couldn't tell you that definitively. But I will tell you that they do exist.

Q. How many?

A. I didn't count.

Q. More than five?

A. More than five, less than ten? Probably. Is that your question?

Q. So between five and ten?

A. I don't know.

Q. What was the last one?

A. I didn't count. So there is something you need to understand. If I didn't count, I can't give you a number. I could say that there probably are more than five and less than fifteen or something in that range, but I didn't count.

Q. Can you specifically recall any of these?

A. That's asked and answered. I said no, I wasn't going to guess at it. And I'm not going to sit here – well, you know what? I can sit here, sir, and go through this [case log] and see if I can recollect. I'd be happy to do that for you right now.

Q. When was the last time –

A. I will go through this –

Q. – that you worked on such a case, sir?

A. – and see if I can recall. It's the same question, isn't it?

Q. So you don't know; is that the answer?

A. I'm not going to guess at it.

The argument dragged on, with Rosenbluth insisting that he needed to review his case files to provide a dependable answer and Green attempting to conclude the back-and-forth by pinning the witness to an "I don't know" answer. By now the deposition was in its fourth hour.

GREEN: There's no way we're finishing today.

LIDDY: I understand you just mentioned that there's no way we're finishing today. Let me tell you, we are going to finish today.

GREEN: Well, not if we keep getting this kind of a response, no. There's no way.

LIDDY: I would suggest – and let me just state for the record that I'm asking counsel to ask their significant and substantive questions early, because we're going to stop the deposition at five o'clock. And that should be adequate time to ask all appropriate and substantive questions. So I'm just giving you fair notice of that.

Green was not happy with the suggestion. His interrogation of Rosenbluth about his past cases and his insistence that the witness answer without reviewing his files were, he told Liddy, "substantive." But "I don't necessarily want to sit here and watch the witness go through all of those pages. I'm perfectly happy with his answer that he doesn't recall. I'd just as soon move on."

ROSENBLUTH: I said I don't recall, and I need to refresh my recollection. Because I can't tell you I recall each and every case and the facts of each and every case.

GREEN: Well –

A. But I can, at least, identify vehicles I think that were in motion when a fire erupted.

Q. Well, that wasn't what I asked you in any event.

A. And now you want to know if they're over 60 miles an hour, right?

Q. Between 65 and 75.

A. That was your question. I know your question very well, Mr. Green.

Q. Well, then you just repeated it incorrectly, sir. It was between 65 and 75. But I don't want you to –

A. I don't know.

Q. – go through this entire list –

A. You might have to have that read back.
Q. I don't want you to go through the entire list right now, because I think you've told us all we need to know about your memory on that. So why don't we move on.
A. Okay. We're talking about my recollection without review of any materials.

The issue was important to both sides. It concerned what is known in product liability cases as "OSI" evidence – proof of "Other Similar Incidents," i.e., similar to the one at issue in the case at bar. It was important to the defense to show, if it could, that Rosenbluth had never been involved in cases, and knew of none, involving fire in moving vehicles under conditions similar to those in *Houck*. Equally, if he had been involved in or was aware of comparable cases and could testify about them during the trial, that could further strengthen the plaintiffs' position.

Green had raised the issue, and Rosenbluth was clearly ready to take whatever time he needed to review his past case records in order to find comparable situations. Green was just as ready to resist, to force Rosenbluth to rely on his memory rather than his written records.

Rosenbluth was unrelenting; he would not answer Green's questions without reviewing his files. Liddy objected that Green's interrogation was "repetitive," and accused the Enterprise lawyer of treating Rosenbluth rudely. Then Green, over Rosenbluth's objections, said he wanted to look at the expert's huge binder of files on the subject and mark it as an exhibit, in which case it might have to be removed, copied and made part of the deposition record.

ROSENBLUTH: I'm not going to lose my binder.
GREEN: We'll have it copied.
ROSENBLUTH: No, I will copy it for you. It does not go with the court reporter – I'll make that crystal clear.
GREEN: Well, we'll talk about that –
ROSENBLUTH: No, we're going to talk about it right now.

When Green attempted to have an exhibit marker put on the binder, Liddy objected, saying he would not permit it to be marked or to leave Rosenbluth's office.

> GREEN: *Well, you can't keep me from marking it as an exhibit. Mark this document as Exhibit 7, Ms. Reporter, please. And then we will – we will have it copied in the original.*
> LIDDY: *No, you're not going to have – it's not going to leave this office. You've gotten your way all day. This is one time you're not going to get your way.*
> GREEN: *You're telling me we can't mark his file as an exhibit –*
> LIDDY: *No. I'm saying –*
> GREEN: *– to this deposition, counsel? That's preposterous, and we're going to do it.*
> LIDDY: *We can refer to it as an exhibit, but we're not going to mark that original. If you want to mark it and agree it's not going to leave the office, that's fine too.*

What he didn't want, Liddy said, was a repeat of "what's happened in the past... notebooks have left the office and come back differently, incomplete or missing documents. So we don't want that to happen in this case." Green finally agreed that the binder would remain in Rosenbluth's office and be copied there, rather than by the court reporter, for the deposition record.

But that hardly put an end to the acrimony. At Green's request Rosenbluth began to summarize the contents of his *Houck* case notebook, but as the summary went on, Green grew impatient, saying he was "not sure I want to listen to all this... I don't want to sit here and have you read this stuff to us, because your lawyer [Liddy] is already trying to cut [the deposition] off, and we need to move on." In that case, Rosenbluth told Green, he shouldn't have asked for the summary; "Nobody's trying to cut you off. If you ask intelligent questions, you'll get intelligent answers."

Rosenbluth reminded Green that he had not yet completed his answer to the Enterprise lawyer's request that he summarize the contents of his case notebook. Green had taken the book away from the witness. Was he going to give it back? Was Green intending to withdraw that request? Green, professing not to recall the earlier question, attempted to ask Rosenbluth about a different document.

ROSENBLUTH: Well, let's not play dumb here.
GREEN: – please – can you please look at the document –
A. No.
Q. – that you pointed out to me?
A. No. We're going to go back and look at the question that wasn't answered, because you wouldn't let me refer to the book.
LIDDY: Let's go back to the question. Maybe we can agree to something else. I think what you asked him was: What's in the book? So he went through and read the table of contents and didn't get through with it. Why don't we stipulate that what's in the book is reflected in the table of contents, which will be attached as an exhibit when it's copied.
GREEN: I'm not stipulating to anything. I just don't want to have him sit there and read the whole table of contents at that pedantic pace that he was doing. It's wasting time. And so what we'd like to do is move on with the deposition.

At about 2 p.m. the deposition recessed for a thirty-minute break. When it resumed, the interrogation proceeded for a while along less combative lines. Green asked Rosenbluth to briefly identify the contents of twelve binders of *Houck* case documents assembled by Rosenbluth's office and relating, among other things, to testimony given by other witnesses in the case, tests carried out by Rosenbluth and Enterprise's experts, billing records, and correspondence. Then the subject of OSIs came up again as Rosenbluth produced two volumes of files – each so large that Green quipped he "might need a forklift to get this one up here"

– documenting crashes involving fire characteristics that Rosenbluth had concluded were similar to those in the Houck crash.

"Show me the ones that represent that they were going at highway speeds, please," Green directed. But as Rosenbluth identified crashes which he believed fit that description, Green repeatedly moved to strike his answers because the crash reports did not literally specify that the speed of the car was "between 65 and 75 miles per hour," the speed range within which the Houck PT Cruiser had probably been travelling before it left the road and crashed. Tempers flared. Rosenbluth told Green he was being "impatient." Liddy objected to Green's "interrupting the witness again and again" and "banging the table."

> GREEN: *I'm not banging the table.*
> LIDDY: *Don't interrupt again. You're interrupting me now. Please stop banging the table, pointing at the witness and standing over the witness. That's not polite.*
> GREEN: *I'm sitting in my chair, counsel, as you can plainly see. Mr. Witness, please show me any alleged other similar incident of an under-hood fire in a PT Cruiser at highway speeds of 65 to 75 miles per hour.*
> ROSENBLUTH: *Now that's a different question.*
> GREEN: *No, that's exactly what I asked you before. Please proceed.*
> LIDDY: *And you just pointed at the witness again.*

Green's agenda was to disqualify each and every OSI that Rosenbluth might cite unless it was documented as involving a vehicle travelling "between 65 and 75 miles per hour." But Rosenbluth's purpose was different; he was seeking to counter earlier claims by Banta, Enterprise's expert, that a fire could not have occurred in the Houck PT Cruiser if it was travelling more than 20 miles per hour. Banta had testified that "a fire could not occur at 60 or 70 miles an hour road speed" or for that matter at any highway speed above 20 miles an hour. Rosenbluth wasn't buying it.

ROSENBLUTH: *I have thirty-three incidents that address what I call dynamic engine compartment fires, but I have none that identify the speed of 65 plus miles per hour. That doesn't mean that that isn't the case.*
GREEN: *You're not aware of any of them –*
A. *But they don't identify it way one or another.*
Q. *So you have no knowledge of any of them in there that – that are at the speed of the vehicle that's involved in this case, correct?*
A. *That you could say one way or the other. There might be. And perhaps these people need to be contacted to get a little bit more information.*
Q. *Have you done that?*
A. *No, sir, I have not.*
Q. *Have you asked anybody to do that?*
A. *No. I thought it was sufficient to know that if a vehicle was going down a highway, going – if they're going in excess of 20 miles an hour, by definition is, according to Mr. Banta, that you cannot have a fire over 20 miles an hour. So if I have one that's going 30 miles an hour, 40 miles an hour and I have a fire, that's – that's where I was going with it.*
Q. *I see. But you don't have a single one in the speed range of the vehicle that's involved in this case, do you?*
LIDDY: *Objection. Argumentative.*
ROSENBLUTH: *I don't know one way or the other. There's none documented –*
GREEN: *You can't point us to a single one?*
ROSENBLUTH: *I understand. I'm trying to – there's none documented in that way. That doesn't mean that some of these people weren't going at that highway speed.*
Q. *It doesn't mean they were either, does it?*
LIDDY: *Objection. Argumentative.*
ROSENBLUTH: *That's my point.*
LIDDY [TO GREEN]: *Would you like to give me a running objection for argumentative?*
GREEN: *No. I'm not giving you a running objection for anything.*

Rosenbluth produced another file of potential OSI's, this one drawn from the North Carolina Accident Database, a records repository maintained by the Highway Safety Research Center at the University of North Carolina and widely used by car crash injury researchers. He told Green the file "identifies incidents that were reported where smoke, fire inside or outside the driver compartment. And it gives us a little synopsis of what these drivers smelled and what they saw. Basically, this goes to the Banta/Guenther testing that nothing gets inside the occupant compartment. Now I did testing that established, in fact, it does." He described the first crash record in the file.

ROSENBLUTH: Vehicle 2 traveling north on U.S. 17. The driver — so 17 means they're going a highway speed, but we don't know what speed. So, again, that goes to your question. But if you're traveling north on U.S. 17, that's a fairly major road. The driver of Vehicle 1 began to notice smoke coming from under the dashboard. The driver then of Vehicle 1 pulled off to the shoulder, exited the vehicle. Vehicle 1 caught fire and began to burn. And he notices the smoke, fire, et cetera, on the inside. So the point of all these is really the inside issue, not the highway issue.
GREEN: Okay. Move to strike as nonresponsive. Do any of these —
A. Oh. Okay.
Q. — involve highway speeds at 65 to 75 miles per hour?
A. In my opinion, going north on U.S. 17 would be in that range.
Q. All right. What's the speed limit on U.S. 17?
A. It's probably 55 or 65.
Q. Do you know?
A. No.
Q. Well, then why are you speculating as to how fast that car was going?
LIDDY: Objection. Argumentative.
ROSENBLUTH: Because a typical highway speed is going to be 55, 65, sometimes 75.

GREEN: Sir, isn't it true that there's no indication of any of these vehicles on this list going 65 to75 miles per hour at the time of an alleged underhood fire? Isn't that true, sir?

A. They only talk about highway speed. Depending on what roadway they're on, if they're with – following traffic, then I think it's fair to assume they're doing a highway speed.

GREEN: Move to strike as –

ROSENBLUTH: They're not on U.S. 17 doing 20 miles an hour.

GREEN: Move to strike as nonresponsive. Are there any of these in their description that say that the vehicle was going between 65 and 75 miles per hour?

A. I only read the first one.

Q. Well, there aren't any, are there, sir?

A. I don't know. I haven't read them.

Q. Then read them and tell us.

A. Okay.

Q. And I don't want to hear any more about what you think they say or what you think people must have. I'm just asking you what does the document say.

A. You want to know –

LIDDY: Well, let me just object to the question as argumentative. Please mark the question.

ROSENBLUTH: You want to know if any of these say 65 miles an hour plus?

GREEN: Sixty-five to 75 miles per hour.

A. Well, 65 plus is easier.

Q. That's fine.

A. So the fact that they're traveling north on I-95, that doesn't give us a number, so you don't want me to count that?

Q. You know that that's correct. Please –

A Okay. Fair enough. I'm just reiterating. Although, the majority indicate highway speeds, none say 65 plus. Actually, there is no speed given in any of these. So you have to assume that, for purposes of my justification

– I know it's not in answer to your question. I just have to assume that if you're traveling on I-95 or 301, you're doing 60, 65 anyway.

GREEN: Move to strike as nonresponsive. Isn't it true, sir, that none of those alleged other similar incidents say that their vehicles were going between 65 and 75 miles per hour? Isn't that true?

A. That's not specifically stated, it's inferred.

Q. Can you show me anywhere in here where there are speed limits – or speeds reported between 65 and 75 miles per hour? Please answer the question, sir.

A. If you're with traffic on I-95, you're doing between 65 and 70.

Q. Sir, can you show me anywhere in this document where it's reported that the speed of the vehicle was between –

A. The speed –

Q. – 65 and 75? It's not reported, is it?

A. The speed is not reported.

Q. Thank you.

A. The conditions are reported, which dictate the speed.

GREEN: Move to strike as nonresponsive. I'm asking you –

LIDDY (TO GREEN): Will you stop pointing? Will you stop pointing at the witness, please? You're pointing your pen. You're poking at his papers. You're poking toward him. Can we just ask him what his opinions are? It's three o'clock.

Q. (By Green) Please answer the question, sir.

LIDDY: He's answered it.

By the time Green's interrogation of Rosenbluth about OSIs ended, the deposition was well into its fifth hour and Wiggins, the Enterprise of San Francisco attorney, had not yet had a chance to ask any questions. Green had done all the interrogating. Other than seeking to discredit any OSI that didn't explicitly use the phrase "65 to 75 miles per hour" in describing a fire-related highway incident, it was not clear why Green had used more than half of the deposition to joust with Rosenbluth over the issue.

So far Green had avoided asking Rosenbluth for his opinions in the case – the subject that usually is the purpose of an expert-witness deposition – but he did so now. What had the witness concluded about the Houck crash on the basis of his extensive test work and analysis? What was he planning to tell the jury at trial about the crash's cause?

Unsurprisingly, Rosenbluth replied with a detailed, damning, point-by-point indictment of the defective vehicle and of Enterprise for having rented it to the Houck sisters. The vehicle was "unreasonably dangerous relative to the potential of a leaking power steering hose"; the "dangerous nature of the vehicle only could have manifested itself if it was rented by Enterprise Rent-A-Car"; the air conditioning was "more likely not in the recirc mode, but in the fresh air mode" at the time of the crash; before leaving the roadway the vehicle was "more likely than not already engaged in heavy smoke and more likely than not open flames"; the initial fire was "caused by the chafing of the high pressure power steering hose with the sharp edge of the differential cover"; the flames were worsened by "released coolant, which ignited given the open flame condition from the power steering fluid already burning"; prior to leaving the roadway "the girls inside the subject vehicle, Raechel and Jacqueline, would have experienced smoke and odor of the engine compartment fire;" the vehicle was "already substantially engulfed in fire within the engine compartment prior to contact with Mr. Woods' Freightliner truck"; the fire origin was "more likely than not at the [vehicle engine's] header assembly, between the exhaust manifold and the catalytic converter."

The bottom line, Rosenbluth concluded, was that it was "extremely negligent of Enterprise to provide a vehicle with a known danger and an outstanding safety recall to any customer. That, basically, is it, yes."

Green questioned the witness at length, trying unsuccessfully to shake his opinions. Then he turned to criticisms of Rosenbluth's test procedures which the Enterprise experts, Guenther and Banta, had made in their earlier depositions. They had questioned whether a test procedure involving real-world measurements of PT Cruiser air flow, followed by bench tests done in a laboratory setting, was reliable. Again the deposition grew contentious.

GREEN: Did you have an engine in the engine compartment in all of your tests that you did? How about all of the bench tests, sir?

ROSENBLUTH: Pardon?

LIDDY: Objection. Argumentative.

GREEN: Did you have an engine in an engine compartment in all of the bench tests you did?

ROSENBLUTH: Every parameter we used for the bench testing was determined by – with an engine in the engine compartment under real world conditions.

GREEN: But when you did the bench tests, there weren't any engine in an engine compartment [sic]. You weren't even in an engine compartment, were you?

LIDDY: Same objection.

ROSENBLUTH: Sir, with all due respect, the parameters for each of the bench tests [were] perfectly acceptable to get those under real world conditions. And the actual test is then under simulated – done under simulated real world conditions in the laboratory. I am totally content, happy and will stand behind the scientific analysis and how we did that – no question.

Q. (By Green) Could you, please, answer my question?

A. I did.

Q. You didn't do those – those bench tests –

A. I did answer your question.

Q. – you told us about weren't done –

A. No, you're trying to take that out of context –

Q. – done in an engine compartment, were they?

A. – and that isn't going to happen.

Q. Those bench tests weren't done –

A. That's not going to happen, sir.

Q. – in an engine compartment, were they, sir?

A. It is not going to happen. I've answered your question.

Q. They were not done in an engine –

A. I've answered your question.

Q. – compartment, were they? And there wasn't an engine there, was it?

LIDDY: Object to the abuse of the witness, the argument and the repetition. [TO GREEN] Would you like to give your colleague [Wiggins] a chance to ask some questions here before we adjourn?

GREEN: Well, you know, we're not going to get finished today. We're going to have to talk about when –

LIDDY: That's a matter of opinion. Would you like to have your colleague ask some questions, so he can have an opportunity, or not?

GREEN: Are you saying that – now we're at 5:15. You told us earlier you were going to quit at 5:00.

LIDDY: That's right.

GREEN: Is your –

LIDDY: I'm just telling you I'm not going to sit here and let you argue with the witness until the cows come home. Would you like to give your colleague a chance to ask questions or not?

GREEN: Well, I'd like to finish my questioning with this witness, and –

LIDDY: If you have any non-argumentative questioning, please feel free to finish.

GREEN: Well, I don't accept –

LIDDY: If you don't, fine.

GREEN: I don't accept the characterization.

LIDDY: I know you don't. I want to give a fair opportunity for the other lawyer to ask questions if he wishes.

GREEN: And we want a fair opportunity to ask the questions about all of his opinions and all of his tests. And we've got a lot of tests and a lot of opinions that he's given, and we're working our way through that.

Over Green's objections, the deposition, which had gone on for eight hours, came to a halt at six p.m. Green wanted at least two more hours to interrogate Rosenbluth, whose testimony he clearly sensed was crucial to the plaintiffs' case; he insisted that a continuance of the deposition be rescheduled "as soon as possible, because of our upcoming trial date." Wiggins complained that he had "not had any chance to make any inquiries of this witness" on behalf of Enterprise of San Francisco, although how his inquiries would have differed from Green's was hardly apparent.

Liddy wouldn't agree to a continuance; the Enterprise lawyers had been given more than enough time to explore Rosenbluth's opinions, he said. If Enterprise tried to get a continuance, he warned, the plaintiffs would seek a court order to prevent it.

Trial was scheduled to begin on June 1, only six weeks away. But before that, the parties were required to meet with Judge Keller and identify all exhibits, evidence and other material they intended to present to the jury. This meant that all the lawyers had to get their trial preparation work completed within four short weeks. There would be no further delays; Keller had made that clear in his order.

17

WHO IS ENTERPRISE, REALLY?

I F "ALL THE world's a stage," the courtroom drama of product-injury lawsuits is reality theater at its most intense. In the tragedy called *Houck v. Enterprise Rent-A-Car, Case HG05220018*, the principal players were two sisters who had died in a catastrophic car crash, their parents, and a huge, impersonal, multinational corporation that had knowingly rented the sisters a dangerously defective automobile.

At trial Cally and Chuck Houck would be palpable presences. But not so what Hannah Arendt called "the doer." A trial, she wrote in "Eichmann in Jerusalem," resembles a play in that both begin and end with the doer, not the victim." But at the *Houck* trial, no witness would appear or speak on behalf of Enterprise's corporate leadership, meaning Jack and Andrew Taylor, the two men who owned and directed the worldwide rental car corporation. Neither had been deposed; their names had not even been mentioned during the hundreds of hours of deposition taken by the Houck and Enterprise lawyers in preparation for trial. Yet the Taylors, father and son, *were* Enterprise Rent-A-Car – and Enterprise was the Taylors.

In "I Shall Raise Thee Up," a book profiling successful business leaders in the context of their Christian commitments, a writer named

Michael Holmes has discerned an almost mystical parallel between Jack and Andrew Taylor and God and Jesus:

> Jesus Himself said, "Most assuredly, I say to you, the Son can do nothing of Himself, but what he sees the Father do; for whatever He does, the Son also does in like manner." In other words, the person under charge will only do what the person in charge is doing. Even now Andy Taylor calls his father the "minister of culture" because when he speaks to him the inevitable question that comes up is, "Andy, are the customers happy?"

Some, possibly the Taylors among them, might see this as laughable or even blasphemous. Nonetheless, the evidence of a strong, special bond between the two men, in which the father wields immense influence over the son, appears in numerous profiles of the Taylors, including one commissioned by Enterprise itself – a slick coffee-table puff piece entitled, "Exceeding Expectations: The Enterprise Rent-A-Car Story." The glossy hardcover book, published in 1997, includes this account of an early father-son collaboration at a time when Jack Taylor's principal business was leasing cars:

> When Andy turned 16 and got his driver's license, Jack quickly immersed him in the business. His first work was doing "repo missions" with Jack, going out at night to repossess cars from customers who had not made their payments... When they went looking for cars, Andy drove the chase car [the car that followed], and Jack took the extra set of keys to bring back the repossessed car. Often the spare keys didn't work – the copies of the early double-sided keys were the worst – and Jack and Andy fumbled in the dark trying to open locked cars... If [Andy's] homework suffered, his intrigue with the car business flourished during these late-night cloak-and-dagger adventures.

Jack Taylor had started Enterprise in 1957, operating it on a shoestring in the basement of a St. Louis Cadillac dealer. As it expanded, Taylor eschewed locating at airport sites, where the major car rental companies had well-established counters, and instead opened up his offices in urban neighborhoods, thus appealing to a local clientele. Enterprise also cemented relations with insurance companies so they would refer policyholders to the rental car agency when their vehicles were in the repair shop after an accident.

Over the next four decades Jack Taylor, following a quintessential American success-story trajectory, built Enterprise into a mammoth complex of businesses that rented and sold cars and trucks, sold coffee and other guest-room items to hotels, and marketed food and personal-care commodities to what the company called the "correctional commissary market," i.e., prisons. Judging from the Enterprise-funded book "Exceeding Expectations," he was grooming Andrew, his only son from a previous marriage, to be his successor from early in the boy's life.

> The leasing business grew steadily during Andy's high school years. Jack frequently brought home a map of St. Louis, which he updated with colored pins to show the location of every car in the leasing fleet... Andy's respect for his father grew, not only because of his nerves of steel repossessing cars in the night, but also because of his success as the owner of a fast-growing business.

After graduating from college and getting married, Andrew Taylor went to work for Jack's brother Paul, who managed a large Lincoln-Mercury dealership in San Francisco that had a vehicle rental-leasing operation. There he "learned the ropes" of the business. "He also had frequent phone conversations with Jack. Jack was both father and mentor for Andy, listening patiently to the customer problems Andy was handling and providing guidance for the tough situations."

Andrew Taylor and his family moved back to St. Louis in 1972, and he began working for his father's company. In 1974 Jack Taylor bought Keefe Coffee, a company that provided in-room coffee equipment to the hotel trade, and named Andrew Taylor to head it. In 1980, according to "Exceeding Expectations," Jack told his son, "I want you to be president of Enterprise."

> Andy, then 33 years old, was, for once, unprepared. His mind got tripped up by his feelings, and he couldn't say anything. Then he blurted out "Wow," and it sounded louder than he meant it to sound. "Thanks," Andy said with a wide grin. Putting to rest Andy's previous insecurities about being the boss's son, Jack replied, "You've earned it."

In 1994, Jack Taylor named his son CEO of Enterprise, and in 2001 Andrew Taylor became chairman of the rental car giant and subsequently of Enterprise Holdings, the umbrella company created in 2009 to oversee all the Taylor business interests.

In a 2007 Q&A interview with *Inc.* magazine, Andrew Taylor described the two men's relationship this way:

> **Who's the smartest you know? Why?**
>
> My father, Jack Taylor, because he was a true entrepreneur, with great values, who listened to his customers and his employees and got this business off the launch pad.
>
> **Who gives you the best advice about your business?**
>
> I have to give the nod to my father again. He's been asking the same questions about our business for 50 years: Are our customers satisfied? Are our employees having fun? Are we doing things the right way?

A less sanguine picture was painted by a disgruntled former Enterprise executive, Larry Underwood, who wrote a book, "Under the Corporate

Microscope," criticizing Andrew Taylor's management of the company. In a review of "Exceeding Expectations" posted on Amazon, he wrote:

> The story is a sanitized version of the company's history, featuring Founding Father Jack Taylor's steadfast commitment to customer service, as the company inexorably grew to mammoth proportions. Mr. Taylor also had a tremendous sense of fairness and loyalty to his employees. While he was the driving force behind the core values his company embodied, there was a strong sense of mutual trust and respect between employees and ownership.
>
> Unfortunately, as Mr. Taylor grew older (he was born in 1922) he gradually turned operating control over to his son, Andrew, who gradually surrounded himself with a huge bureaucratic management team of humorless, micro-managing, untrustworthy drones. The transition to this culture of fear seemed to correspond to the time when Enterprise had finally taken over the top spot in the car rental market (mid '90s). That's about the time the wonderful company Jack Taylor had founded in 1957 began to act like a "big company", with all its devious trappings and hidden agendas.

In 2006, *Fortune* profiled the Taylors and their empire, prompted, the magazine wrote, by the "face-off" between Enterprise and Hertz, whose dominance in the rental car business had been usurped by the Taylors. Promising to "lift the curtain" and provide an "inside view" of Enterprise, "this very private entity," the profile began by contrasting the seemingly self-effacing founder with the size of his family's fortune:

> Says the tall, lean, and sharply dressed Jack Taylor, retired now from active management but an ardent tracker of all that transpires in the company: "Enterprise sort of grew by itself. I never thought it would be more than a small to medium-sized business. I knew I wanted to live reasonably comfortably and to get a couple of new cars every two or three years, and I thought that

if I was really successful, I would have maybe a condominium in Florida and a reasonably nice house here in St. Louis."

He could buy a major slice of either place. The Taylors, who own almost all of Enterprise, do not publicly disclose how much it makes. But *Fortune*'s interviews and various triangulations allow us to estimate with some confidence that profits this fiscal year, on that $9 billion in revenues, will be upwards of $700 million. That compares with the $378 million that Hertz made in 2005, which was its best year ever.

Until 2009, Enterprise's vehicle safety infractions had largely stayed out of the public eye. Even the Houck sisters' crash and the subsequent litigation generated by it received scant press coverage, none of it at the national level. Then, in August 2009, ten months before the *Houck* trial was scheduled to take place, a prominent Midwestern newspaper published an in-depth investigative story that quickly went national: Enterprise Rent-A-Car had been renting and selling General Motors cars from which, at Enterprise's direction, standard-equipment side air bags had been omitted.

The Kansas City *Star* report disclosed that Enterprise had placed the safety-debilitated vehicles in the hands of both their rental customers and purchasers of Enterprise used cars, and had even falsely claimed in on-line advertising that the cars were equipped with "F & R" – front and rear – "Side Air Bags."

Enterprise Rent-A-Car, the nation's largest private buyer of new cars and seller of used ones, chose to "delete" a standard safety feature from thousands of Chevrolet Impala fleet vehicles, saving millions of dollars. After the company rented out those 2006-08 model vehicles, Enterprise and countless dealers nationwide offered them for sale on the open market — minus the side-curtain air bags that have been shown to dramatically reduce highway deaths.

What's more, a Kansas City *Star* investigation found that hundreds of Impalas already sold were incorrectly advertised on Enterprise's Web site as having the very head-protecting feature that the rental company opted to exclude on General Motors' factory floor.

According to the *Star,* the rental car company had saved $175 on each of the Impalas from which GM, at Enterprise's direction, deleted the side air bags. The deletions netted Enterprise a total savings of $11.5 million. In defense of its actions, Enterprise told the *Star* it has not violated any federal regulatory mandate; although GM had provided the side air bags as standard features on the Impalas, it had not been required to do so by Federal safety standards.

"But the St. Louis-based company admitted making a mistake in its online advertising," the *Star* report said. 'There's definitely a glitch in the system,' Christy Conrad, Enterprise's vice president for corporate communications, acknowledged when the *Star* informed Enterprise of the misleading Web postings. After checking data on past sales, the company determined that 745 Impalas— model years 2006 through 2008 — sold from Enterprise's used-car lots 'were marked incorrectly, only online, as having side air bags and they did not,' Conrad said."

The prestigious Insurance Institute for Highway Safety told the *Star* that "side impacts are the second-most common fatal accident, after frontal crashes. The institute said more than 8,000 people were killed in side-impact collisions in 2007. Studies have shown that side air bags with head protection reduce highway deaths 45 percent among drivers in cars struck on the driver's side." The Institute was critical of Enterprise's deletion of the safety feature from the Impalas, the *Star* reported:

A spokesman for the Insurance Institute, Russ Rader, called the discovery astonishing. "Fleet buyers are actually given the option to delete a safety feature that otherwise comes standard? I've never heard of that," Rader said "My personal view is that the liability concern alone would raise a lot of red flags if I were an official at Enterprise, looking to purchase cars that would be rented" by unknowing customers.

Rader also said "this presents a big problem for consumers" who consider buying used fleet vehicles, commonly known as program cars. "If you look up crash-test ratings before buying, you'll find that the 2006-08 Impalas were rated by the Insurance Institute as 'good' in front-impact and side-impact tests. But that's a test that included the side air bags. No vehicle has earned a 'good' rating for side-impact protection without the side air bags," Rader said.

Shortly after the story appeared in the *Star,* Enterprise sought to control the damage by offering to buy back the defective Impalas at cost plus. By then the story had been picked up by the national media, with coverage on CBS, ABC, and Fox affiliates and by McClatchy, Huffington Post, CNET and Consumer Reports news services, among others. Around that time a car crash injury believed to have resulted from Enterprise's dereliction came to light: an Iraq war veteran reportedly became a quadriplegic after his 2005 Impala, made by GM of Canada and purchased from Enterprise, was struck by another vehicle. He sustained devastating neck injuries that experts said would have been prevented or lessened had the car been equipped with side air bags. He sued GM and Enterprise. The case was settled for an undisclosed amount.

Meanwhile, a class action suit was filed against the rental car company on behalf of people who had purchased the air bag-lacking cars. It settled a year later when Enterprise agreed to give the cars' purchasers a $100 coupon toward renting or buying another vehicle from the company. It also agreed to distribute "NO SIDE AIRBAG" warning stickers which owners could place on their vehicles at time of sale.

To some safety advocates, the agreement represented barely a feather-tap on the knuckles, one appallingly incommensurate with the seriousness of Enterprise's offense. For one buyer of a safety-deficient

Impala from Enterprise, the agreement was almost a joke. "I don't know how the people at Enterprise can live with themselves," she told the Star. "My husband rides as a passenger with his eyes closed."

Eventually the story died down, but Enterprise had now had a taste of the negative national publicity that can befall a major business when it is caught putting profits before its customers' safety. It came at a portentous moment – the point in time at which Enterprise was beginning to assess its end-game strategy for defending itself before a jury in the *Houck* litigation and minimizing the likelihood of negative-publicity fallout from the trial.

18

AN INSULTING OFFER

A FEW MONTHS BEFORE the trial date, Grassini and Wrinkle scheduled a meeting with the Houck parents to brief them on the status of the case. When Cally and Chuck arrived at the lawyers' offices, they found that Grassini's workroom had been taken over by dozens of accordion file folders of *Houck v Enterprise* case documents that would be used at trial to wage a full-scale product-liability assault on the rental car company, including hundreds of thousands of pages of expert depositions taken over the preceding five years.

Cally recalled that the meeting began with Wrinkle describing the crash-causation findings of the plaintiffs' experts, Rosenbluth, Romig and Irwin. He showed them the plastic overflow container on which Romig had identified an incriminating burn pattern, and walked them through the reconstruction opinions of the three experts. The briefing "took quite a long time. I think we were probably there three-four hours. There was a lot of technical information." The lawyers told the Houcks that "Enterprise, as a result of this new information, had hired a new lawyer, James Yukevich, who was more specialized in negotiations and settlements and that sort of thing."

Enterprise was proposing another settlement meeting, the lawyers told her, and she would need to be available in case there was a viable settlement offer. A few weeks later the settlement meeting was held at in

Los Angeles. Grassini, Wrinkle and Yukevich attended. While the lawyers conferred, Cally waited outside.

"At the end of the day," she recalled, "probably two-three o'clock in the afternoon, Larry and Roland came out and took me into a little side office and explained to me that Enterprise's settlement was basically insulting – they were insulted by it, I got that very clearly – and that we're going to trial. I said okay, and I don't think I even asked what their offer was. I don't remember any figures." She did recall, though, that the offer had been conditioned on the Houcks' signing a non-disclosure agreement – a legally binding agreement preventing them from publicly revealing any information about the case, the cause of their daughters' deaths, or the amount of the settlement.

Cally was undismayed by the meeting's outcome. She and Chuck had agreed that their commitment to finally getting the facts of Enterprise's wrongdoing "out in the open" would preclude them from accepting what some people might consider a positive settlement, i.e. a few million dollars tied to a non-disclosure agreement. It would take a full-blown trial to expose Enterprise's misconduct to public scrutiny, she believed.

It was late afternoon and growing dark by the time Cally got in her car for the two-hour drive back to Ojai. When she turned on the ignition she saw that the lighted dashboard clock read "5:55". "I didn't really think anything of that 555," she said, "except that Raechel, whenever it would happen that all the digits on the clock were the same, would say, 'Make that number of wishes.' So I made five wishes, one of which was 'I hope this is over soon, hope it's coming to an end!'"

19

A Stunning Admission

IN EARLY 2010, two new characters joined the cast of leading legal play-ers in *Houck v Enterprise* – California Superior Court Judge Richard Keller, assigned to oversee the trial, and James Yukevich, the Los Angeles attorney retained by Enterprise at the last minute to defend it before a jury. Yukevich, not Green or Wiggins, was now calling the legal shots on behalf of the rental car company.

Keller, 62, was in his twelfth year as a Superior Court judge trying criminal and, more recently, civil cases. He "keeps a messy desk and acknowledges a conservative rep among some criminal court attorneys," one legal newsletter had written, noting that the judge had a sign on his desk that read, "Einstein had a messy desk too." In person Keller was low-key and affable, a good listener. Lawyers on both sides of criminal court cases believed he was fair, if no-nonsense, in his rulings. By his own admission he did not brook legal pettifogging: "I do not deal well with petty arguments over discovery," he told an interviewer.

The disposition of cases tried before Keller since he had moved from the criminal to the civil bench in 2007 gave scant indication of how he might render rulings in *Houck*. In 2007 and 2008 he had adju-dicated a contentious dispute between the University of California at Berkeley and a group of tree-sitting protestors occupying a grove where the school planned to cut down trees so that it could build a high-tech gym. His rulings had been balanced, meaning they gave neither side an unqualified victory; he held that the tree-sitters were unlawfully occupying campus property but prohibited the university from dislodging them forcibly since that might endanger their lives. Also in 2008 he had ruled in favor of low-income tenants of the California Hotel, a historic property in Oakland whose non-profit owner, Oakland Community Housing, Inc., was attempting over their objections to evict them. According to a newspaper report, Keller believed OCHI was running a "shell game" in which they were enjoying "ungodly credits and tax benefits" at the expense of tenants.

In 2009 he had presided over a jury trial in *Gersten v. Asbestos Corporation Ltd., et al,* a product liability case in which a 73 year old pleural mesothelioma sufferer alleged that the corporation was responsible for his illness because he had been exposed to asbestos while working in facilities operated by his employer, Combustion Engineering, an affiliate of the defendant, in the late 1950s. The defense won the case after a factual dispute arose over when the plaintiff had actually worked for Combustion Engineering.

Enterprise's new attorney, James Yukevich, headed the Los Angeles corporate-defense firm of Yukevich Calfo & Cavanaugh, whose client list also included a number of auto manufacturers, among them Ford, Honda, Hyundai, and Subaru. Like Larry Grassini, he was an east coast transplant to California.

According to a consulting group that annually evaluated defense-attorney law practices, Yukevich Calfo was one of the "most feared law firms in the nation... They have a take-no-prisoners attitude, and they don't contemplate not winning." On its website, the Yukevich firm's sales promise to prospective corporate customers was that it would "defend your interests, your reputation and your clients.

"We understand that when your products are under examination, so is the reputation of your company. We ensure you have all the resources you need to control the story, and convey the message that keeps your integrity intact, and your business growing… we help you honestly assess the situation and develop effective strategies that achieve the results you want whether it is a defense verdict or a favorable settlement."

Presumably Enterprise was banking on Yukevich to craft a *Houck* trial strategy that would get "the results you want" for the rental car industry's alpha-dog – a jury verdict against the Houcks

On Monday, May 3, less than a month before the trial date, at a court-ordered meeting between the attorneys for Enterprise and the Houck family, Yukevich's strategy was unveiled. Its impact on *Houck v Enterprise* was stunning.

The meeting's purpose was to "exchange and work out all required trial documents," including exhibits, evidence, and witness lists. Trial briefs – summaries of the positions each side would take before the jury – were to be submitted to the judge. As directed by the court, the Houck family's attorneys showed up with detailed lists of their planned trial exhibits, including Rosenbluth's cutaway PT Cruisers, extensive photos and videos from the crash scene, and videos of the Rosenbluth-Romig tests. The Enterprise attorneys showed up empty-handed, with no exhibits, evidence, or briefs. Instead, Yukevich announced that his client would, in effect, plead guilty. Enterprise, he said, was admitting that its actions had caused the deaths of the Houck sisters. Specifically, Enterprise Rent-A-Car of St. Louis – "headquarters" – and Enterprise Rent-A-Car of San Francisco were informing the court that rather than attempting to defend themselves at trial, they would:

"…admit that Raechel Veronique Houck and Jacqueline Marie Houck died instantaneously as a direct result of the collision between a PT Cruiser which they occupied and had rented from Enterprise Rent-A-Car of San Francisco, LLC, and a semi-trailer truck on October 7, 2004;

"…admit that they were negligent and that their negligence was the sole proximate cause of the fatal injuries of Raechel Veronique Houck and Jacqueline Marie Houck;

"...withdraw all prior denials that may be inconsistent with this admission of liability and withdraw all affirmative defenses."

All that was left to be decided, it seemed, was the amount of monetary damages that Enterprise should pay the Houck family for the wrenching losses it had suffered due to the violent deaths of Raechel and Jacqueline.

What appeared to be a simple issue, however, turned out to be anything but. The Enterprise defendants had not admitted their wrongdoing out of a newly-discovered sense of remorse; they had done so as a carefully-calculated tactic to limit their losses. As Yukevich put it in one of his many pre-trial filings, "given the developments in this case" and the "highly emotional nature" of the Houck sisters' deaths, the defendants had "decided that an admission of fault is the most advantageous position available to them in this litigation." Loss-control tactics, not contrition, were behind Enterprise's guilty plea.

Yukevich now proceeded to attempt a resolution of the case favorable to his client. He would again propose to the Houcks that they accept a lowball settlement offer and, in exchange, sign a non-disclosure agreement under which no information about the litigation, Enterprise's bad behavior, or the company's admissions of liability would ever be made public. Thus he would make good, at least partially, on his pledge to the client to "help you honestly assess the situation and develop effective strategies that achieve the results you want whether it is a defense verdict or a favorable settlement." The cost of damages to the multi-billion dollar rental car giant would be miniscule and, most importantly, there would be no trial, no embarrassing publicity, no historical footprint left by *Houck v. Enterprise.*

In short, after five years of unyielding insistence that the Houck crash was Raechel's fault, not its own, Enterprise had totally reversed course and was now ready to admit that its wrongdoing had killed the sisters – but only as a means of keeping that wrongdoing out of the public eye forever.

Looking back on Yukevich's guilty-plea strategy a few years later, both Roland Wrinkle and Judge Keller concluded that Enterprise had no other choice.

If the facts of the girls' deaths were presented to a jury, Wrinkle believed, the jurors would "jump out of the box and ring (Enterprise's) neck, they'd get so angry. And somebody" – Yukevich – "was finally smart enough to figure that out," but only after Enterprise had put the Houcks "through hell."

"So – the five years it took, couldn't get a trial date, Chuck's case against Chrysler, the Chrysler bankruptcy, *and* it was this massive defense, all these experts, to prove it had nothing to do with the defect, it was all the fault of your daughter, who killed herself and killed her sister, and then somebody finally figured out that a jury's going to get livid at this type of presentation. Very unusual that they would admit liability and everything else, but it would have been worse [for Enterprise] if a jury had found out about all that."

Why had the rental car company persisted in its "massive defense" for so long? "They did it to beat the people down, so they'll say, 'I can't take it anymore, I gotta get out of this' – abandon the case or settle it on Enterprise's terms." As Wrinkle saw it, "everything was against the Houcks" until Enterprise pled guilty.

To Judge Keller, the admission-of-liability strategy was one of Enterprise's "smarter moves... If I were the (defendants') trial attorney, the last thing in the world I would have wanted the jurors to hear was about the nature of the crash, the fire, the pictures – those pictures would have been devastating, I think."

Right after his admission of Enterprise's liability, Yukevich approached Grassini with an offer to settle the case for three million dollars and a confidentiality agreement. The Houcks quickly rejected the offer; they "wanted the story to be told," Grassini recalled, "and we knew we really couldn't tell the story unless we went to trial, got a verdict, and then they couldn't force confidentiality on us. Cally and Chuck made the decision to go forward... so they could then let the public know what was going on in the rental industry." The Houcks "couldn't do what they needed to do by settling the case, and they couldn't do what they needed to do by the trial itself, but they needed to go through the trial so then they could talk about what really happened. That's why the trial was so important, because it got them to that next step."

But it also meant re-experiencing the deaths of Raechel and Jacqueline yet again; it was "not an easy trial for them to go through."

Trial remained scheduled for June 1; a jury would decide the amount of damages. It would hear testimony from the family and friends of the sisters about the two girls' lives, endeavors, plans and dreams.

For Enterprise it was a major setback. At this point its only option was to attempt to place restraints on the content and volume of information about the Houck crash that would be shown to the jury and included in the public record of the trial. To do this it turned to a legal tool, the *in limine* motion. The Latin term translates as "on the threshold; at the outset." In jurisprudence, it describes one party's motion, made before a trial begins, to limit the admissibility of evidence by an opposing party.

Yukevich launched a barrage of *in limine* motions designed to squelch any attempt by the Houck attorneys to introduce "evidence regarding the circumstances of the accident or the culpability of defendants." All such evidence "must be excluded," he argued. For the jury to hear about the accident or about Enterprise's role in causing it would be "unduly prejudicial" to the rental car company. Yukevich cited California cases where, in similar trials, courts had excluded evidence that would "necessitate undue consumption of time or... create substantial danger of undue prejudice, of confusing the issues, or of misleading the jury."

Although Enterprise had admitted its responsibility for the Houck sisters' deaths, the language of the motions seemed at times to be suggesting that the court should feel sympathy for the rental car company. Yukevich described the plaintiffs' "allegations" and "claims" – a PT Cruiser power steering hose defect that caused a fire, smoke in the passenger compartment, and driver loss of control – as "extremely complicated theories." Enterprise had needed to conduct "a thorough and earnest analysis of plaintiffs' complex claims. This analysis took a great deal of time, effort and resources." Its decision to admit liability "was not made lightly." (In a response, Grassini and Wrinkle quoted a California appellate court decision referring to the "classic example of chutzpah—the person who murders his father and mother and then asks for mercy on the ground he is an orphan.")

Even though Enterprise's "thorough and earnest analysis" had consumed nearly five years and cost both parties millions of dollars in legal and expert fees, the Houck attorneys should not be allowed to "unfairly characterize defendants as dawdlers or obstructionists," Yukevich contended. The plaintiffs should only be permitted to show the jury evidence bearing on three issues: the "present value of future contributions" by the deceased to the survivors, the value of "personal service, advice or timing that would probably have been given" by the deceased to the survivors, and the "value of the deceased's society and companionship" to the survivors.

Clearly the first issue did not apply to the Houck family's losses; the sisters had been young women still partially dependent on their parents' support. The second and third, however, did apply. The violent deaths of Raechel and Jacqueline in effect had "wiped out the Houck family," in Larry Grassini's words. Whether Yukevich objected or not, the "value of the deceased's society and companionship" to the Houck family was at the heart of damages question, and the contributions of the sisters' "personal service" to society, whether as future artists, teachers or in other capacities, were not irrelevant.

As the trial date loomed, attorneys for the two sides made their arguments to Judge Keller over the most contentious of the *in limine* motions, meanwhile working out agreements to modify or drop others. What remained would be considered by the court at time of trial in *Houck,* now only days away. The upshot would be exclusion of evidence relating to the details of the crash and Enterprise's specific wrongdoing but allowance of testimony from family and friends of the sisters – testimony essential to humanizing Raechel and Jacqueline so that the jurors would have a sense of the excruciating impact of their deaths on those close to them.

20

VOIR DIRE

THE FIRST PHASE of the trial in *Houck v Enterprise* began on the morning of Tuesday, June 1, 2010 in Courtroom 608 of the Fremont Hall of Justice, an unremarkable low-rise building in downtown Fremont, California.

The windowless courtroom, small and government-issue contemporary in layout and decor, was dominated by the purple of its upholstery and the light maple tone of its woodwork. At its front, on a slightly raised dais, was the judge's bench. To the left of the bench were seats for the witness and court reporter; to its right, arrayed along one wall of the room, were the jurors' seats – the so-called jury box. Facing the judge were tables for counsel and a lectern for the attorney addressing the court. Behind the tables were seats for spectators. One door to the courtroom led from the public corridor through a foyer which was flanked by a waiting room for witnesses. Another, behind the judge's bench, led to a rear hallway that connected all the courtrooms, judges' chambers, and jury rooms on the floor.

The trial's first order of business was *voir dire* of prospective jurors. *Voir dire* – from the French for "speak the truth" – is the process in which, at the outset of a jury trial, prospective jurors are questioned by the judge and by counsel for the opposing parties in order to reveal their biases or other impediments to impartiality. "When attorneys are allowed to conduct the *voir dire*," one authority states, "they often try to ask questions that will reveal individuals' personalities and political or cultural persuasions. In cases where the facts are shocking or the evidence is difficult to view, attorneys may also use *voir dire* as a way to introduce the issues so that the eventual jurors are prepared for what will happen at trial." Based on a prospective juror's answers, either attorney may challenge that person's fitness to serve, either for cause or peremptorily. The judge rules on these challenges, and can himself exclude someone from the jury based on his own concerns.

Shortly after 9 a.m. a panel of seventy-four prospective jurors was shown into the courtroom. Keller introduced the attorneys for the two sides to the jury candidates: Larry Grassini, Roland Wrinkle, and Larry Grassini's attorney daughter Kathleen for the Houck family, and Yukevich and two associates from his firm, Cristina Ciminelli and Monique Youngquist, for Enterprise. Grassini introduced Cally and Chuck Houck to the panel, thus putting a human face on the plaintiffs' case. The prospective jurors filled out questionnaires about themselves, which Keller reviewed. He excused twelve of the panel from further jury duty for hardship reasons and directed the rest to return to the courtroom the following day for continued *voir dire*. The trial was adjourned midday.

The following morning, Wednesday, June 2, the remaining prospective jurors returned to the courtroom. Eighteen were randomly called and seated in the jury box to be questioned by Keller, Grassini and Yukevich. The process would continue through the next day until a jury of twelve members and an alternate had been chosen. Each attorney would frame his questions so as to identify jury candidates who might be inclined for or against his client's position, and also would use the opportunity to subtly or not-so-subtly advance that position. Judge Keller would attempt to clarify the task that the jurors, once seated, would be charged with carrying out.

During the *voir dire* the prospective jurors were encouraged by the judge to voice their questions and concerns about the case. Repeatedly they asked whether they eventually would be told the facts of the Houck sisters' death – why and how they had been killed by Enterprise. Repeatedly Keller was compelled to tell them they would not. There would be no testimony on the subject, he warned. The only information the jury would receive was "what the plaintiffs claim are their losses as a result of that and you're going to hear why they are claiming that, what they are basing their claim on. You're going to hear what the defendant's response to that is. So you're not going to be deciding in a vacuum. What you are simply not going to be doing is hearing 'why' because it's not an issue. The 'why' has already been answered" by Enterprise's guilty plea.

The trial was "not an action now to punish the defendants," Keller said; Enterprise had already admitted responsibility. Rather, it was "to find out what amount, if any, the plaintiffs have proven to you is their actual economic loss or non-economic loss in this particular case. In other words, the loss of comfort, the loss of companionship..." Neither he nor the law could provide guidance on what those figures should be, he said. "It is up to the jury using its life experiences, its common sense, to say here's what [they] think is the dollar value, if any, to be placed on this loss. Nobody's claiming that, you know, dollars are ever going to bring anybody back; they are not." The civil justice system "doesn't have the ability to do that. All it has the ability to do is ask you to put a dollar sign on it." It's "almost asking juries to say how many angels dance on the head of a pin," he said, but it's "the only system we have."

The jury's task in that system was "not easy," Keller said. "In this case, it is going to be, I am sure, emotional and hard. But the decisions this jury makes cannot be made based upon sympathy. They have to be based upon the facts of the case. They have to be based upon simply the evidence that you hear in the courtroom and then putting that all together with your own experiences as, you know, adults. And I don't mean to, and I am not – I feel very confident there is going to be more than one tear shed in this courtroom when you hear the testimony and that's understood. The question is after that has happened can you sit down and without letting emotion carry the day decide what a fair verdict would be? And I don't know how else to put it."

The trial would be a difficult one for the jury, Keller was warning; he also was cautioning that the jurors needed to understand the role of the lawyers who were appearing before them. He said his experience with Grassini and Yukevich "has been very good, they are very nice people." Nonetheless, although in *voir dire* "attorneys will tell you, and I think they have in this case, they just want people that can be fair and impartial to both sides, I will tell you that's not true. They may believe it, but they want people that are going to be sympathetic to their side. I am the only person that's participating in this portion of [the trial] that has to be worried about both sides. Their job is not to be worried about the other side. Their job is to be worried about their client."

The lawyers' job, in other words, was to determine whether and to what extent prospective jurors would favor one party or the other in deciding how much Enterprise should be required to pay the Houcks for their losses. To Keller, as he told Grassini and Yukevich out of the presence of the jury candidates, there was little doubt about where jurors would be coming from at the outset; it was "a given that everybody's going to favor the plaintiff in this case" because Enterprise had admitted it caused the girls' deaths. "So the question is not if they are going to favor the plaintiffs, but are they going to unfairly favor them or are they going to take into consideration emotions which they are going to be told they are not to consider. Those are the things I have to look at, not whether they are going to favor the plaintiff, because the plaintiff is already favored because of the admission of liability."

The Houck attorneys were not encouraged by the early results of the *voir dire*. "Things looked a little bleak for us," Wrinkle recalled of the first day. To Grassini, the prospective jurors seemed at first impression to be "a tough crowd, a real tough crowd... one of the difficult things for jurors to understand is a wrongful death case." Jurors "want to say, you know, 'How can money replace a child?' and it's kind of an easy out for a juror because they go, 'I don't want to have to think about that. I really don't want to think about losing a child.'" Moreover, "We weren't allowed to say anything about the case, how it happened, how they died, about when Enterprise admitted liability, about what we went through with discovery, it was just, 'We're here to ask you for damages for the loss of their children, and the defendants have admitted they caused the deaths.'"

As the *voir dire* process unfolded, the very different agendas of the plaintiffs and the defendants became apparent. Grassini's questions centered on the devastating impact of the Houck sisters' violent deaths upon the parents, and on the meaning of Enterprise's unequivocal admission of responsibility for those deaths. Yukevich's stressed that the trial was not meant to "punish" Enterprise for its admission but only to award "fair and reasonable" monetary damages to those survivors.

More than once Grassini said that in effect, the trial was about not one but four cases – one for each death and one for each parent. "...it's unusual in that this is just not one case, because it's for the deaths of two daughters. Both daughters were killed in this accident. And it's also a case for the mother who lost her older daughter, Raechel, and her younger daughter, Jackie, and for the dad, Chuck, who lost his older daughter, Rachael, and his younger daughter, Jackie. So it's basically four cases."

He did not want Enterprise to get "some kind of gold medal" for admitting liability, he stressed. Repeatedly he reminded the prospective jurors that Enterprise had admitted it was the "sole cause" of the two girls' wrongful deaths. "I have said it so many times now. They've admitted they were the sole cause of the deaths of these girls. Are there any of you that are sitting there and saying, well, maybe they really weren't and I have to take that into consideration? Is everybody willing to accept that statement from the defendants, even though you won't know any of the underlying facts? But the reason I am – I keep asking these questions, because I see some – some questions in people's eyes, and I just want to make sure that everybody understands exactly what's been admitted to in this case and what your job will be."

Yukevich, while acknowledging that the Houck parents were "lovely people" and their daughters were "lovely, lovely young women," returned time and again to the central themes of his questioning, i.e., that the jury should award no more than "fair and reasonable" damages, and that their decision should not be directed at "punishing" Enterprise for the unexplained wrongdoing to which it already had admitted. Nor should it be driven by sympathy for the Houcks; he was seeking to weed out jurors who "would let their emotions override a considered rational judgment" in reaching their decision – a process that Judge Keller had earlier warned would be "emotional and hard."

By the end of the final day of *voir dire*, the prospects for the plaintiffs seemed more encouraging. Lois Heaney was a highly experienced trial consultant retained by Grassini and Wrinkle to observe the *voir dire*, analyze the responses of prospective jurors to the attorneys' questions, and evaluate their strengths and weaknesses. As the *voir dire* process came to a close and Judge Keller made a final selection of jurors, she felt optimistic about the jury's make-up and the trial's probable outcome.

Enterprise's admission of liability had made the trial easier for the plaintiffs, Heaney knew. "The jury could then just really focus on 'what's the tragedy here.'" But there were still hurdles to cross. Of Enterprise's "damage control" tactic of admitting fault, Heaney concluded that the rental car company had been "hoping that a bunch of the evidence of their wrongdoing will somehow not be as amplified before the jury and the jury won't get as mad. And therefore the jury will just be looking at, 'So okay, it's very sad, but what's the value [of the losses of life]?'"

Still, she thought, Enterprise's tactic could backfire. "Juries are really motivated by questions of 'what good will this do?' In many ways people want to feel that their damage award really accomplishes something more than just saying to the parents, 'We're very sorry and here's a lot of money.' They want it to accomplish something, to have some kind of a purpose." Heaney called *Houck* "an 'every-person's case'... a middle-class person's problem. I would guess that many or most middle-class people who've been on vacation have rented a car. So it is a situation that people can identify with, and that's a piece of what we were looking for" in jury selection.

It was likely that Enterprise was hoping for conservative jurors, Heaney thought; about half of the *Houck* trial jury members were Asian-Americans. The defense "usually is thrilled to have Asians," Heaney said, "because they're very typically and notoriously conservative, frugal, high on individual responsibility, good defense jurors. I think [Enterprise] ignored, to their detriment, things that some of these jurors were actually saying. They were persuaded that because they were Asian-American and some of them young, they were going to fit their defense stereotype."

As it turned out, Heaney said, some of the supposedly "conservative" jurors were "pretty anti-corporate – which is something that [plaintiffs] like going in to these sort of things. We were looking for people who were somewhat anti-corporate and also who had strong relationships with family members – with their parents, with their children – and understood that bond. And people who had a sense of – you know, more conservative people, in a certain way, are motivated by a notion of following the rule. Well, the rules here would say, if you've got notice there's something wrong with this car and it's under recall, then you have a duty not to keep renting it out."

The end result was "the right mix of jurors," Heaney said. "Ordinarily you see a lot of people saying, 'Well, I'm kind of suspicious of plaintiffs, they're here for a lot of money, I don't know if this is a legitimate lawsuit,'" but the *Houck* jurors "thought this was a legitimate and real case. The obvious thing was this was a rental car, that there'd been an accident, and that Enterprise was acknowledging responsibility, that two young girls were dead, and that therefore, even if inferentially, there's something wrong with the car, that there's some reason that Enterprise thinks they have screwed up.

"So the jury understands that and the jury understands that this is the sort of thing that Enterprise really doesn't have a whole lot to say about what caused this accident. All Enterprise can do, really, is get up and say, 'We're very sorry, but they don't deserve a whole lot of money.'"

21

REMEMBERING THE SISTERS

O N THURSDAY, JUNE 3, 2010, after three days of *voir dire*, Judge Keller completed his final jury selection. The trial would enter its decisive final phase the next day. And, as Lois Heaney had predicted, Enterprise's lawyer Yukevich would "get up and say, 'We're very sorry, but the Houck parents don't deserve a whole lot of money.'"

Cally Houck and her companion, Carl Nienaber, were staying at a nearby Marriott, where Grassini's office had arranged to house the Houck family members and friends who would appear as witnesses during the trial's pivotal days. Some arrived by car, others by plane. Cally shuttled between the hotel, the courthouse and nearby San Jose Airport, picking up and dropping off witnesses.

Cally was "was more than ready for the trial," but she was "disappointed that the jury wasn't going to hear the whole story. I was still stung by the fact that Enterprise had tried to blame Raechel. I was offended." Her overall feeling as the trial got underway was, "Let's get this over with, we've been waiting five years." But she was having a hard time with the trial's focus on money. "I knew they were going to rule on damages, but I had a disconnect with that. 'Award of money' – it's such a weird term, like it's blood money." Her repugnance at the thought of "blood money" as a surrogate for her daughters' lives would remain long after the trial was over.

On the morning of Friday, June 4, the final phase of the trial in *Houck v. Enterprise* began with opening statements by the opposing attorneys. The courtroom's spectator seats were largely filled with family and friends of the Houck sisters who had shown up to lend support to Cally and Chuck and, if called upon, to testify about their recollections of Raechel and Jacqueline. A smaller section was taken up by a contingent of lawyers and executives from Enterprise. Cally was seated next to Lois Heaney; the jury consultant's assurances, she recalled, gave her confidence as the trial began.

As had their *voir dire* questions, the two attorneys' opening statements demonstrated the stark difference in what each was urging the jury to determine should be Enterprise's compensation to the Houcks for taking their daughters' lives.

Yukevich, while reiterating his formulaic and obligatory *voir dire* admission that Enterprise's negligence was "the sole proximate cause of the happening of this accident," told the jury that the rental car corporation believed no more than "three to four millions dollars total amount" would be a "fair and reasonable amount of money" for Enterprise to pay the Houcks in redress of its wrongdoing in causing their daughters' deaths. He reinforced the defense's firmness on that figure by adding that he was "not trying to give you a number which is some – of a low number, something that you can move from." It appeared to be Enterprise's idea of the maximum amount of damages that the jury should allow the Houck parents to receive – a figure virtually the same as the one with which Enterprise had attempted to settle the case with a confidentiality agreement before the trial. Yukevich reiterated three times that "three to four million dollars is a fair and reasonable compensation."

Grassini began by posing a rhetorical question to the jury: What were the Houcks seeking from this trial? "Justice," he answered – justice in terms of "what the consequences should be for wrongfully killing these two girls." The "biggest worry that a parent has is that they are going to get a phone call like the Houcks got," because "our biggest job as parents is to provide the safety of our children." Thus the jury's job was to "determine the consequences [to Enterprise] for taking that away from the Houcks from the day they got that phone call October 7, 2004 through the six-and-a-half years they waited to have you make this decision... this is the most unspeakable thing that can happen."

He displayed poster-sized pictures of Raechel and Jacqueline as he continued:

"...Raechel, beautiful, lovely, talented, 24 years old when she was killed. She fit a lot into her life. She loved to write. She loved music. She loved children. She learned fluent Italian... She was a dancer. She was a singer... Cally lost Raechel. Chuck lost Raechel...

"Jackie... a little over 20... very much into horses... an excellent rider... a spectacular artist.... Like her sister, she loved kids... wanted to go down to Costa Rica and work with the youth down there... Cally lost Jackie. Chuck lost Jackie...

"I am incapable of explaining to you what that loss would be. I think you can all understand that the loss of one child under these type of circumstances would be terrible. The loss of two is incomprehensible. The greatest tragedy that can befall a parent is to lose a child. Chuck and Cally lost two six-and-a-half years ago, and they have waited and waited patiently for this day and – these few days where you twelve folks will get the opportunity to tell the defendants what the consequences of their acts should be. The defendants shouldn't determine what the consequences of their acts should be."

A "fair and reasonable figure," Grassini said, would be $12 million for each of the losses – Cally's of each daughter and Chuck's of each daughter, or $48 million. "That's what I say," Grassini told the jury, "But you are the sole judges of that. You are the voice of the community. You are going to tell this community, these defendants, what the consequence is of killing two beautiful lovely girls."

Over the next two days, eight of the sisters' friends took the witness stand. Under questioning by Grassini they told the jury about the lives of

Raechel and Jacqueline Houck, showed photos and videos of the sisters, and described their special place in the hearts and memories of the witnesses. Raechel was remembered as "caring, loving, nurturing... sweet and bouncy... energetic, enthusiastic, passionate... a beautiful writer... a dancer... a singer." Jacqueline was "a free spirit... loved nature... a painter... loved to make people laugh... had a huge empathy for animals and kids... a leader... a tremendously fabulous" horsewoman. The two girls "loved travel... loved each other... mothered one another...if one of them had gone [died in the crash] without the other one, it would almost have been too much for the other one to handle."

On the stand, in the jury box and among the spectators, copious tears were shed – it was, as Keller had foreseen, "emotional and hard" to hear the dead girls' violently foreshortened lives memorialized. To Cally, the trial was "like a five-day funeral." But she didn't break down. "My tears had flowed five years before. Now it was time to carry on."

When Greg Houck, the sisters' younger brother, took the stand, his testimony was, for Cally, "the hardest part" of the trial. "He was so stoic. He broke down a couple of times and they kept asking him whether he wanted to take a break and he said, 'No, I'm going to be fine,' and he went forward with his testimony."

"I miss them to death," Greg told the jury. "It doesn't get much easier. You just miss them more and more. They were my mentors." Raechel had been "very nurturing... she taught me music with her singing and playing keyboard to me." Jacqueline was "the artist with her painting, and I learned that from Jackie, too." His sisters had urged him to "strive for my talents" and had "taught me to use my imagination." From them he had learned "a hundred percent" to "speak my mind and believe in whatever I believe in and just keep striving for that." He had been "so distraught" when his sisters moved to Santa Cruz, but at least he could then look forward to their visits home. But now he could "no longer wait for them to come."

Cally and Chuck Houck were the trial's final witnesses.

Praying she could be "the voice of my daughters," Cally had brought to the trial photos and videos of Raechel and Jacqueline taken over their lifetimes, some with each other, some with friends, some with their parents and brother. As she showed these to the jury she described her daughters and her relationship to them: "We were like a triad, the three of us... They were my strength. They were my best friends."

During the girls' childhood, Cally had been "a stay-at-home mom by choice...actively involved in my children's daily life." She had been "a carpool mom, a team mom, a homeroom mom." She had been "in awe of my kids. I know it sounds kind of crazy. Sometimes I couldn't believe they were mine because they were incredible to me." She had "loved being in their space...wanted to be where they were all the time." That "never stopped, and it doesn't stop now, really."

She and Chuck had been "very lucky." The girls "always seemed to like us. They always seemed to want to be around us, which is kind of unusual, even as teenagers." And at the same time "their devotion to one another was profound. If I have anything to be proud of as a parent, it's that our children truly loved and liked each other" and were "always looking out for one another."

Growing up, Cally said, Raechel had been "mama's helper. She always took the big sister approach with her sister. Jackie always looked up to her big sister. Jackie was Peter Pan girl and Raechel was mom's help girl...their love for one another and for their brother is something I am very proud of."

Early in 2004, while she was working as an *au pair* for a family in Italy, Raechel had sent Cally an email which Grassini asked her to read to the jury. In it the daughter had written to her mother:

"Thank you for being an example of truth, charity, and good humanity. I think you are an authentic soul who taught me more than most... Please know that without you and your planted seeds I would be a shallow non-person being swayed by the wind. Thank you for giving me roots and strength of mind, body, soul, and spirit. Your intellect inspires me to strive to be the same every day. I love you all the time, even the times I yell. And I wish you a year with open gates ahead beckoning for the future of a woman who really ran with the wolves. Talk to you soon. Love, your first born."

"Jackie had a way with animals and art and Raechel had a way with words and music and dance," Cally told the jury. And like Cally, both had "lots of passion for whatever they did. I saw the child in me in Jackie and I saw the mom in me in Raechel."

On the afternoon of June 7, Chuck Houck took the stand as the trial's final witness.

He had strived to keep his daughters "safe and to take care of them, and to show them the world," he told the jury. Most of all, he stressed, as children "they would always come first" to him.

Their childhoods had been "great times." He recalled taking Raechel to the beach as an infant; "she would go running down to chase the birds and you had to be quick because she'd just go right in the water. She didn't know she couldn't swim." Raechel was "adventurous, wanted to travel, wanted to get out...see the world, every inch of it and meet every person and speak every language." Jacqueline was "kind of that free spirit... She would tell you everything going on in [her] life, everything that she thought about."

The sisters "looked out for each other, always took care of each other." They "got along great." They were "kind...bright...out to do the world." Chuck's "greatest moments," he said, were when the girls were home, when "everybody was under one roof."

"I can't touch them now. I can't hold them. I can't protect them. And I worry about them. And I want them at peace. And I want the world to know the horrific thing that has been done to my daughters," Chuck Houck told the jury.

As he said this, he looked over at an Enterprise attorney who, apparently unmoved, was polishing her nails. It was too much for the grieving father. "I mean, you got to be kidding me," he erupted at the woman. "What is wrong with you?"

It was, as Roland Wrinkle said later, "dramatic, very dramatic." Was it dramatic enough to unfairly bias the jury against Enterprise? Yukevich thought so. He seized on the incident as an opportunity to ask Judge Keller to declare a mistrial, which would mean going through the arduous, costly process of trying *Houck v. Enterprise* all over again. Perhaps this would be so discouraging to the plaintiffs that they would settle the case on Enterprise's terms.

Out of the presence of the jury, Yukevich argued that a mistrial was justified "based upon Mr. Houck's comments at the end of this trial… Certainly, the comments at the end, looking over at my table or my client and asking what was wrong with us, talking about horrific things that were done to his daughters, I am sorry to even have to stand up at the end of this trial with all the witnesses that has gone before, but this is exactly what we were worried about. This is exactly what's happened. So, unfortunately, on behalf of Defense I move for mistrial at this point."

Opposing Yukevich's motion, Grassini told the judge that every one of his witnesses, including Chuck Houck, had been "instructed not to go into the facts of the accident, not to go into how the girls were killed, not to go into the recall, not to go into the foundation, not to go into the five-and-a-half years that the Defendants decided to put these folks through a big fight on liability.

"Now, two weeks ago they [Enterprise] decide to come in here and admit liability. We have done everything we possibly could. And all that dad did at the end of this thing is look over and say, 'Why did you commit that horrific act, the killing of two children,' which they admitted is a horrific act. There is not a juror there that doesn't think it is. And there was no – there was no violation of any court order as far as talking about any of the events of it. And certainly after going through all of these witnesses, keeping as tight a control as the Court did on it, I can't imagine that that one comment would justify throwing all of that out…. the father's reaction to that question certainly wasn't intentional, wasn't planned, and I don't think it was in any way damaging to the Defendant's position."

Yukevich persisted. Chuck's comments should be deemed "inflammatory, they're intended to inflame the passions of the jury, they are intended to increase the amount of damages in this case." They were "provocative and may have a significant effect on the way the jury views this case... I just have no choice but on behalf of my client to move for a mistrial."

There would be no mistrial. In his view, Keller said, there is "enough emotion in this case that that one comment is not sufficient for me to justify a mistrial." He would instruct the jury to ignore Chuck's comment, he said, but he would not accede to Yukevich's motion. Enterprise, Yukevich's client, had "acknowledged liability...this is, you know, part of what the parents are going through. But I think, you know, this is not a case about, you know, infliction of emotional distress or anything. It has to do with what the loss is. I – so I am not prepared to grant the motion."

A few moments later the jury was brought back into the courtroom and Keller gave it a "cautionary note" about Chuck's outburst. "The final comment that Mr. Houck made is not – does not go to anything you are going to have to decide. Defendants have already admitted liability in regard to it... I am going to ask you to please disregard the last comment that Mr. Houck made."

The next day, Grassini and Yukevich made their closing arguments. Each reiterated their damage claim proposals– Grassini's for $48 million, Yukevich's for $3 million. As he had in his opening statement, Grassini asked the juror to "give justice" to the Houcks for their losses. "And when I ask for justice, I am not asking you for half justice because half justice is half injustice. Chuck and Cally Houck don't deserve any more injustice than they've already had starting October 7, 2004." Yukevich, he warned, would ask that the jury to "be fair to Enterprise." It's "the catch phrase that they used throughout this trial... be reasonable to Enterprise," even though Enterprise had been unreasonable in the way they had taken the Houck sisters' lives. The Houcks weren't seeking sympathy. "Believe me, the Houcks have had plenty of sympathy. What they need is your justice. The defendants are the ones who are saying, 'We admit that we're responsible. We admit that we're responsible.' Responsibility without accountability is nothing...

"Consequences. There are consequences to killing two young beautiful girls, two human beings. Accountability. They need to be accountable. That's what this case is all about."

During the trial, one of the witnesses had read aloud a poem written by Raechel to her parents when she was 17 years old. It illustrated, Grassini said, "how Raechel and Jackie were," and "the type of parents that Chuck and Cally were." Entitled "Yin and Yang," it described the parents this way:

"My father taught me independence. My mother taught me harmony. Together they taught me youth... My father helps me avoid mistakes. My mother helps me learn from them. Together they taught me giving. Together they taught me compassion... Father taught me sacrifice, discipline. Mom taught me freedom and ideas. Together they taught me companionship... My mother taught me to dream, and my father taught me how to wake up...together they taught me I was a gift."

Yukevich, Grassini concluded, was telling the jury not to hurt Enterprise simply because it was a corporation. "But the Houcks didn't make a decision as to who was going to cause the deaths of their daughters... their loss would be just as great if it was an individual who had caused that wrongful death... They've suffered, and they are to be compensated for that suffering, the suffering of the loss of the love, affection, companionship, and all those words, but all it means is their two lovely daughters were ripped from them. That's all. Grief and sorrow, that's what you suffer immediately and get over, but you never, ever, ever get over the loss of the love of your daughter."

Yukevich's opening statement had implied that Enterprise believed its $3 million was the highest amount the jury should consider; it was "not a low number, something you can move from." He tried now to back away from that implication. "I didn't tell you this is a number, not a penny more. I am not telling you now." What he had meant, he said, was that "in negotiations sometimes people start high, start low, work their way to the middle... I'm suggesting to you that that's not what you should do... it's your decision as to what's fair and reasonable... What I am asking you to do is be fair to both sides...if you're not fair to both sides, that results in injustice. You don't punish individuals, corporations for injustices that could not be prevented."

Grassini's use of the terms "consequences, accountability," Yukevich asserted, "the way it's said, it's code word, it's courtroom-speak for punishment, and it's not allowed... He said the courtroom is the great equalizer. That's where little people can take on big corporations. Exactly what you're not supposed to do in this case. That's not it. This is not David and Goliath. It's a company that's admitted liability and has asked for a fair trial."

He concluded by thanking the jury for "listening to a case that involves such sadness and tragedy." Curiously, despite his insistence a few moments earlier that the case "is not David and Goliath," he now said it "involves an individual versus a corporation."

The trial was at an end; the jury, which Enterprise had successfully blocked from learning the horrendous details of the crash that killed Raechel and Jacqueline, would deliberate until it reached a verdict.

20

VERDICT

MIDMORNING OF JUNE 9, 2010, the jury in *Houck v. Enterprise* announced its verdict. Enterprise would be required to pay compensation of $15 million to the Houck parents for their loss of comfort and companionship caused by their daughters' deaths.

Cally earlier had told Carl and her friend Nancy Mason that she felt the outcome of the trial somehow would involve the "5-5-5" sequence that had first showed up on her dashboard clock after the failed settlement meeting in Los Angeles a few months earlier. Now, she saw the judgment – $15 million on June 9, "6 + 9" – as a sign from her daughters.

The trial had been "excruciating" for Cally, but its conclusion brought "relief at five years of litigation and waiting coming to an end," she said. Following the verdict, family, friends and lawyers gathered in the hallway outside the courtroom. Judge Keller joined them, Cally recalled, with "tears in his eyes".

Cally and Carl left right after that for the long drive home. Greg had given his mother a bouquet of flowers with a blue butterfly balloon tied to it; she decided to drive to Ojai on a route that would take them past the site of the PT Cruiser crash in which Raechel and Jacqueline had died, so that Cally could place the bouquet there. She had avoided driving on that section of highway 101 since the day of the crash but now felt "brave enough to make the trip – I was driving." But as they neared the site, "I had a meltdown. I pulled over, hands were shaking, I was sweating, clammy, I was crying... It wasn't just that this represented this big dark hole in my life that I never got too close to the edge of, but it was also the relief of five years of litigation being over. So it was an accumulation of all of that."

Bouquet in hand, Carl got out of the car and ran across two lanes of traffic. At a place in the median where the crash had taken place, he laid the bouquet and balloon in the grass. Then he returned to the car and sat with Cally, comforting her until she calmed down. It was the last time Cally would travel on that section of 101; henceforth on trips north she would avoid it even at the cost of long detours. The place "haunts me," she said; "there's something evil about that place."

Cally found herself weeping often in the days following the trial. Partly it centered on what she thought of as "the blood money" aspect of the jury decision. "It represented – and it didn't matter how much it was – the lives of my daughters. It was a really hard thing for me to reconcile with." Friends told her this was what the girls would have wanted, and she hoped they were right. But she was troubled by other things as well. The voices of witnesses talking about the girls at the trial "kept coming back." And she had wanted Enteprise to admit publicly that Reachel, "this girl you implied was suicidal or alcoholic or whatever, none of it was true, it was so far from reality. I wanted that exoneration."

Adding to her pain was the finality of it all; it was "officially over." As long as the litigation had been in progress and the trial was still pending, there was something to do, some action to be taken about her daughters' deaths. "But when the trial was ended, it was like, 'Now what?' I couldn't let go, because there was something else to get done. The payment of money was like, 'Alright, so what?' But the mom in me knew there were going to be other kids, and by golly, I wasn't going to let Raechel and Jackie die in vain."

A few years earlier Cally had created a small foundation in the girls' memory. Celebrating their love of travel and "the wonder of different cultures," the Raechel & Jackie Foundation would work to "encourage creative expression and environmental stewardship that improves the quality of life for youth and preserves cultural heritage and natural resources for generations to come." After deductions for legal costs, Cally received $4.2 million as her share of $15 million judgment against Enterprise. She donated a third to the foundation.

Shortly after the verdict, the Grassini-Wrinkle law firm issued a press release (see appendix) detailing the facts of the PT Cruiser crash that had killed the Houck sisters – the recall, Enterprise's failure to correct the defect, the rental car company's insistence that the crash was caused by the driver, and its attempts to settle the case with a confidentiality agreement. Attached to the release were key documents that demonstrated Enterprise's culpability for the crash, including the Matias declaration, notice of the defect received by Enterprise but not acted on, the PT Cruiser recall itself, and customer contracts showing that Enterprise had rented out the defective car three times before renting it to the Houck sisters. The release quoted Larry Grassini as saying, "I was so inspired by the bravery of Chuck and Carol, who refused to take any amount of money in exchange for muzzling them from exposing Enterprise's business practice of renting recalled cars."

About that time Cally, still in emotional distress and wondering whether she would "ever be at peace" again, recalled reading something that the dean of Vanderbilt Divinity School had written in response to a grieving parent:

"What's really happening when someone turns from grief to activism is about encountering a life changing event that causes one to think of one's own life differently. You ask the question that every mother, father and brother asks in these sudden death instances, 'How do we redeem the loss?'"

It was, she said, "absolutely spot on for me." Henceforth she would devote herself to redeeming the loss of her daughters at Enterprise's hands.

AFTERWORD

S HORTLY AFTER THE trial in *Houck v. Enterprise,* Cally Houck embarked
on a mission to give meaning to the loss of her daughters. Working
with safety advocacy groups, most prominently the California-based
Consumers for Auto Reliability and Safety (CARS) and the Washington-
based Center for Auto Safety (CAS), she began a campaign to win pas-
sage of laws prohibiting rental car companies from putting unrepaired
recalled vehicles into their customers' hands.

Early in 2011, California Assemblyman William Monning introduced such a proposal in the state legislature. Monning, a Democrat,
had a special commitment to the Houcks. He represented the state assembly district that included Santa Cruz – the town where Raechel and
Jacqueline Houck were living at the time of the crash, and where they
had rented the lethal PT Cruiser from Enterprise. Although Monning's
bill would apply only to cars rented in California, if passed it would
represent a huge incentive toward getting other states, and possibly the
federal government, to take similar action.

Hearings on the Monning bill, at which Cally and representatives
of the advocacy groups testified, attracted considerable media coverage. But they also revealed that the rental car industry was opposed
to any such laws and, using campaign contributions and political
influence, would lobby to defeat them. Ironically and inexplicably,
Enterprise was the most vehement opponent of the bill. It argued that
the Houck tragedy was an isolated instance of a defective Enterprise

rental car killing or injuring its occupants. Of course, past crashes of Enterprise-owned cars that had been recalled but not repaired probably would have gone undetected. The Houck crash, indeed, would have been chalked up to "driver error" had the parents not happened to discover the PT Cruiser's defect history. And it was close to certain that any previous lawsuits against Enterprise for similar "wrongful deaths" caused by unrepaired recalled vehicles would have been settled with confidentiality agreements – and therefore never made public.

Enterprise's argument was difficult to rebut. If it knew of other cases it was not about to disclose them. Monning's bill passed the California assembly but was unable to withstand the rental car industry's oppositional lobbying in the state Senate, where it was put on hold indefinitely and eventually died.

Meanwhile, federal legislators had taken an interest in the issue, again with the stimulus of Cally Houck and the consumer groups with which she was working. Democratic Senators Charles Schumer of New York and Barbara Boxer of California began introducing bills to prevent auto rental companies from putting their customers behind the wheels of recalled but unrepaired defective vehicles. For a while the rental car industry continued to oppose the measures but a breakthrough came early in 2012 when Hertz, Enterprise's leading competitor, broke ranks with the industry and agreed to support the bills. With the industry oppositional front collapsing, Enterprise soon announced that it too would support the bill, and followed up by vigorously lobbying for its enactment. Whether from a belated sense of remorse for its role in the deaths of the Houck sisters or for self-serving "corporate image" purposes, its about-face won the approval of Cally Houck. She stated:

"As we moved forward toward legislation, our former opponents in the rental car industry, and specifically Enterprise, became vital and important allies in our continued efforts to make rental car safety a law. Some corporations will support campaigns because it's good for public relations. However, Enterprise's sincere endorsement, and later unequivocal support and assistance in our efforts, is an example of what corporations should do when they realize their business policies are not good for the consumer. Enterprise's engagement and commitment in seeing this cause through to the successful end is, in fact, its genuine redemption."

On October 1, 2012, eight years after the deaths of the Houck sisters, Enterprise CEO Andrew Taylor finally wrote a letter of apology to Cally Houck, for "all the difficulty and sadness the accident... has caused you and your family." On December 4, 2015, the Raechel and Jacqueline Houck Safe Rental Car Act was signed into law.

APPENDIX: GRASSINI & WRINKLE POST-TRIAL PRESS RELEASE*

ENTERPRISE RENT-A-CAR ADMITS TO RENTING TWO YOUNG SISTERS A CAR WHICH HAD BEEN RECALLED A MONTH EARLIER FOR UNDERHOOD FIRES AND CAUSING THEIR WRONGFUL AND UNREASONABLE DEATHS.

I N A CIVIL lawsuit for wrongful death recently concluded in Alameda County Superior Court, Enterprise Rent-A-Car Company and Enterprise Rent-A-Car Company of San Francisco each admitted they caused the wrongful and unreasonable deaths of Raechel Houck, age 24, and her younger sister Jacqueline Houck, age 20, on October 7, 2004, by renting them a 2004 PT Cruiser which was the subject of a recall by Chrysler because of potentially dangerous and unsafe power steering hoses which, if they fail, "can result in an underhood fire." After receiving the recall notice a month earlier on September 9, 2004, Enterprise went ahead and rented the unfixed vehicle to three customers prior to renting it to Raechel Houck. The young women died in a fiery crash while traveling northbound on Highway 101 in Monterey County outside of King City. The girls' parents, Carol Houck and Charles Houck, filed a wrongful death lawsuit in Alameda County Superior Court. Enterprise fought the case for five years after hiring a team of lawyers and expert witnesses, claiming that the accident was caused by the bad driving of Raechel Houck.

On the eve of the trial, which started June 1st, the two Enterprise entities finally admitted that "they were negligent and that their negligence was the sole proximate cause of the fatal injuries of Raechel V. Houck and Jacqueline M. Houck."

Enterprise Rent-A-Car purchases seven percent of all new automobiles sold in the United States, making it, and its 840,000 fleet of cars and $6.4 billion in revenues, the largest rental car company in North America. Enterprise also owns Alamo and National car rental companies.

During the lawsuit, a former Area Manager for Enterprise Rent-A-Car Company of San Francisco, Mark Matias, who was in charge of the

Capitola Enterprise branch which rented the fatal vehicle, testified: "At the branch level, managers and employees intentionally rented recalled vehicles to the public." According to Mr. Matias, managers "authorized the rental of recalled vehicles, even with safety recalls." "If the only vehicle left on the lot was a recalled vehicle, the branch would rent that vehicle to a customer." Mr. Matias further testified that, "I can guarantee that if any of those vehicles on the lot [at the Capitola branch] are recalled, at least one is going to be rented out" and that "[a]t the corporate level, their philosophy was that, 'If all you have are recalled vehicles on the lot, you rent them out.' It was a given. The whole company did it."

Both of the managers-in-training who rented the PT Cruiser to the Houck sisters provided statements to the parents' lawyers saying that Enterpriser intentionally overbooked vehicles "to get customers in the front door" and knowingly rented out vehicles in need of service and maintenance. The recalled PT Cruiser rented to Raechel Houck was the last car on the lot and was represented to her as a "free upgrade."

Thomas Moulton, who is the Group Vehicle Repair Manager for Enterprise of San Francisco and is in charge of handling recalls, testified in a deposition that he never "considered the possibility that Enterprise should not rent cars to the public after they have received recall notices form the manufacturer." According to Moulton's testimony, he has "no idea" whether "it's a good idea . . . to rent cars that can catch fire to the public." He also had no idea if anybody at Enterprise did anything about the notice of recall received on the PT Cruiser which was rented to the Houck sisters.

Enterprise's Vice President of Service Operations, Thomas Gieseking, testified in a deposition that he was unaware of any changes Enterprise plans for the way it handles recalled vehicles.

By admitting that they unreasonably caused the wrongful death of the Houck girls, Enterprise was able to keep this evidence of its business practices from the jury. Nevertheless, the jury awarded damages of $15,000,000.00.

Enterprise claimed the defect in the recalled vehicle did not cause the fiery crash, but argued that the Houcks' daughters were killed because Raechel was a bad driver. Raechel's mother, Carol Houck, said, "For five and a half years, Enterprise hammered us with a team of 'experts' who kept saying our oldest daughter was responsible for killing herself and her baby sister, and then admitted that it was Enterprise who was responsible just before the trial started."

The sisters' father found it very difficult to keep fighting Enterprise for the five years but did so because "No amount of money will bring our two angels back to us, but I wanted the world to know what Enterprise did to my family."

Enterprise offered the parents $3 million if they would agree to keep the matter "confidential." They refused. "All the money in the world could not make up for the risk that this could happen again to somebody else's kids," said the girls' mother.

Larry Grassini of the Woodland Hills, California law firm of Grassini & Wrinkle remarked, "I was so inspired by the bravery of Chuck and Carol, who refused to take any amount of money in exchange for muzzling them from exposing Enterprise's business practice of renting recalled cars."

We have included copies of the following important documents which were uncovered during the course of our investigation of Enterprise's business practice and in discovery during the lawsuit:

1. Photographs of the accident scene and the PT Cruiser.
2. Internal Enterprise documents showing when and how Enterprise learned of Safety Recall D18 and that the issue was still unresolved as of May 5, 2007 ($2^1/_2$ years later).
3. The Safety Recall D18 itself.
4. The three rental contracts where the subject PT Cruiser was rented out after getting notice of the recall.
5. The Houck rental contract (i.e., the fourth after getting notice).
6. The declaration of Mark Matias.
7. A survey of complaints relating to the D18 recall.

8.   A photograph of Raechel, Jacquie and little brother Greg.
9.   A photograph of Raechel.
10. A photograph of Jacquie.
11. A photograph of Raechel and Jacquie.

PLAINTIFF'S EXHIBIT
li&i*e..5014490
140
Agnew, Bob J

From: gsbll@daimlerchrysler.com
Sent: Thursday, September 09, 2004 12:41 PM
To: bfabian@wheels.com; jross@ hertz.com; jcreeden@budgetgroup.
com;
randy.rawlinsonOthrifty.com; calhounb@nationalcar.com; MuscatoF
ancrental.com;
rtaylor@donlen.com; bcarlson@cleverett.wa.us; stevea.smith@fleet.
gecapitalcom; jamesiessig@gsa.gov; Agnew, Bob J; james.litwin@gsa.
gov;
tommy@theleasingcompany.com; Muehleisen, Christian J; steve.
smock@verizon.com; tom.wall@metrokc.gov; gsprinkel allstateleas-
ing.com; amold.nelson@ncmail.net; roy.williams dge.state. ia.us;
kathy.shannon dgs.state.la. us; joseph. such dot.state.wi.us; linda.
gladem@doa.state.wi.us; fannie.robertsedtag.com; clarkrm@ldsch-
urch.org; maintm@mikealbert.com; service Omikealbert.com; timg0
mikealbert.com;
jpjohnston ITIMM.COM, cread@arifleet.com; sdombrowski@dollar.
com; larry.fewis@sce.com; srg@dunhamexpress.com; mary.warren@
thrifty.com; becky.stocker@thrifty.com; neil.fisher@phh.com; ray.
gebhardt@phh.com; nxm2@pge.com;
alchanchorena@ verizon.com; Christopher_Powers@dom.com; jgpl@
dcx.com; rmlowe duke-energy.com; warranty@comcast.net; dziehm
eaubumhills.org; Todd. Boutefle@doa.state.wi.us; AHWilson@lasd.
org; sminier@emkay.com; davidm@budgetbuffaio.com; kathyb@
budgetbuffalo.com; joef budgetbuffalo.com; gage.wagoner@phil-
ips.com; bhansson eamileasing.com; MiltonDOchesterfield.gov;
Maung.thant@cendant.com; Marc.Martine@cendant.com; Thomas.

Tittmann@cendant.com; Robert.McManus@cendant.com; Ipavek@ agstar.com; ken.mckenney@verizon.com; kenneth.taite us.ngrid.com
Cc: GSB11 daimlerchrysler.com
Subject: DCX • Safety Recall D18 — Power Steering Pressure Hose:
Attachments: D18.pdf

To all this may concern

The attached file contains the dealer *and* owner letters for Safety Recall D18 -- Power Steering Pressure Hose.

This recall affects 2001 through 2004 model year Chrysler PT Cruiser and 2005 model year Chrysler PT Cruiser Convertible (PT) vehicles equipped with a non-turbocharged 2.4L engine and an automatic transaxle.

The dealer letters will be mailed during the week of September 13th. The owner letters will be mailed during the week of September 20th.

If there are any questions please feel free to contact me.

Thanks - Greg

Greg Burks
DaimlerChrysler National Fleet Service
2301 Featherstone Road • CIMS 429-08-10
Auburn Hills, Michigan 48326
Phone: 248/512-7960 Fax: 512-7999
Tieline: 722- 'E-mail: gsb11@dcx.com

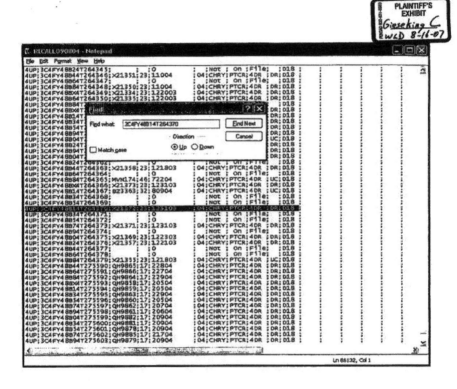

```
___ File  Options  Commands  Programs  Exit(X)  Help   11:23:07  5/01/07
Logical                    QuestView (TM)              Pg: __1  of 1.
File: EA005P01__   FA OPEN RECALL HISTORY LOG FILE BY UNIT #/RECALL
Libr: ELLIB_____   Fmt: EA005ED1__                     ............  Display
Mbr : EA005P01__   Rec: _____17,041 of 166,160   Scan: _____

Position to . . . , UNIT NO.: X21372
          RECALL CAMPAIGN: D1B
MANUFACTURER : CHRY                   ADDED BY EMPL.: _____
UNIT NO. .. . .: X21372               CHANGE TIME   :      0
VIN .. . .. . .: 3C4FY4BB14I264370    CHANGE DATE   :      0
RECALL CAMPAI.: D1B                   CHANGED BY PR:
CAMPAIGN DESC: POWER STEERING PRESSURE HOSE
DEACTIVATION :        0               CHANGED BY EM:
DEACTIVATION :        0
DEACTIVATION :
DEACTIVATION :
ADD TIME ... : 35223
ADD DATE ... : 20040910
ADDED BY PROG: EAJ008A001

2=Exit            4=Prompt      5=Refresh     6=Command pr.   7=Position
16=Services       19=A01        10=Actions    11=Inquiry      24=More keys

H        >                        A                          1/1
```

```
___ File  Options  Commands  Programs  Exit(X)  Help   11:23:57  5/01/07
Logical                    QuestView (TM)              Pg: __1  of 1.
File: EA007P00__   FA OPEN RECALL CAMPAIGN FILE BY MFR/RECALL
Libr: ELLIB_____   Fmt: EA007E00__                    ............  Display
Mbr : EA007P00__   Rec: _____45 of 592              Scan: _____

Position to: MANUFACTURER: CHRY
          RECALL CAMPAIGN: D1B
MANUFACTURER : CHRY                   CHANGED BY EM: 91209
PRIORITY OR N: Y
RECALL CAMPAI: D1B
CAMPAIGN DESC: POWER STEERING PRESSURE HOSE
CHRYSLER ACTI: 20040909
ADD TIME ... :  60212
ADD DATE ... : 20040608
ADDED BY PROG: FAJ003A002
ADDED BY EMPL:
CHANGE TIME  : 132303
CHANGE DATE  : 20040909
CHANGED BY PR: EAS007A001

2=Exit            4=Prompt      5=Refresh     6=Command pr.   7=Position
16=Services       19=A01        10=Actions    11=Inquiry      24=More keys

H        >                        A                          7/30
```

```
 ___File__Options__Commands__Programs__Exit(X)__Help___11:28:06_5/01/07
Logical                   QuestView (TM)                    Pg: _1_of 2_
File: BACHIST___  ECR: Rental Unit History
Libr: ELLIB_____  Fmt: BL0ACHIS__                              Display
Mbr : BACHIST___  Rec: 44,449,253  of 281627845  Scan: .................

Position to . . . .  HUNIT: X21372
                       YR: _4
                      MON: _9
                      DAY: 11
                    MTIME: 1031
  HUNIT  MON  DAY  YR  TIME  TIMEAP MSG
  X21372   9   11   4  1031   AM    2370  D755371  OPENED   MADDOX*   K  95172
  X21372   9   11   4  1040   AM    2370  D755159  CLOSED   SHOCK*    TE 6226X
  X21372   9   27   4   424   PM    2370  D755371  CLOSED   MADDOX*   K  6226X
  X21372   9   27   4   425   PM    2370  D755371  PENDED   MADDOX*   K  6226X
  X21372   9   27   4   445   PM    2370  D755600  OPENED   TEMME*    CA 7848V
  X21372   9   29   4  1049   AM    2370  D755600  CLOSED   TEMME*    CA 4529W
  X21372   9   29   4   101   PM    2370  D755630  OPENED   CUMMINGS* 7848V
  X21372   9   29   4   112   PM    LAST LOC  RENTED                  4529W +

F3=Exit        F4=Prompt     F5=Refresh    F6=Customize     F7=Position
F8=Options     F9=List       F10=Actions   F11=Info         F24=More Keys

 1      >                         A                              7/30
```

```
 ___File__Options__Commands__Programs__Exit(X)__Help___11:28:28_5/01/07
Logical                   QuestView (TM)                    Pg: _1_of 2_
File: BACHIST___  ECR: Rental Unit History
Libr: ELLIB_____  Fmt: BL0ACHIS__                              Display
Mbr : BACHIST___  Rec: 46,722,107  of 281627845  Scan: .................

Position to . . . .  HUNIT: X21372
                       YR: _4
                      MON: 10
                      DAY: _2
                    MTIME: 1059
  HUNIT  MON  DAY  YR  TIME  TIMEAP MSG
  X21372  10    2   4  1059   AM    2370  D755630  CLOSED   CUMMINGS* 2274H
  X21372  10    2   4  1256   PM    LAST LOC  TEST DRIVE 6TA           2274H
  X21372  10    4   4   735   AM    LAST LOC  2370                     2274H
  X21372  10    4   4   811   AM    LAST LOC  ALI RENTING              2274H
  X21372  10    4   4   824   AM    2370  D755686  OPENED   HOUCK*  RA 6226X
  X21372  10    7   4  1128   AM    DX76C56 TOTALED                    4529N
  X21372  10    7   4   524   PM    2370  D755686  CLOSED   HOUCK*  RA 6226X
  X21372  10    7   4   524   PM    LAST LOC  UNKNOWN                  6226X +

F3=Exit        F4=Prompt     F5=Refresh    F6=Customize     F7=Position
F8=Options     F9=List       F10=Actions   F11=Info         F24=More Keys

 1      >                         A                              7/30
```

From: Gleseking. Thomas A
Sent: Friday, May 28.2004 6:13 PM
To: #Business Managers; #Vehicle
Repair; #Loss Control Mgr/Supr
Cc: #General Managers; #RVP: #Vehicle Acquisition
Subject: Recall Automation Update
U.S. & Canada

PLAINTIFF'S, EXHIBIT -
tlasefeLf
wet "-Vic

Beginning June 1, 2004. any SAFETY RECALLS Issued by General Motors, Ford, and Chrysler will be automatically entered Into the ECARS system. This includes all Buick. Cadillac, Chevrolet. GMC, Oldsmobile, Pontiac, Ford, Lincoln, Mercury, Chrysler, Dodge, and Jeep divisions.

Vehicles NOT INCLUDED *In* this project at file time are all of the import manufacturers, as well as Saturn.

The way the process will work is corporate will receive an electronic file from the manufacturer when a recall is released. The file we receive will be used to download new recalls into ECARS. The branches will receive the same notification that they currently receive today. The only difference is that corporate will now be electronically replacing the manual process you currently follow. You will still receive notifications by mail. This is an NHTSA requirement. We suggest that you follow your current procedures minus entering the recall Into ECARS.

AGAIN, ALL IMPORT MANUFACTURERS, SATURNS, AND NON-SAFETY RECALLS WILL STILL HAVE TO BE MANUALLY ENTERED INTO ECARS. We will continue to work with these manufacturers to help automate their recall process and we will keep you updated on our progress. This will not affect any safety recalls issued prior to June 1st. Those recalls will still have to be manually entered.

Needless to say, we are excited about this new process and we hope it brings some value to your groups and regions. If you nave any questions. please contact Bob Agnew, John Ward, or me.
Tom Gleseking

Received Aug-00-2007 04:20pm From-0200010706To-GRASSINI & WRINKLE Page 014

DAIMLERCHRYSLER
SAFETY RECALL - POWER STEERING HOSE

Dear: (Name)

This notice is sent to you in accordance with the requirements of the National Traffic and Motor Vehicle Safety Act.

DaimlerChrysler Corporation has decided that a defect, which re-lates to motor vehicle safety, exists in some **2001 through 2004 model year Chrysler PT Cruiser and 2005 model year Chrysler PT Cruiser Convertible vehicles equipped** with a **2.41, non-turbocharged engine and an automatic transaxle.**

The problem is...   **The power steering pressure hose on your PT Cruiser** (VIN: xxxxxxxxxxxxxxxx) **may contact the transaxle differ-ential cover. Prolonged power steering hose contact can cause the hose to rub through and leak power steering fluid. Power steering fluid leakage in the presence of an ignition source can result in an under-hood fire.**

What your dealer **DaimlerChrysler will repair your vehicle free of charge (parts and labor). To do** *will do...* this, your dealer will inspect and re-position the power steering hose. Any damaged hoses will be replaced. The inspection and repositioning will take about $^1/_2$ hour to complete. Hose replacement, if necessary, will require another hour. However, ad-ditional time may be necessary depending on how dealer appointments are scheduled and processed.

What you must   Simply **contact your dealer** right away to schedule a ser-vice appointment.
do to ensure

your safety   **Remember to bring this letter with you to your dealer.**

If you need   If you have questions or concerns which your dealer is unable to resolve, please

help...   contact DaimlerChrysler at 1-800-853-1403.

Please *help* us update our records, by filling out the enclosed pre-paid postcard, if any of the conditions listed on the card apply to you or your vehicle. Be sure to print the last eight (8) characters of the VIN (VVVVVVVV) and notification code D18 on the postcard. If you have already experienced this condition and have paid to have it repaired, you may send your original receipts and/or other adequate proof of payment to the following address for reimbursement: DaimlerChrysler, P.O. Box 610207, Port Huron, **MI** 48061-0207, Attention: Reimbursement.

If your dealer fails or is unable to remedy this defect without charge and within **a reasonable** time, you may submit a written complaint to the Administrator, National Highway Traffic Safety Administration, 400 Seventh Street, S.W., Washington, DC 20590, or call the toll-free Auto Safety Hotline at 1-888-327-4236.

We're sorry for any inconvenience, but we are sincerely concerned about your safety. Thank you for your attention to this important matter.

Note to lessors receiving this recall: *Federal regulation requires that you forward this recall notice to the lessee within 10 days.*

hI$_i$

NHTSA　　　　　　**Office of Defects Investigation**
Recalls - Search Results

Report Date : **October 4, 2005 at** *02:11 PM*
SEARCH TYPE : **VEHICLE**
Make : **CHRYSLER**
Model : **PT CRUISER**

Type : **ANY.**　　　　110-4●●●●●●●●●●●●●●●　　　　**14.0●111.01.4.**

Make : CHRYSLER **Model :** PT CRUISER **Year :** 2004
Manufacturer : DAIMLERCHRYSLER CORPORATION
NHTSA CAMPAIGN ID Number : 04V268000 **Mfg's Report Date :**
JUN 02, 2004
Component: STEERING:HYDRAULIC POWER ASSIST:HOSE,
PIPING, AND CONNECTIONS
Potential Number Of Units Affected : 438391
Summary:
ON CERTAIN PASSENGER VEHICLES EQUIPPED WITH 2.4L NON-
TURBOCHARGED ENGINES AND AUTOMATIC TRANSAXLES,
THE POWER STEERING PRESSURE HOSE MAY CONTACT THE
AUTOMATIC TRANSAXLE DIFFERENTIAL COVER, POTENTIALLY
DAMAGING THE HOSE.
Consequence:
POWER STEERING FLUID LEAKAGE IN THE PRESENCE OF AN
IGNITION SOURCE CAN RESULT IN AN UNDERHOOD FIRE.
Remedy:
DEALERS WILL INSPECT AND RELOCATE, OR REPLACE AS
NECESSARY, **THE POWER STEERING HOSE** AND CONFIRM
TORQUE OF THE HOSE FASTENER AT THE STEERING GEAR

END. THE RECALL BEGAN ON SEPTEMBER 20, 2004. OWNERS SHOULD CONTACT DAIMLERCHRYSLER AT 1-800-853-1403.

Notes:

DAIMLERCHRYSLER RECALL NO. D18. CUSTOMERS CAN ALSO CONTACT THE NATIONAL HIGHWAY TRAFFIC SAFETY ADMINISTRATIONOS AUTO SAFETY HOTLINE AT 1-888-DASH-2-DOT (1-888-327-4236).

DAIMLERCHRYSLER
September 2004
Dealer Service Instructions for:
Safety Recall D18
Power Steering Pressure Hose

Models

2001-2004	**(PT) Chrysler PT Cruiser**
2005	**(PT) Chrysler PT Cruiser Convertible**

*NOTE: This recall applies only to the above vehicles equipped with a 2.4L non-turbocharged engine (**"B" in the 8th VIN Position**) and an automatic transaxle (Sales Code **DGB) built through April 26, 2004 (MDH 042613).***

IMPORTANT: Some of the involved vehicles may be in dealer new vehicle inventory. Federal law requires you to stop sale and complete this recall service on these vehicles before retail delivery. Dealers should also consider this requirement to apply to used vehicle inventory and should perform this recall on vehicles in for service. Involved vehicles can be determined by using the VIP inquiry process.

Subject
The power steering pressure hose on about 435,000 of the above vehicles may contact the transaxle differential cover. Prolonged power steering hose contact can cause the hose to rub through and leak power steering fluid. Power steering fluid leakage in the presence of an ignition source can result in an underhood fire.

Repair

The power steering pressure hose must be inspected and repositioned. Pressure hoses that are damaged must be replaced.

Safety Recall D18 — Power Steering Pressure Hose Alternate Transportation

Dealers should attempt to minimize customer inconvenience by placing the owner in a loaner vehicle if inspection determines that power steering hose replacement is required and the vehicle must be held overnight.

Parts Information

<u>Part Number Description (Model Year Application)</u>
CBTBD181 Power Steering Pressure Hose (Late-2002 through 2005 Model Years)
CBTKD182 Power Steering Pressure Hose (2001 through Early-2002 Model Years)

<u>Each dealer</u> to whom vehicles in the recall were invoiced will receive ONE (1) of each power steering pressure hose to service vehicles as necessary. Additional power steering hoses may be ordered as required. *Very few vehicles are expected to require power steering hose replacement.*

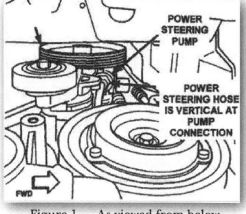

IMPORTANT: <u>The power steering hose to pump connection orientation changed late in the 2002 model year.</u> **For 2002 model year vehicles, inspect the hose connection orientation to determine the proper replacement hose. For hoses with a vertical orientation, order P/N CBTKD182 (Figure 1). For hoses with an angled orientation, order P/N CBTBD181. The two hoses are not interchangeable.**

Figure 1 — As viewed from below

Safety Recall D18 — Power Steering Pressure Hose Service Procedure

A. Inspect Power Steering Pressure Hose:

1. Raise the vehicle on an appropriate hoist.

2. Inspect the section of power steering pressure hose closest to the transaxle differential cover (near the left rear of the engine) (Figure 2).W

3. • **If the power steering hose is cut or worn such that the hose reinforcement cords are visible,** the power steering hose must be replaced. **Continue with Section B. — Replace Power Steering Pressure Hose.**

    • **If the hose section of the power steering hose is NOT cut or worn, or if the hose reinforcement cords are not visible,** continue with Step 4.

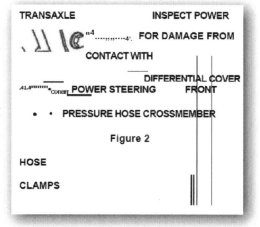

TRANSAXLE   INSPECT POWER
FOR DAMAGE FROM
CONTACT WITH
DIFFERENTIAL COVER
POWER STEERING   FRONT
• • PRESSURE HOSE CROSSMEMBER
Figure 2
HOSE
CLAMPS

4. Mark the location on the power steering hose of the two (2) clamps that secure the power steering hose to the rear of the engine (Figure 3).

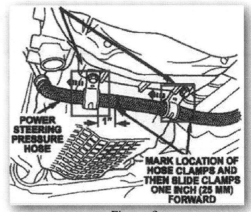

Figure 3

**Safety Recall D18 — Power Steering Pressure Hose
Service Procedure (continued)**

5. Disconnect the two (2) clamps that secure the hose to the rear of the engine (Figure 3).
6. Loosen the power steering hose-to-steering gear connection (Figure 4).
7. Slide both hose clamps forward one (1) inch each on the hose (Figure 3).
8. Attach the two (2) hose clamps to the engine and tighten to 75 in-lbs (8.5 N-m).
9. Reorient the hose so that:

The foam donut on the hose (2004/2005 model years) just contacts the front crossmember, or;

The hose has 1/2" (12.5 mm) clearance to the front crossmember (2001-2003 model years) (Figure 5).

NOTE: For 2001 through 2003 model year vehicles, place a folded shop towel between the hose and the crossmember to maintain the %" clearance while tightening.

10. While keeping the hose in position, tighten the power steering hose-to-steering gear connection to 28 ft-lbs (38 N-m) (Figure **4**).

NOTE: Use a $^3/_8$" torque wrench with a 1" extension and a crow's foot socket to tighten the steering gear connection.

11. Lower the vehicle and return it to the customer.

**Safety Recall DIS — Power Steering Pressure Hose
Service Procedure (continued)**

B.. Replace the Power Steering _Pressure_ Hose:

NOTE: Only damaged power steering pressure hoses, as determined by the inspection in Section A, require replacement. Very few vehicles are expected to require power steering hose replacement.

1. Lower the veΩhicle.
2. Open the hood.
3. Siphon as much fluid as possible from the power steering reservoir.
4. Raise the vehicle on the hoist to working level.
5. Remove the right front wheel and tire assembly.

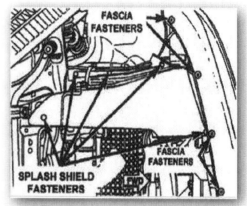

Figure 6 — Viewed from below

6. Remove the right front lower wheel well/drive belt splash shield (Figure 6).

7. Remove the air conditioning (A/C) compressor drive belt (Figure 7).

Figure 7

8. Disconnect the two (2) A/C compressor electrical connectors (Figure 7).

9. Remove the four (4) A/C compressor bracket bolts (Figure 7) and set the compressor aside.

10. Fully raise the vehicle.

Safety Recall D18 — Power Steering Pressure Hose
Service Procedure (continued)

11. Disconnect the power steering pressure hose from the steering gear and drain the fluid (Figure 8).

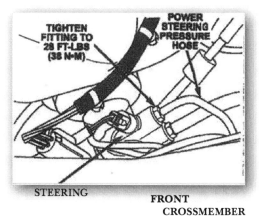

Figure 8

12. Disconnect the two (2) power steering hose clamps from the rear of the engine (Figure 9).

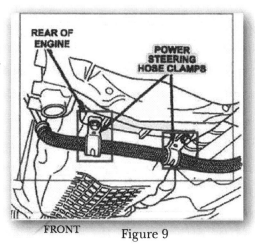

Figure 9

**Safety Recall D18 — Power Steering Pressure Hose
Service Procedure (continued)**

13. Disconnect the power steering hose support bracket from the front of the engine (Figure 10).
14. Disconnect the power steering hose from the power steering pump (Figure 10).

NOTE: For 2001 and 2002 model year vehicles, place a shop towel between the pump pulley and the power steering hose to protect the pulley from damage due to tool contact.

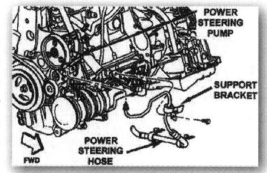

Figure 10

15. Remove the power steering hose and discard it.
16. Loosely connect the new power steering hose to the power steering pump.
17. Install the power steering hose support bracket to the front of the engine (Figure 10). Tighten the bracket fastener to 70 in-lbs (8 N-m).
18. Tighten the power steering hose-to-pump connection to 275 in-lbs (31 N-m) (Figure 10).
19. Install the A/C compressor (Figure 7). Tighten the compressor bracket bolts to 250 in-lbs (28 N-m).
20. Connect the two (2) A/C compressor electrical connectors (Figure 7).
21. Install the A/C compressor belt.
22. Install the lower wheel well/drive belt splash shield (Figure 6).

23, Route the power steering hose around the rear of the engine and install the two clamps to the rear of the engine (Figure 9). Tighten the clamps to 75 in-lbs (8.5 N-m).

24. Loosely connect the power steering hose to the steering gear (Figure 8).

Safety Recall D18 — Power Steering Pressure Hose
Service Procedure (continued)

25. Orient the hose so that:
    - The foam donut on the hose (2003-2005 model years) just contacts the front crossmember, or;
    - The hose has Y2" (12.5 mm) clearance to the front crossrnember (2001-2002 model years) (Figure 11).

NOTE: For 2001 through 2002 model year vehicles, place a folded shop towel between the hose and the crossmember to maintain the 'A" clearance while tightening.

26. While keeping the hose in position, tighten the power steering hose-to-steering gear connection to 28 ft-lbs (38 N-m) (Figure **8).**

NOTE: Use a $^3/_8$" torque wrench with a 1" extension and a crow's foot socket to tighten the steering gear connection.

27. Lower the vehicle to working level.
28. Install the right front wheel and tire assembly. Tighten the lug nuts to 95 ft-lbs (130 N•m).
29. Lower the vehicle until the front wheels are just off of the ground.
30. Fill the power steering reservoir with Mopar **ATF+4 (P/N 05013457AA).**
31. **Turn the steering wheel from lock-to-lock twenty (20) times.**
32. **Start the engine and then turn it off.**
33. **Top off the fluid in the power steering reservoir.**

Safety Recall D18 — Power Steering Pressure Hose

O   Service Procedure (continued)

34. Turn the steering wheel from lock-to-lock eight (8) more times.
35. Start the engine, verify that there are no leaks and then turn it off.
36. Top off the fluid in the power steering reservoir again.
37. Lower the vehicle completely.

Completion Reporting and Reimbursement

Claims for vehicles that have been serviced must be submitted on the DealerCONNECT Claim Entry Screen located on the Service tab. Claims submitted will be used by DaimlerChrysler to record recall service completions and provide dealer payments.

Use one of the following labor operation numbers and time allowances:

Labor Operation Number	Time Allowance
Inspect and reposition power steering pressure hose	19-D1-81-82 0.2 hours
Inspect and replace power steering pressure hose	19-D1-81-83 1.0 hours

Add the cost of the recall part, if necessary, plus applicable dealer allowance to your claim.

NOTE: See the Warranty Administration Manual, Recall Claim Processing Section, for complete recall claim processing instructions.

Parts Returned

Not required.

Dealer Notification and Vehicle List

All dealers will receive a copy of this dealer recall notification letter by first class mail. Two additional copies will be sent through the DCMMS. DealerCONNECT will be updated to include this recall in the near future.

Safety Recall D18 — Power Steering Pressure Hose
Vehicle Lists. Global Recall System, VIP and Dealer Fellow up

All involved vehicles have been entered into the DealerCONNECT Global Recall System (GRS) and Vehicle Information Plus (VIP) for dealer inquiry as needed. Involved dealers were also mailed a copy of their vehicle (VIN) list with the dealer recall notification letter.

GRS provides involved dealers with an <u>updated</u> VIN list of <u>their incomplete</u> vehicles. The owner's name, address and phone number are listed if known. Completed vehicles are removed from GRS within several days of repair claim submission.

To use this system, click on the "Service" tab and then click on "Global Recall System." Your dealer's VIN list for each recall displayed can be sorted by: those vehicles that were unsold at recall launch, those with a phone number, city, zip code, or VIN sequence.

Dealers must perform this repair on all unsold vehicles *before* retail delivery. Dealers should also use the VIN list to follow up with all owners to schedule appointments for this repair.

Recall VIN lists may contain confidential, restricted owner name and address information that was obtained from the Department of Motor Vehicles of various states. Use of this information is permitted for this recall only and is strictly prohibited from all other use.

Owner Notification end Service Scheduling

All involved vehicle owners known to DaimlerChrysler are being notified of the service requirement by first class mail. They are requested to schedule appointments for this service with their dealers. A generic copy of the owner letter is attached.

Enclosed with each owner letter is an Owner Notification postcard to allow owners to update our records if applicable.

Additional Information

If you have any questions or need assistance in completing this action, please contact your Service and Parts District Manager.

Customer Services Field Operations DaimlerChrysler Corporation

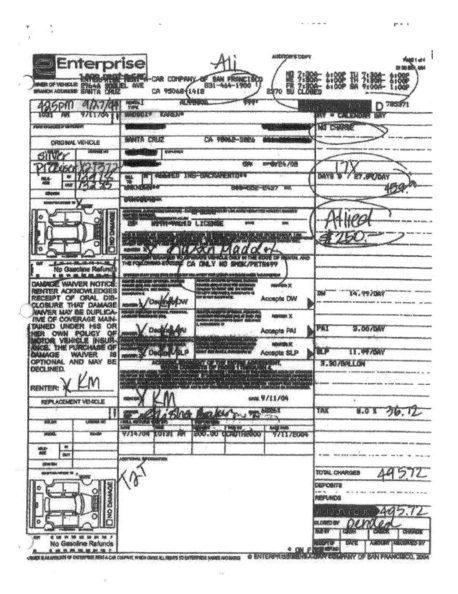

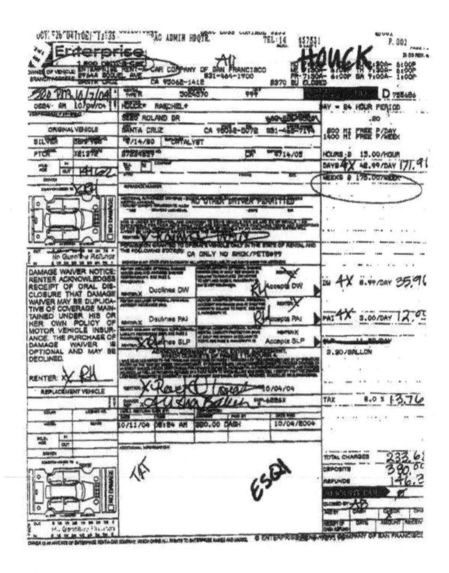

DECLARATION OF MARK MATIAS

I, Mark Matias, have personal knowledge of the facts stated in this declaration and, if called as a witness, I could and would testify competently thereto under oath. I declare as follows:

1. I am over 18 years of age, and I reside in San Jose, California.
2. I was employed as an Area Manager, at Enterprise Rental Car of San Francisco, for 11 years, from 1994 until December 2004. As an Area Manager, I was in charge of the general operations of seven Enterprise offices (including Capitola), located in northern California, referred to as Region W.
3. As an Area Manager, my duties included: visiting each Enterprise office daily; reviewing daily reports to ensure that inventory was accurate; reviewing billing records; and ensuring that all aspects of the business operations were running properly.
4. I am familiar with the facts regarding this matter; specifically, that Raechel Houck rented a recalled PT Cruiser from Enterprise's Capitola, California branch, on October 4, 2004, and was subsequently involved in a fatal vehicle accident, involving the PT Cruiser, along with her sister, Jacqueline Houck, on October 7, 2004; however, at no time during my employment, as an Area Manager, at Enterprise, prior to this accident, was I aware that the PT Cruiser was a recalled vehicle.
5. I was contacted by a legal representative, on behalf of Enterprise, regarding this matter, and was asked not to speak with anyone about this case. But it is important to me to tell the truth.
6. I have no specific knowledge of how the Enterprise offices, at the corporate level (corporate, regional, or group headquarters), may have failed to prevent the rental of the recalled PT Cruiser to Ms. Houck on October 4, 2004; however, at the branch level, managers and employees intentionally rented recalled vehicles to the public.

7. I know that Enterprise Branch Managers, within Region W, authorized the rental of recalled vehicles, even with safety recalls. Safety recalls are referred to as priority recalls. When the fleet was short, and there was demand for vehicles, these recalled vehicles would be rented to the public.

8. As an Area Manager, I knew how operations were handled. When demand called, we rented out recalled vehicles. It happened; I won't lie. If the only vehicle left on the lot was a recalled vehicle, the branch would rent that vehicle to a customer.

9. I am aware of instances where employees knowingly rented recalled vehicles to customers without a manager's approval, when there was a shortage of vehicles on the lot.

10. To my knowledge, the managers and/or employees who knowingly rented recalled vehicles were never reprimanded by Enterprise executives; however, I am not sure whether corporate headquarters had knowledge of these instances.

11. I am familiar with former Enterprise Branch Manager, Andrea Acevilla, who was employed as a Branch Manager at Capitola's office location, in October 2004. Ms. Acevilla reported directly to me. She had trouble running rental operations, because she ran a tight operation; "tight," meaning that she would overbook rental cars; and as a result, there would be a shortage of rental vehicles on the lot. I can guarantee that if any of those vehicles on the lot are recalled, at least one is going to be rented out.

12. She also had trouble maintaining her accounts with dealerships, because of the constant shortage of vehicles on the lot. Additionally, I would notice that Ms. Avecilla's billing invoices did not always match up correctly, and she did not always properly document her billing invoices.

13. Enterprise, at the corporate level, pressed the local offices to run a tight operation. Their philosophy was that, "You've got to keep booking, because you don't know when you are going to get a car back." But then of course, you run short on vehicles, and if

all you have are recalled vehicles on the lot, you rent them out. It was a given. The whole company did it. Enterprise's corporate offices looked the other way regarding this fact.

14. Many times the recall warning attached to a vehicle's unit number on the computer Screen, did not say safety recall or priority recall. Only when that vehicle was taken into the dealership, and the dealership ran the VIN number, would specific information about this recall become available.

15. I also have knowledge of instances where Enterprise employees rented recalled vehicles, because they failed to pay attention to the recall warning attached to the vehicle's unit number on the computer system, which registers when closing out a rental contract; however I cannot recall any specific examples at this time.

16. When a recall warning does come up on the screen that says priority recall, the respective employee is required to take the key of that vehicle, and place that key in an area designated for non-rentals; however, here is where the procedure is too loose, and mistakes can happen. An employee is only required to write the word "recall" on a post-it-note, which is placed on the keys. There is nothing in place that keeps an employee from renting that car. The computer system doesn't lock up. There is nothing to prevent an employee from taking those keys, and renting that vehicle out to the next customer.

17. Enterprise employees and management also had an opportunity to gain notice of a recall through other resources, such as daily reports, the unit history report for each specific vehicle, and the maintenance report; however, these reports were printed at the Branch Manager's discretion. There was no specific policy requiring that these reports be printed out at specific times.

I declare under the penalty of perjury under the laws of the State of California that the foregoing is true and correct.

Executed this_____day of_____2008, in _____, California.

_____

Mark Matias, Declarant

AUTOMOTIVE CONSULTING SERVICES, INC.
4747 SOUTH LAKESHORE DRIVE, SUITE 101
TEMPE, ARIZONA 85282
(480) 890-1000
FACSIMILE (480) 456-3805

OTHER SIMILAR INCIDENTS
CONSUMER COMPLAINTS OF BURNING OR FIRES IN PT
CRUISER VEHICLES
OCCURRING ON OR SINCE 01/16/07
HOUCK V DAIMLERCHRYSLER CORP.
ACS 04-1118B
04/15/10
RED = ENGINE COMPARTMENT FIRE — 5 TOTAL
BLUE = HVAC VENT SMOKE — 3 TOTAL

ODI #	INCIDENT DATE	INCIDENT LOCATION	VEHICLE MAKE	VEHICLE SPEED	ACCIDENT NARRATIVE
10181068	01/29/07	Lindsay, Canada	On 2003 PT Cruiser	0	WHILE LETTING MY CAR WARM UP, WITH THE HEATED SEATS ON LOW, THE DRIVERS SEAT STARTED SMOLDERING, AND FILLED THE CAR WITH SMOKE. I PHONED 911 FOR THE FIRE TRUCK. THE CUSHION UNDER THE LEATHER UPHOLSTERY DISINTEGRATED UNDER THE HEAT. THE CAR IS A 2003 PT CRUISER GT TURBO, WITH ONLY 23000 KM. I HAVE NOT CONTACTED MY DEALER, YET. VIN UNAVAILABLE
10184202	02/22/07	Hampton, VA	2003 PT Cruiser	45	THE CONTACT STATED THAT WHILE DRIVING THE 2002 CHRYSLER PT CRUISER AT 45 MPH SHE SMELLED SMOKE. AFTER DRIVING TWO MILES MORE THERE WERE FLAMES AND ASHES COMING FROM UNDER THE HOOD. THE CONTACT STATED SHE PULLED OFF THE ROAD, EXITED THE VEHICLE, AND REMOVED HER PERSONAL BELONGINGS. AT

					APPROXIMATELY 15 SECONDS LATER THE VEHICLE WAS COMPLETED ENGULFED IN FLAMES. THE ROADS WERE CLEAR. THE CONTACT STATED THERE WAS A FIRE DEPARTMENT REPORT AVAILABLE. THE FIRE MARSHALL WAS UNABLE TO INSPECT THE VEHICLE TO DETERMINE TO THE CAUSE OF THE FIRE. THE VEHICLE WAS DECLARED A TOTAL LOSS BY THE INSURANCE COMPANY SHE RECEIVED A RECALL NOTICE FOR THE FUEL PUMP MODULE SECONDARY SEAL ON AUGUST 30 2004 AND HAD IT REPLACED AT 8900 MILES. ALSO, HE CONTACT STATED SHERECEIVED A RECALL FOR POWER STEERING PRESSURE HOSE ON AUGUST 11TH 2005 AT 14000 MILES. THE CONTACTWAS UNSURE IF THE POWER STEERING PRESSURE HOSE WAS REPLACED, ADJUSTED OR INSPECTED. THE VEHICLE HAD 20000 MILES AT THE TIME OF THE FIRE. VIN: 3C4FY48B12T
10195403	06/12/07	Pottstown, PA	2003 PT Cruiser	10	AS MY WIFE WAS DRIVING THE CAR SHE NOTICED A SUDDEN LOSS OF POWER ASSIST IN THE STEERING. SHE WAS ABLE TO DIRECT THE CAR INTO A PARKING SPACE, AND UPON EXITING, NOTICED LARGE AMOUNTS OF SMOKE COMING FROM UNDER THE CAR. SHE ASKED OTHERS TO CALL THE FIRE DEPARTMENT, AND BY THE TIME THEY ARRIVED, THE CAR WAS TOTALLY ENGULFED IN FLAMES. UPON REVIEW AT THE ACCIDENT SCENE THERE WAS A NOTICEABLE TRAIL OF POWER STEERING FLUID ON THE ROAD BED FOR APPROXIMATEI x A 500 FEET BEFORE SHE CAME TO A STOP. VIN: 3C8FY68B23T
10194142	06/15/07	Las Vegas, NV	2003 PT Cruiser	20	ON THE STREET ENGINE STOPPED, POWER STEERING INOPERATIVE, SMOKE APPEARED FROM UNDER THE HOOD. TURNED THE KEY OFF. RAISED THE HOOD, HAD FIRE BENEATH THE BATTERY AREA. DEALER STATED THAT A MISROUTED CABLE BETWEEN THE BATTERY AND STARTER SHORTED OUT, CAUSING THE FIRE WHICH RUINED THE CABLING, BATTERY AND STARTER. CHRYSLER'S EXTENDED WARRANTY WILL NOT COVER THIS DAMAGE BECAUSE THE
					BATTERY CABLE WAS NOT COVERED. VIN: 3C4FY58B63T
10196014	07/06/07	Merritt Island, FL	2002 PT Cruiser	N/A	FIRE IN ENGINE DEPARTMENT. VIN: 3C4FY48B12T
10264883	09/26/07	Pasadena, CA	2003 PT Cruiser	0	I PURCHASED A 2003 CHRYSLER PT CRUISER IN JULY 2008 IN OCT. WE NOTICED LIGHTS FLICKERING HEADLIGHT SWITCH STARTED BURNING FOG LIGHTS CAME ON DIDN'T WORK BEFORE TOOK IT DODGE NEW SWITCH AND 22 PIN CONNECTOR. NEW PCM REPROGRAMMED IT STILL SAME PROBLEM LIGHTS FLICKER AND CHECK ENGINE LIGHT STAYS ON. VIN: 3C8FY78G73T
10248988	02/04/08	Kenwood, CA	2001 PT Cruiser	0	MULTIFUNCTION SWITCH FOR TURN SIGNAL, HEADLIGHTS AND FOG LIGHTS IS DEFECTIVE. ELECTRICAL FAILURE CAUSES MELTING, SMOKE, BURNING AND MALFUNCTION. VIN: '3C8FY4BB41T
10220571	03/01/08	Neeah, WI	2001 PT Cruiser	25	THE CONTACT OWNS A 2001 CHRYSLER PT CRUISER. THE VEHICLE SPEED CONTROL WAS PREVIOUSLY DISCONNECTED. WHILE DRIVING 25 MPH, THE CONTACT NOTICED SMOKE COMING FROM THE STEERING COLUMN. THE DEALER STATED THAT THE FAILURE WAS ELECTRICAL AND RELATED TO THE VEHICLE SPEED CONTROL. THE HIGH AND LOW BEAM SWITCH WAS ALSO BURNED. THE MANUFACTURER STATED THAT THERE WAS NO EXISTING RECALL.THE CONTACT ALLOWED THE VEHICLE TO COOL DOWN AND WAS ABLE TO DRIVE HOME. A MECHANIC WILL REPAIR THE VEHICLE SINCE THE MANUFACTURER STATED THAT THEY WERE UNABLE TO OFFER ANY ASSISTANCE. SHE IS UNABLE TO DRIVE THE VEHICLE DUE TO THE SAFETY RISK INVOLVED. THE FAILURE MILEAGE WAS 65,000 AND CURRENT MILEAGE WAS 65,100. VIN: 3C8FY4BBO1T

10238410	07/12/08	St. Clair Shores, MI	2002 PT Cruiser	55	THE CONTACT OWNS A 2002 CHRYSLER PT CRUISER. WHILE DRIVING 55 MPH, THE CONTACT NOTICED SMOKE UNDER THE HOOD OF THE VEHICLE. SHE THEN NOTICED FLAMES UNDER THE HOOD THROUGH THE DASHBOARD OF THE VEHICLE. THE ENGINE TURNED OFF, WHICH FORCED THE CONTACT TO COAST THE VEHICLE TO A STOP. THE PASSENGER OF THE VEHICLE INJURED HER NOSE AND WRIST WHILE ATTEMPTING TO EXIT THE VEHICLE. THE DRIVER WAS NOT INJURED. THE VEHICLE WAS DIAGNOSED BY THE MANUFACTURER AND THEY STATED THAT THE FAILURE WAS NOT CAUSED BY A VEHICLE DEFECT. THE FIRE DEPARTMENT EXTINGUISHED THE FIRE AND A POLICE REPORT WAS FILED. THERE WERE NO WARNINGS PRIOR TO THE FAILURE. THE CURRENT AND FAILURE MILEAGES WERE 71,300. VIN: 3C8 FY68 B42T
10237755	08/01/08	Madera, CA	2002 PT Cruiser	25	2002 PT CRUISER, WAS SERVICED ABOUT 3-4 MOS PRIOR, RUNNING FINE, ALL OF A SUDDEN SMOKE WAS COMING OUT OF THE INSIDE OF THE CAR VENTS, I PULLED OVER WHEN I EXIT THE CAR, I SAW SMOKE AND HEARD SOMETHING IGNITE IN THE HOOD. THERE WAS NO WARNING OF ANYTHING WAS WRONG WITH THE CAR, THERE WERE NO WARNING LIGHTS, THERE WAS NO STALLING OF THE CAR, NOTHING. VIN: 3C8FY68B42T
10246099	09/04/08	Corona, NY	2006 PT Cruiser	0	THE CONTACT OWNS A 2006 CHRYSLER PT CRUISER. WHILE THE ENGINE WAS TURNED ON AND THE AIR CONDITIONER WAS ACTIVATED, THE VEHICLE WOULD OVERHEAT. HE NOTICED SMOKE COMING FROM THE ENGINE COMPARTMENT. THE DEALER INSPECTED THE VEHICLE AND FOUND NO FAILURES. THE MANUFACTURER HAS NOT BEEN NOTIFIED. THE CURRENT MILEAGE WAS APPROXIMATELY 30,000 AND FAILURE MILEAGE WAS APPROXIMATELY 29,000. VIN: 3A4FY48B96T
10254109	01/02/09	Chapel Hill, NC	2004 PT Cruiser	35	THE CONTACT OWNS A 2004 CHRYSLER PT CRUISER. WHILE DRIVING 35 MPH, THE CONTACT SMELLED AN ELECTRICAL BURNING SMELL COMING FROM THE INSTRUMENT PANEL. SHORTLY AFTERWARDS, THE INSTRUMENT PANEL INDICATORS STOPPED WORKING. THE CONTACT THEN SMELLED BURNING PLASTIC. THE CHRYSLER DEALER PULLED THE INSTRUMENT CLUSTER AND DISCOVERED THAT THE CLUSTER CIRCUIT WAS BURNED. THE DEALER REPLACED THE INSTRUMENT CLUSTER WITH A NEW PART AND THEY RETAINED THE OLD PART. THE FAILURE MILEAGE WAS 74,600. VIN: 3C8FY78G64T
10293383	05/04/09	Port Orchard, WA	2003 PT Cruiser	0	1. I GENERALLY DRIVE OUR 2003 CHRYSLER PT CRUISER WITH THE FOG LIGHTS ON DURING THE DAY, AND THE HEADLIGHTS AT NIGHT. THIS MEANS I WAS TURNING THE FOG LIGHT SWITCH ON THE TURN SIGNAL UNIT SEVERAL TIMES A DAY. 2. BEGINNING EARLY IN 2009 I EXPERIENCED TIMES WHEN THE FOG LIGHTS WOULD NOT TURN OFF WITH THE SWITCH WITHOUT A LOT OF CYCLING, OR THE FOG LIGHTS WOULD TURN THEMSELVES ON WHEN THE DOOR CLOSED. THE VIBRATION OF THE VEHICLE MADE THAT HAPPEN. THEN, WHEN TRYING TO GET THE FOG LIGHTS TO TURN OFF, THE SWITCH BEGAN TO SMOKE. TURNING OFF THE CAR CLEARED THAT, SO I STOPPED USING THE FOG LIGHTS. THE TURN SIGNALS AND HEADLIGHT PORTION OF THE SWITCH WORKED FINE. 3. I CONTACTED THE CHRYSLER DEALERSHIP AND WAS TOLD THEY WERE OUT OF THE SWITCH. I THEN CONTACTED A LOCAL AUTO MAINTENANCE COMPANY I HAVE USED IN THE PAST AND TRUST. THEY QUOTED ME A BETTER SERVICE PRICE, AND THAT THE SWITCH WAS BACKORDERED. THERE WERE OVER 5000 SWITCHES ON BACKORDER AND IT WAS SIX MONTHS AFTER THE ORDER WAS PLACED BEFORE WE RECEIVED THE SWITCH AND HAD IT INSTALLED. MY CONCERN IS TWO FOLD: 1. THE 5000 MAY WELL HAVE BEEN THE TIP OF THE ICEBERG IN TERMS OF FAILURES, AND 2. IF I HAD NOT BEEN SITTING THERE, WOULD THE LIGHTS, AFTER COMING ON BY THEMSELVES HAVE CAUSE THE SWITCH TO ACTUALLY

					CATCH THE VEHICLE ON FIRE? I THOUGHT THAT THE BRIEF TIME I WAS SMOKE SHOULD HAVE BEEN ENOUGH TO BLOW THE FUSE, BUT IT DIDN'T. VIN: 3C8FY78G83T
10268600	05/12/09	Brookeland Center, MN	2004 PT Cruiser	25	THE CONTACT OWNS A 2004 CHRYSLER PT CRUISER. WHILE DRIVING 25 MPH, THE CONTACT NOTICED SMOKE COMING FROM THE HEADLIGHT SWITCH. HE INVESTIGATED FURTHER AND NOTICED THAT THE SWITCH WAS MELTING AND SMOKING. HE EXITED THE VEHICLE AND PROCEEDED TO DISCONNECT THE BATTERY TO STOP A FIRE FROM OCCURRING. THE HEADLIGHTS CANNOT BE USED BECAUSE THE SWITCH FAILED; THEREFORE, HE CANNOT DRIVE THE VEHICLE AT NIGHT. THE CONTACT CALLED THE DEALER AND WAS INFORMED THAT THEY WERE AWARE OF THE ISSUE, BUT THERE WERE NO CURRENT REPLACEMENT PARTS TO REPAIR THE FAILURE. THE PART THAT THEY BELIEVE WILL CORRECT THE FAILURE IS ON BACK ORDER. THE VEHICLE HAS NOT BEEN REPAIRED. THE CONTACT IS IN THE PROCESS OF NOTIFYING THE MANUFACTURER. THE VIN WAS UNAVAILABLE. THE FAILURE MILEAGE WAS 75,000 AND CURRENT MILEAGE WAS 75,600. VIN UNAVAILABLE
10303235	08/17/09	Boise, ID	2007 PT Cruiser	50	WE HAVE A 2007 IN NOVEMBER 2007 THE IGNITION SWITCH FUSE STARTED TO BLOW OUT ONCE EVERY 3 MONTHS. IT GOT WORSE IN AUGUST 16, 2009 IT WOULD NOT STOP BLOWING SO WE TOOK IT TO LARRY MILLER DODGE TO HAVE IT CHECK AND THEY SAID IT WAS THE IGNITION SWITCH AND IT MELTED SOME WIRE UNDER THE DASHBOARD. HAD IT ALL REPLACED AND DROVE AROUND FOR A FEW DAYS STARTED DOING IT AGAIN. I TOOK IT BACK AND THEY HOOKED IT UP TO THERE MACHINE AND DIDN'T FIND ANYTHING WRONG SO I LEFT IT THEY TOLD ME THAT IT NEEDED TO DO IT IN FRONT OF THEM AND IT DID STARTED BLOWING THE IGNITION FUSE RIGHT THERE I LEFT THE CAR WITH THEM AND THE NEXT DAY THEY TOLD ME IT STOPPED DOING IT A DAY LATER IT
					DID IT AGAIN SO I CALLED THE MAIN OFFICE OF LARRY MILLER AND THEY TOLD ME THEY WOULD LOOK INTO IT TO STAY BY THE PHONE AND THEY WOULD CALL ME ON WHAT TO DO I DID. 2 MONTHS LATER WENT BY AND I CALLED THEM AND THEY SAID THAT THE GUY THAT WAS HELPING ME GOT FIRED AND THAT THEY CLOSED THE CASE I HAVE BEEN CALLING THEM ABOUT EVERY DAY ABOUT THIS AND THEY SAID IT IS MY PROBLEM NOT THEIRS.AND NOW THE COOLING FAN IS NOT WORKING THERE IS SOMETHING WRONG WITH THE ELECTRICAL SYSTEM WITH THIS CAR. I AM AFRAID TO DRIVE IT BECAUSE I HAVE A LITTLE BOY WITH ME AND AM WORRIED SOMETHING IS GOING TO CATCH FIRE. VIN: 3A4FY48B07T
10297622	09/25/09	Stafford, CT	2002 PT Cruiser	0	I WAS DRIVING MY 2002 PT CRUISER, I WAS STOPPED AND NOTICED FLAMES COMING FROM UNDER THE HOOD. I GOT OUT AND WITHIN A MINUTE THE CAR WAS FULLY ENGULFED. THE CAR WAS COMPLETELY DESTROYED. I HAVE PICTURES OF THE CAR AFTER THE DAMAGE. VIN UNAVAILABLE
10315950	12/24/09	San Paolo	2005 PT Cruiser	90	MALFUNCTION ON THE HEADLIGHT/FOG LIGHT MULTIFUNCTION SWITCH ON A CHRYSLER PT CRUISER 2005, VIN NUMBER 1C8FYB8B85T564682 (EXPORT VEHICLE, RUNS IN BRAZIL). IT STARTED UNWITTINGLY TURNING ON THE FOG LIGHTS EVEN WHEN THE CAR IGNITION WAS OFF, IT LEAD TO DRAIN CAR BATTERIES AND FOR ME TO THINK AT FIRST THAT WAS A PROBLEM WITH MY BATTERY, SINCE WHEN I SAW THE CAR THE FOG LIGHTS WERE OFF BECAUSE IT DRAINED THE POWER. THEN, AFTER A HOT DAY I WAS DRIVING AT NIGHT ON A RAINY AND DANGEROUS HIGHWAY AND MY FOG LIGHTS WENT OFF AND I FELT A SMELL OF BURN CABLE AND SMOKE INSIDE THE CAR, SO I STOPPED THE VEHICLE AND SAW SMOKE COMING OUT OF THE MULTIFUNCTION SWITCH AND GOT REALLY SCARED. AFTER SO MANY DAYS AND SEARCHING ON THE INTERNET I FINALLY DISCOVERED THAT THE BATTERY DRAIN HAD TO DO WITH THE FOG LIGHTS

					SWITCH. I TOKE ALMOST 6 MONTHS TO DISCOVER IT AND SO MY FOG LIGHTS REFLECTOR STARTED TO MELT AND LOOSE THERE FLEXIBILITY. I WENT TO CHRYSLER DEALERS IN BRAZIL AND THEY SAID THEY CANT DO NOTHING FOR ME SINCE THE CAR IS NO LONGER IN WARRANTY. THE THING IS, THERE IS MORE THAN 550 COMPLAINTS (AND COUNTING) ON A WEBSITE EXPLAINING THE PROBLEM AND WHAT THE MANY DANGEROUS POSSIBLE CONSEQUENCES. AND 95% OF THE CARS IN THOSE COMPLAINTS ARE NOT UNDER WARRANTY FROM CHRYSLER MANUFACTURE. NOW I ACTUALLY RUN WITH THE CAR WITHOUT THE FUSE RESPONSIBLE TO FOG LIGHTS. IT COST ME A BRAND NEW BATTERY AND 2 DAMAGED FOG LIGHT REFLECTORS AND THE OBLIGATION OF RUNNING WITHOUT FOG LIGHTS ON HIGHWAYS. (THAT ARE EXTREMELY DANGEROUS WITHOUT THE PROPER ILLUMINATION! HTTP://WVVW.TO P IX COM/F0 RUM/AUTOS/CH RYSLE R-PT-CRUISERTTF61KHBDLDVT92AH2 VIN: 1C8FYB8B85T564682
10300424	01/20/09	Nashville, TN	2002 PT Cruiser	35	THE CONTACT OWNS A 2002 CHRYSLER PT CRUISER. WHILE DRIVING VARIOUS SPEEDS WITH THE FOG LAMP LIGHT ILLUMINATED THERE WAS A BURNING RUBBER SMELL. THE FOLLOWING DAY, WHILE DRIVING APPROXIMATELY 35 MPH SHE ALSO SMELLED BURNING RUBBER; HOWEVER, AFTER SHE PARKED THE VEHICLE SMOKE WAS COMING FROM THE VEHICLE. THE DEALER WAS CONTACTED AND THEY STATED THAT SEVERAL PT CRUISERS EXHIBITED THE IDENTICAL FAILURE WHICH WAS CAUSED BY A SWITCH IN THE STEERING COLUMN. THE MANUFACTURER STATED THAT THEIR SPECIAL INVESTIGATION UNIT WILL CONTACT HER TO SEE WHAT CAUSED THE SMOKE. THEY ALSO ADVISED HER NOT TO HAVE THE VEHICLE REPAIRED OR TOWED. THE FAILURE AND CURRENT MILEAGES WERE 51,000. VIN UNAVAILABLE

ACKNOWLEDGMENTS

S PACE IS INADEQUATE to name all those who have given support and en-
couragement to the writing of "Death By Rental Car." But I would
be remiss if I failed to express my gratitude at least to Cally Houck, Carl
Nienaber, Larry Grassini, Roland Wrinkle, Ralph Nader, Philip Spitzer,
Clarence Ditlow, Bert Kelley, Tom Field, Susan Baker, Donald Slavik,
Leon Robertson, and David Michaels. To them and many others, my
thanks.

SOURCES

SOURCES FOR EACH chapter are identified below. Where the source is fully identified in the text, it is not listed here.

Preface

Transcript and Videotape, Senate Commerce, Science and Transportation Subcommittee on Consumer Protection, Product Safety and Insurance: April 2, 2014 Hearing, General Motors Ignition Switch Recall

Chapter One

Letter of August 13, 2008, from Batza & Associates to Grassini and Wrinkle Law Firm reporting on August 7, 2008 interview of Ian Burnham

Letter of August 13, 2008, from Batza & Associates to Grassini and Wrinkle Law Firm reporting on August 8, 2008 interview of Alisha Jensen

June 6, 2006 deposition of Charles T. Houck, *Charles T. Houck and Carol S. Houck, surviving heirs to Raechel Veronique Houck and Jacqueline Marie Houck, Deceased, Plaintiffs, vs. DaimlerChrysler Corporation, et al., Defendants*

http://www.edmunds.com/chrysler/pt-cruiser/2004/

http://www.cars.com/chrysler/pt-cruiser/2004/expert-reviews

June 6, 2006 deposition of Carol S. Houck, *Charles T. Houck and Carol S. Houck, surviving heirs to Raechel Veronique Houck and Jacqueline Marie Houck, Deceased, Plaintiffs, vs. DaimlerChrysler Corporation, et al., Defendants*

Chapter Two

August 12, 2008 deposition of Jesus Francisco Trevino, *Charles T. Houck and Carol S. Houck, surviving heirs to Raechel Veronique Houck and Jacqueline Marie Houck, Deceased, Plaintiffs, vs. DaimlerChrysler Corporation, et al., Defendants*

http://www-odi.nhtsa.dot.gov/cars/problems/defect/results.cfm?action_number=PE04028&SearchType=QuickSearch&summary=true

http://www.gpo.gov/fdsys/pkg/STATUTE-80/pdf/STATUTE-80-Pg718.pdf

http://www-odi.nhtsa.dot.gov/recalls/recallprocess.cfm

E-mail of September 9, 2004 from gsbl1@daimlerchrysler.com (Greg Burks, DaimlerChrysler National Fleet Service)

Chapter Three

June 6, 2006 deposition of Charles T. Houck, *Charles T. Houck and Carol S. Houck, surviving heirs to Raechel Veronique Houck and Jacqueline Marie Houck, Deceased, Plaintiffs, vs. DaimlerChrysler Corporation, et al., Defendants*

September 9, 2006 deposition of Carlos Woods, *Charles T. Houck and Carol S. Houck, surviving heirs to Raechel Veronique Houck and Jacqueline Marie Houck, Deceased, Plaintiffs, vs. DaimlerChrysler Corporation, et al., Defendants*

August 30, 2006 deposition of Esther Kosty, *Charles T. Houck and Carol S. Houck, surviving heirs to Raechel Veronique Houck and Jacqueline Marie Houck, Deceased, Plaintiffs, vs. DaimlerChrysler Corporation, et al., Defendants*

June 12, 2006 deposition of Denise Schafer, *Charles T. Houck and Carol S. Houck, surviving heirs to Raechel Veronique Houck and Jacqueline Marie Houck, Deceased, Plaintiffs, vs. DaimlerChrysler Corporation, et al., Defendants*

August 29, 2006 deposition of Russell Deases, *Charles T. Houck and Carol S. Houck, surviving heirs to Raechel Veronique Houck and Jacqueline Marie Houck, Deceased, Plaintiffs, vs. DaimlerChrysler Corporation, et al., Defendants*

August 30, 2006 deposition of Douglas Michael Finch, *Charles T. Houck and Carol S. Houck, surviving heirs to Raechel Veronique Houck and Jacqueline Marie Houck, Deceased, Plaintiffs, vs. DaimlerChrysler Corporation, et al., Defendants*

August 29, 2006 deposition of Darrell Robert Mackinga, *Charles T. Houck and Carol S. Houck, surviving heirs to Raechel Veronique Houck and Jacqueline Marie Houck, Deceased, Plaintiffs, vs. DaimlerChrysler Corporation, et al., Defendants*

August 20, 2006 deposition of William Stratman, *Charles T. Houck and Carol S. Houck, surviving heirs to Raechel Veronique Houck and Jacqueline*

Marie Houck, Deceased, Plaintiffs, vs. DaimlerChrysler Corporation, et al., Defendants

July 28, 2008, deposition of Anthony McFarland, *Charles T. Houck and Carol S. Houck, surviving heirs to Raechel Veronique Houck and Jacqueline Marie Houck, Deceased, Plaintiffs, vs. DaimlerChrysler Corporation, et al., Defendants*

August 29,2006, deposition of Michael R. Schad, *Charles T. Houck and Carol S. Houck, surviving heirs to Raechel Veronique Houck and Jacqueline Marie Houck, Deceased, Plaintiffs, vs. DaimlerChrysler Corporation, et al., Defendants*

Chapter Four

June 6, 2006 deposition of Carol S. Houck, *Charles T. Houck and Carol S. Houck, surviving heirs to Raechel Veronique Houck and Jacqueline Marie Houck, Deceased, Plaintiffs, vs. DaimlerChrysler Corporation, et al., Defendants*

Testimony of Nancy Mason, June 4, 2010, *In The Superior Court Of The State Of California, County Of Alameda, Before Honorable Richard O. Keller, Judge, Department 608, Charles T. Houck and Carol S. Houck, Plaintiffs, vs. Enterprise Rent-A-Car Company Of San Francisco And Enterprise Rent-A-Car Company, Et Al., Defendants, Case No. HG05220018*

Testimony of Blair Whitten, June 7, 2010, *In The Superior Court Of The State Of California, County Of Alameda, Before Honorable Richard O. Keller, Judge, Department 608, Charles T. Houck and Carol S. Houck, Plaintiffs, vs. Enterprise Rent-A-Car Company Of San Francisco And Enterprise Rent-A-Car Company, Et Al., Defendants, Case No. HG05220018*

June 6, 2006 deposition of Charles T. Houck, *Charles T. Houck and Carol S. Houck, surviving heirs to Raechel Veronique Houck and Jacqueline*

Marie Houck, Deceased, Plaintiffs, vs. DaimlerChrysler Corporation, et al., Defendants

October 13, 2004 e-mail from Jessica Standley Cairrns to Carol Houck

Chapter five

Author's Interview, Larry Grassini and Roland Wrinkle, December 12, 2011

Author's Interviews, Kathleen Grassini, December 22, 2011, August 5, 2013

Author's Interview, Carol Houck, January 29, 2013

Chapter six

Plaintiffs' Principal Trial Brief, February 24, 1997, *Iscela Ornelas et al. v. Chrysler Corporation et al., Superior Court of California, Case No. BC 141099*

Roy Haeusler, Chief Engineer, Auto Safety, Chrysler Corporation, "Recent Developments in Car Design for Injury Reduction," October 27, 1965

New York Times, "U.S., Chrysler Reported Near Deal on Safety," by James Bennett, March 27, 1995

Statement of Clarence Ditlow, director, Center for Auto Safety, "Retrofits for GM Firebomb Pickups," April 23, 2001

Mother Jones, "Side-Saddle Madness," by Suzie Larsen, February 24, 1998

New York Times, "Chrysler Plans To Replace Van Latches," by James Bennett, March 28, 1995

Open Letter from Clarence Ditlow to Chrysler Minivan Owners, January, 2001

New York Times, "Chrysler Seeks to Quiet Mini-Vans' Safety Critic," by James Bennett, February 17, 1995

Detroit News, "Safety Firebrand Refuses to Relent: Fired Employee Battles Chrysler in Courtroom," Bill Vlasic, July 13, 2003

Chapter Seven

Author's Interview, Larry Grassini and Roland Wrinkle, December 12, 2011

Chapter Eight

June 6, 2006 deposition of Charles T. Houck, *Charles T. Houck and Carol S. Houck, surviving heirs to Raechel Veronique Houck and Jacqueline Marie Houck, Deceased, Plaintiffs, vs. DaimlerChrysler Corporation, et al., Defendants*

June 6, 2006 deposition of Carol S. Houck, *Charles T. Houck and Carol S. Houck, surviving heirs to Raechel Veronique Houck and Jacqueline Marie Houck, Deceased, Plaintiffs, vs. DaimlerChrysler Corporation, et al., Defendants*

http://www.sedgwicklaw.com/Publications/detail.aspx?pub=3908

http://www.selmanbreitman.com/About-Us.shtml

Author's Interview, Carol Houck, January 29, 2013

Chapter Nine

"Alternative Cause Strategies in Product Liability Litigation: The Need for Alternative Defenses," Sean Overland, American Society of Trial Consultants, September 2009

"Why Do Jurors Blame The Victim?" Quentin Brogdon, *Trial,* December1, 2003

"Accidents and Acts of God: A History of Terms," Loimer, H; Guarnieri, M, American Journal of Public Health, 1996, 86:101–107

"Victim-Blaming: A New Term for an Old Trend," Schoellkopf, Julia Churchill, Lesbian Gay Bisexual Transgender Queer Center, Paper 33, 2012.

"The Richest Man in Town: The Twelve Commandments of Wealth," Randall Jones, Hatchette Book Group, 2009

September 13, 2006 deposition of Brenna (Carlson) Furness, *Charles T. Houck and Carol S. Houck, surviving heirs to Raechel Veronique Houck and Jacqueline Marie Houck, Deceased, Plaintiffs, vs. DaimlerChrysler Corporation, et al., Defendants*

August 30, 2006, deposition of Chad Hogan, *Charles T. Houck and Carol S. Houck, surviving heirs to Raechel Veronique Houck and Jacqueline Marie Houck, Deceased, Plaintiffs, vs. DaimlerChrysler Corporation, et al., Defendants*

July 17, 2008, deposition of Nicolle Pinto Echevarria, *Charles T. Houck and Carol S. Houck, surviving heirs to Raechel Veronique Houck and Jacqueline Marie Houck, Deceased, Plaintiffs, vs. DaimlerChrysler Corporation, et al., Defendants*

November 2, 2006, deposition of Arthur John Mora, *Charles T. Houck and Carol S. Houck, surviving heirs to Raechel Veronique Houck and Jacqueline Marie Houck, Deceased, Plaintiffs, vs. DaimlerChrysler Corporation, et al., Defendants*

Coroner's Report, Case Number 04-295, Raechel Houck, November 2, 2004

California Highway Patrol Traffic Collision Report, Local Report No. 2004100008, October 21, 2004

Chapter Ten

http://www.exponent.com/capabilities/

"Doubt Is Their Product," David Michaels, Oxford University Press, 2008

"The Expert Witness Scam," Leon Robertson, 2006

Exponent 2010 Annual Report

February 3, 2009, deposition of Douglas E. Young, Ph.D., *Charles T. Houck and Carol S. Houck, surviving heirs to Raechel Veronique Houck and Jacqueline Marie Houck, Deceased, Plaintiffs, vs. DaimlerChrysler Corporation, et al., Defendants*

Chapter Eleven

Author's Interview, Carol Houck, January 29, 2013

Author's Interview, Carol Houck, July 6, 2013

Author's Interview, Larry Grassini and Roland Wrinkle, December 12, 2011

Chapter Twelve

Author's Interview, Larry Grassini and Roland Wrinkle, December 12, 2011

http://www.enterpriseholdings.com/press-room/enterprise-rent-a-car-neighborhood-network-advancing-local-mobility-sustainability.html

May 16, 2007, deposition of Thomas Moulton, *Charles T. Houck and Carol S. Houck, surviving heirs to Raechel Veronique Houck and Jacqueline Marie Houck, Deceased, Plaintiffs, vs. DaimlerChrysler Corporation, et al., Defendants*

August 16, 2007, deposition of Thomas Gieseking, *Charles T. Houck and Carol S. Houck, surviving heirs to Raechel Veronique Houck and Jacqueline Marie Houck, Deceased, Plaintiffs, vs. DaimlerChrysler Corporation, et al., Defendants*

Chapter Thirteen

http://www.enterpriseholdings.com

www.aboutus.enterprise.com

Letter of August 13, 2008, from Batza & Associates to Grassini and Wrinkle Law Firm reporting on August 7, 2008 interview of Ian Burnham

Letter of August 13, 2008, from Batza & Associates to Grassini and Wrinkle Law Firm reporting on August 8, 2008 interview of Alisha Jensen

Letter of August 6, 2008, from Batza & Associates to Grassini and Wrinkle Law Firm reporting on August 8, 2008 interview of Andrea Avecilla

Letter of August 27, 2008, from Batza & Associates to Grassini and Wrinkle Law Firm reporting on August 8, 2008 interview of, and declaration by, Mark Matias

Letter of September 3, 2008, from Batza & Associates to Grassini and Wrinkle Law Firm reporting on August 8, 2008 interview of Michael Fortino

December 8, 2009, deposition of Lloyd D. Rae, *Charles T. Houck and Carol S. Houck, surviving heirs to Raechel Veronique Houck and Jacqueline Marie Houck, Deceased, Plaintiffs, vs. DaimlerChrysler Corporation, et al., Defendants*

January 5, 2010, deposition of Robert Cunitz, Ph.D., *Charles T. Houck and Carol S. Houck, surviving heirs to Raechel Veronique Houck and Jacqueline Marie Houck, Deceased, Plaintiffs, vs. DaimlerChrysler Corporation, et al., Defendants*

Chapter Fourteen

"Expert Witness Mental Health Testimony: Handling Deposition And Trial Traps," Donald A. Eisner, Ph.D., J.D., American Journal Of Forensic Psychology, Volume 28, Issue 1, 2010

January 20, 2010, deposition of Gregory D. Stephens, *Charles T. Houck and Carol S. Houck, surviving heirs to Raechel Veronique Houck and Jacqueline Marie Houck, Deceased, Plaintiffs, vs. DaimlerChrysler Corporation, et al., Defendants*

January 13, 2010, deposition of Andrew Irwin, *Charles T. Houck and Carol S. Houck, surviving heirs to Raechel Veronique Houck and Jacqueline Marie Houck, Deceased, Plaintiffs, vs. DaimlerChrysler Corporation, et al., Defendants*

Chapter Fifteen

October 28, 2009, deposition of Robert D. Banta, *Charles T. Houck and Carol S. Houck, surviving heirs to Raechel Veronique Houck and Jacqueline Marie Houck, Deceased, Plaintiffs, vs. DaimlerChrysler Corporation, et al., Defendants*

December 18, 2009, deposition of Dennis A. Guenther, Ph.D., P.E., *Charles T. Houck and Carol S. Houck, surviving heirs to Raechel Veronique Houck and Jacqueline Marie Houck, Deceased, Plaintiffs, vs. DaimlerChrysler Corporation, et al., Defendants*

Chapter Sixteen

October 20, 2008, deposition of Joseph Howard Romig, Ph.D., *Charles T. Houck and Carol S. Houck, surviving heirs to Raechel Veronique Houck and Jacqueline Marie Houck, Deceased, Plaintiffs, vs. DaimlerChrysler Corporation, et al., Defendants*

April 15, 2010, deposition of Gerald Rosenbluth, Ph.D., *Charles T. Houck and Carol S. Houck, surviving heirs to Raechel Veronique Houck and Jacqueline Marie Houck, Deceased, Plaintiffs, vs. DaimlerChrysler Corporation, et al., Defendants*

Chapter Seventeen

"The Big Surprise Is Enterprise: Quietly Beating Out Rivals Hertz And Avis, This Privately Held Outfit Reigns As The No. 1 Car-Rental Company In America, And The Taylor Family Aims To Keep It On Top," Carol J. Loomis, Fortune, July 14, 2006

"10 Questions for Andy Taylor," Inc.com, November 1, 2007

"Enterprise Rent-A-Car Sold Chevies Without Standard Air Bags," Rick Montgomery and Dan Margolies, The Kansas City Star, August 16, 2009

"Class Claims Enterprise Lied About Cars," Courthouse News Service, April 30, 2010

Chapter Eighteen

Author's Interview, Carol Houck, May 2, 2013

Chapter Nineteen

Author's Interview, Hon. Richard Keller, August 8, 2013

"University Fences In a Berkeley Protest, and a New One Arises," Jesse McKinley, New York Times, September 13, 2007

"UC, Tree-Sitter Clashes Continue in Court, Grove," Richard Brenneman, The Berkeley Daily Planet, July 3, 2008

"Big Victory for California Hotel Tenants," Lynda Carson, indybay. org, October 29, 2008

Author's Interview, Larry Grassini and Roland Wrinkle, December 12, 2011

Chapter Twenty

Voir Dire Transcript, June 1-3, 2010, *In The Superior Court Of The State Of California, County Of Alameda, Before Honorable Richard O. Keller, Judge, Department 608, Charles T. Houck and Carol S. Houck, Plaintiffs, vs. Enterprise Rent-A-Car Company Of San Francisco And Enterprise, Rent-A-Car Company, Et Al., Defendants, Case No. HG05220018*

Author's Interview, Larry Grassini and Roland Wrinkle, December 12, 2011

Author's Interview, Lois Heaney, August 28, 2013

Chapter Twenty-One

Author's Interview, Carol Houck, April 6, 2014

Trial Transcript, June 4-9, 2010, *In The Superior Court Of The State Of California, County Of Alameda, Before Honorable Richard O. Keller, Judge, Department 608, Charles T. Houck and Carol S. Houck, Plaintiffs, vs. Enterprise Rent-A-Car Company Of San Francisco And Enterprise, Rent-A-Car Company, Et Al., Defendants, Case No. HG05220018*

"Enterprise Rent-A-Car Admits To Renting Two Young Sisters A Car Which Had Been Recalled A Month Earlier For Underhood Fires And Causing Their Wrongful And Unreasonable Deaths," Grassini & Wrinkle, undated press release

Afterword

"Calif. Assembly Approves Rental Car Recall Bill," Adam Weintraub, Associated Press, April 28, 2011

"Ojai Mother Of Two Crash Victims Crusades For Rental-Car Law," Cindy Von Quednow, Ventura County Star, May 4, 2011

"Assemblyman Bill Monning," Santa Cruz Good Times, April 26, 2011

"New 'Used' Car Rentals May Have Serious Safety Problems," Paul A. Eisenstein, The Detroit Bureau, NBC, May 19, 2014. http://www.nbcnews.com/storyline/gm-recall/new-used-cars-rentals-may-have-serious-safety-problems-n109281

INDEX

Subaru, 194

Syngenta, 82

Taylor, Jack and Andrew, 70, 99,
    100, 182-186, 222
Temme, Kathy, 114
Trevino, Jesus Francisco, 7-12, 14
"Turning Lead Into Gold: How
    the Bush Administration is
    Poisoning the Lead Advisory
    Committee at CDC," 82, 83

"Under the Corporate
    Microscope," 186
Underwood, Larry, 185
Unintended acceleration, 83,
    84, 85, 87
USA Today, 85
Ventura, 5, 15, 23, 24, 71,
    72, 93, 94

Voir dire, 200, 201, 203, 204,
    205, 207, 208

Wheeler, Daniel, 18, 19,
    25, 161
Wheeler, Daniel, 25
Wiggins, Troy, 86, 101-104, 108, 111,
    121, 123, 124, 133, 138, 139, 140,
    148, 150, 157, 158, 162, 177, 180,
    181, 193
Wrinkle, Roland, 28, 30-34, 35-37, 39,
    41-43, 45-47, 49, 51, 94-98, 100,
    106, 114, 115, 120, 138, 156, 159,
    191, 192, 196-198, 201, 203, 205,
    212, 240

Young, Douglas, 77, 85
Youngquist, Monique, 201
Yukevich, James, 162, 191-199,
    201-204, 207, 208, 212- 216

Made in the USA
Middletown, DE
12 September 2021